CALIFORNIA:

The New Society

Also by REMI NADEAU

City-Makers

The Water Seekers

The Ghost Towns of California

Los Angeles: From Mission to Modern City

CALIFORNIA:

The New Society

by REMI NADEAU

DAVID McKAY COMPANY, INC.
New York

CALIFORNIA: The New Society

LIBRARY OF CONGRESS CATALOG CARD NUMBER: 63-19338

MANUFACTURED IN THE UNITED STATES OF AMERICA

VAN REES PRESS • NEW YORK

TO MARGARET

Foreword

This is a book about Californians as people, and California as a society. It is not about public affairs, but private lives. Not a guidebook for newcomers, but an inquiry into the way Californians think and act, the kind of culture they are creating, and the implications for the future of California and the country.

My indebtedness to those who have added substance to this book is immeasurable. They include patient librarians who have helped me find the pertinent reports, books, and other publications; reporters, most of them unknown to me, who write for the many newspapers throughout the state whose pages were studied; my wife and several other close observers of the California scene who read all or part of the manuscript and made invaluable suggestions to improve its marksmanship; many strangers, both children and adults, who unknowingly contributed to this book through unguarded remarks that did not fall unnoted; and many friends who may henceforth watch their tongues in my presence, since they discover here that "A chiel's amang you takin' notes, And faith he'll prent it."

Contents

CALIFORNIA:

The New Society

Map of California

California: A New Society?

1.

At the height of the 1849 Gold Rush, the Californians couldn't wait for Congress to approve their application for statehood. They drafted a constitution, elected a governor and legislature, sent two congressmen and two senators to Washington—months before the United States decided to admit California.

Little more than a century later the Californians couldn't wait for the Census Bureau to proclaim theirs the most populous state in the Union. They served notice that on December 21, 1962, California would surpass New York. Asked one disgruntled New York official, "Didn't they give the hour of the day?"

Rambunctious, impetuous, incurably optimistic—these are some of the qualities that have made Californians a source of wonder to other Americans. In a sense they now have what they always wanted—the recognition that cannot be denied to the biggest. But this also thrusts them into a role of national leadership that they never sought. The question is whether they hear this summons to greatness, or whether they still heed, in Thoreau's phrase, "a different drummer."

One Friday afternoon, I was standing in an elevator next to a business acquaintance—an older man—and by way of being pleasant, asked, "Going to have an exciting weekend?"

The answer was slow and measured, without a turn of the head. "I hope not."

I felt like telling him that if he didn't like California he should go back where he came from. Most of us are going to have an exciting weekend, even if we have to lie about it.

"When I first came out here I was shocked," a corporate executive once told me. "On Friday night employees will leave town for the weekend and won't think one thought about their company till they return."

I have news for this man. A number of Californians don't think much about their work during the week, either. In the average California office, Wednesday is "hump day"—you're over the hump. By Friday, you're mentally already on the weekend. Friday night the going-home traffic is clogged not only with commuters, but with house trailers, campers, boats-on-wheels, pickups carrying motorcycles or midget racers, autos with anything from skis to surfboards strapped on top. In the summer, churches go on half schedules and some shut down altogether. Job absenteeism may not be much worse in California, but one large company found too many vacationing employees were phoning in to say they couldn't make it back on time—would need an extra day.

"We had to post an order," said a personnel official, "that anybody who didn't get back from vacation on time would be laid off. That did it."

Not everybody clears out of town on weekends. The California house is considered a sort of do-it-yourself resort, complete with swimming pool and private sun deck. Many large apartments and tract developments play up "resort living" with community pools, tennis courts, putting greens, even

2

cocktail lounges. As one tract advertises, "This permanent private community was designed for vacationtime informality 365 days a year." The new senior-citizen developments are centered around a program of "active retirement," with a full range of hobby and sports activities under a paid recreation director. A housing development in Huntington Beach offers outdoor showers to "leave sand and salt outside" and a boat door at the rear of the garage so you can "move your craft into the backyard for storage or maintenance." Subdivisions on the north shore of San Francisco Bay and along the Sacramento River are offering private dock facilities. The incorporated city of Palos Verdes Estates operates a country club, partly through tax funds; when one of the lounges was refurbished, one citizen commented, "There aren't many cities with barstools in the budget." Californians express this general frame of mind in their favorite parting words: "Have fun!" or "Don't work too hard!"

The fact is that California, perhaps more than any other state, is really a fulfillment of the American dream. Except for some areas of blight, here is the good life—considerable comfort, escape from drudgery and hardship, reasonable leisure time, and the environment to make the most of it. Is this not the American promise—freedom to enjoy life as the fruit of honest labor? Following the American tradition to its ultimate, California is really a sort of secular Kingdom Come.

It is perhaps natural, then, that the Californian would resign from society and succumb to what the sociologists call "privatism." There is in California a sense of individuality but little sense of community. In Los Angeles County, where the family moves an average of every four years, the movement of population works against community attachments. Even among San Franciscans, who have an unabashed love of city, newcomers from the East find few neighbors to talk to, since everybody is pursuing his interests about town, and they wrongly conclude that San Francisco is unfriendly. Says a young San Francisco newcomer, "Everyone is so concerned with 'having fun'—sometimes I think there's nobody here with even one foot on the ground."

True, many of the new tract neighborhoods exhibit close social activity, but such neighborliness seldom extends beyond a block and is interrupted by the high moving rate. In hillside developments where front-yard gossiping is often physically impossible, neighbors can be near strangers. When two important things happened to my closest neighbor—he became a grandfather and his wife's car was stolen—it was a week before I heard about either. In one San Joaquin Valley town the merchants scarcely knew those operating across the street until they formed a service club.

In short, California living tends to be compartmented—each family pursuing its own activities with little awareness of others. Obligation to the community, and to a nebulous thing called society is some sort of school-room myth. Explains one comparative newcomer, "There is a feeling of detachment from the problems of the world. I found myself fading into the scene pretty fast. All I can hear is the splash of the pool."

Like the early Spanish Californians with their Christmas *piñata*, the modern Californians have taken a stick to life itself and are beating it till the last goody falls out. Without making a noise about it, they quietly subscribe to the philosophy of Auntie Mame: Life is a banquet, and a lot of poor suckers are starving to death.

3.

Is all this necessarily bad? One company personnel officer says not. "We don't want 'em to think about work on their days off. We want 'em to come back refreshed."

Besides, doesn't the family draw closer together through

4

mutual hobbies and sports? In Pomona, the son of a motor-cycling father started riding his own machine (presumably a midget version) at the age of eighteen months. One tract advertisement in San Fernando Valley shows the family and apparently some neighbors lounging around in shorts and bathing suits, drinks in hand, while the children romp in the pool. "Why does the husband stay home in Woodland Oaks?" it asks.

"He entertains at home because he prefers his own wet bar to the one at the club . . . He's at home in the kitchen . . . (He calls the built-in double oven 'His and Hers'!)"

If the Californians did not invent togetherness, they are at least the first to make it a religion.

Moreover, tolerance for others is a natural corollary to the Californian's preoccupation with self. One has difficulty doing as one pleases in a society of busybodies or bigots.

California's individuality has therefore worked against conformity. Long before Los Angeles became noted for its crackpots, San Franciscans were humoring the boulevard eccentric, treasuring him for his contribution to local color, taking pride in him as evidence of their cosmopolitan big-ness of heart.

But in addition to the obvious screwballs, Californians also value more respectable nonconformity. Being a "character" is a social asset, and many a hostess prides herself on bring-ing together "interesting people." Californians readily cross denominational lines in religion. In one of the largest churches in San Fernando Valley, most of the members are from other denominational backgrounds. Politicians who might elsewhere be able to deliver large voting blocs are sadly aware that California has an extremely high propor-tion of independent voters (approximately one-third) who put more importance on issues and candidates than on party affiliation. California politics are consequently more free-wheeling, unpredictable, and unmanageable than those of any other state.

It is this very tolerance, in fact, that explains California's tradition of health faddists, faith healers, occultists, political quacks, and economic medicine men. Open minds are not always intellectual. They will give a hearing to gimcrackery as well as to logic.

This form of credulity finds vindication in the California environment. It is a state of extremes, superlatives, and near miracles. The classic postcard showing palm and orange trees against a background of snowy mountains is no curiosity, but a California commonplace. The climate varies from the arid Mojave Desert to the rain forest of the Redwood coast. Scenery ranges from the rugged, wave-splashed cliffs of the coastline to some of the jaggedest mountains in the world.

As if nature itself did not stretch one's credulity enough, the state's dynamic growth has been equally unbelievable. Its American history began with the greatest rush of people, migrating as individuals, ever recorded up to that time. The coming of the railroads and the automobile kept the human tide running high until California became the most populous state in the Union. Colossal fortunes were made in gold mining, railroads, petroleum, the movies. Spurred by the energy of real estate promoters, whole towns (today, whole cities) have sprung up virtually overnight. Water to serve these new millions was brought over mountains and plains in several of the longest aqueducts on the globe. Hydroelectric power was transmitted over longer distances than anywhere in the world. No engineering challenge—railroads over the Sierra, bridges over San Francisco Bay—was avoided.

One could not be in California long without catching this fever. Nothing is impossible. Someone claims a new revelation from God? Maybe so. Beat the Depression by giving money to the old folks? Tell us more. Invent a new idea and make a million? Many have done it in California's dynamic economy. A few are still doing it.

All of this spurs the Californian's inclination to gimmick solutions. California itself, as a lure to the dissatisfied of other states, is a gimmick. Many Americans consider California the easy answer to their problems. Are they in ill health? They come to California. Are they unhappy in their jobs? Come to California. Is their marriage in trouble? A change of environment, a new start in California.

As citizens, they tend to apply the same technique to the business of the state. They do not regard society as a group career, requiring continual attention. They tend to believe they can do as they please, on their own, and when public problems arise they can solve them on the spur of the moment with a gimmick. During the Depression they came close to adopting several schemes to pull the California economy up by its own bootstraps, by giving money to people and making them spend it. With the rise of the Communist challenge since the war, some of them have met the issue by displaying the American flag in front of their houses every day, demanding more loyalty oaths of more people, or forming quasi-military organizations to prepare for guerrilla warfare. These are extreme cases, but they are natural products of a state that has an unusual proportion of citizens predisposed to gimmick solutions.

In short, the Californian is preoccupied with private affairs, at the expense of public affairs. He is a passionate individualist, but not in the French sense of political individualism. His individualism is, rather, the type foreseen by Tocqueville in his *Democracy in America*—an individualism "which disposes each member of the community to sever himself from the mass of his fellows, and to draw apart with his family and his friends; so that, after he has thus formed a little circle of his own, he willingly leaves society at large to itself." Tocqueville hoped Americans would be diverted from this

7

tendency by their governmental processes, which forced them into mutual concern and cooperation. He reckoned without the Californians.

4.

All of this is a glimpse of what is known as "California Living." It is not the life of all 17,000,000 Californians. There are obvious pockets of resistance, not only in out-of-the-way localities, but even in some metropolitan suburbs. In these exceptions, life is still that of today's small town in the Middle West, or of nearly all of California two generations ago. But elsewhere the strenuous, self-oriented life—what has been called the "fun morality"—is the dominant mode in California and has been pushed to a farther extreme than in almost any society of comparable size in the world.

Is all this very important? California has always been a renegade among states, populated by renegades among people. But it is now the most populous in the Union. It has more inhabitants than Canada and more than the whole population of the United States as late as 1840. It is still growing at headlong pace—17,000,000 in 1963, an estimated 25,000,000 by 1975. This is more than the individual populations of some ninety foreign countries.

California has also been a pacesetter and an exporter of culture. The tract home, the backyard barbecue, the private swimming pool, the drive-in, the supermarket, the house trailer, the sports car, the suntan, the bare midriff, the get-rich-quick scheme, the get-with-God scheme—all these either originated in, or were converted into a craze by, California.

In the past, these were considered quaint customs brought back from the American frontier. California was out in the provinces; she was absorbed in winning an empire; and she had little of enduring substance to say to the rest of the world.

8

Today California has become big time. The Continental Tilt, as writer Frank McCulloch labeled it, has now tilted so far that California may soon be not the outpost but the wellspring of American culture. So if the Californians are developing a new society—some might call it an antisociety—the effect on the nation may be more than incidental.

Generalizations about California are always risky. For at least five generations it has been in continual change, and the rate of change is, if anything, accelerating. It exhibits a variety of climate, geography, and peoples that is unequaled by any other state (and that make it a true microcosm of the nation). Few statements about California are completely true, or are even approximately true for very long.

But it must also be said that California, through this very change and diversity, is a forcing house of national character. Having left behind the social inhibitions of his old hometown, the Californian is a sort of American in the making. What the American is becoming, the Californian is already. Like the microbe that the scientist has succeeded in isolating, California is a social organism that is unprotected by a screen of custom and conformity. It is a magically honest and sometimes frightening mirror at the other end of the microscope. As one startled newcomer put it, "Every national evil can be studied more clearly here." So, it must be added, can every national good.

CHAPTER II

The Metropolites

1.

"For some obscure reason, most suicides off the Golden Gate bridge jump back toward the city rather than toward the Pacific."

"One of the odd things about suicides from the bridge . . . was that the jumpers always turned their backs toward San Francisco, never faced it."

Arguing over these contradictory quotes from national magazines is beside the point. The main thing is that they epitomized the trauma of present-day San Francisco. It wants to be loved, even by suicides. It is finding out, with great shock, that it is sometimes hated.

Until recently, it could almost be said that San Francisco was everybody's favorite city. The case was well put in the title of a magazine article, "Our National Love Affair with San Francisco." One couple on a round-the-world trip went from Tacoma, Washington, to Tokyo by way of San Francisco. When asked why they detoured so far, they answered, logically, "You can't go around the world without seeing San Francisco." Even its ancient rivalry with Los Angeles vanished after World War II—at least from L.A.'s standpoint.

Says one of my Angeleno friends, "If I could make a living anywhere, I most probably would live in San Francisco." Whenever San Francisco is mentioned, someone is certain to say, dreamily, "Oooh, I love that city."

Maybe this accounts for the reaction that is beginning to appear. Today it has suddenly become chic to knock San Francisco. In 1959, columnist Gene Sherman of the *Los Angeles Times* apparently launched the movement by returning from a trip to the northern city and announcing his disenchantment. "I saw San Francisco falter, like an embarrassed old lady, and I turned away." More recently I encountered the same attitude in another Angeleno. "The last time I was up there," he said, "there was an air of decline about the place." By the 1960's, the onslaught was in full cry. Commented a leading stage actor, "San Francisco spends too much time telling itself how wonderful it is." A young newcomer observed, "Los Angeles may be lunatic, but San Francisco just pretends to be so *satisfied* with itself." Repeating this charge of abnormal narcissism, a national magazine writer concluded, "Contemporary San Francisco is an ingratiating failure." Another referred to the place as "a sort of Disneyland for drunks."

All of this has produced outraged howls from San Franciscans, who, despite their cultivated sophistication and disdain for provincialism, are actually among the greatest local boosters anywhere. But the truth is that San Franciscans themselves are beginning to doubt. In what was once the principal port on the American Pacific, they have watched the decline in shipping as Los Angeles and Seattle took away some of the business, and the embargo on Red China disposed of more. Since San Francisco was built on commerce and finance, rather than manufacturing, this was alarming. Would their beloved city fade quietly away and finally sit on its hillside throne in elegant decay?

But at the same time San Franciscans see evidence of her

essential vitality in the new modern skyscrapers on lower Market Street, the rise of gleaming new apartments in the old Western Addition, the invasion of freeways and parking lots to handle her busy auto traffic. Suddenly they realize that the old landmarks are falling under the demolition rams and power shovels. They see the San Francisco they loved disappearing—or so they think. They are quietly panicked with the thought that they must choose between the past and the future. As Herb Caen, their favorite columnist, sadly put it, "I don't know if we can sustain the myth of San Francisco much longer."

The remarkable thing is that San Franciscans think they need a myth. In most other parts of the world, the inhabitants accept their physical environment as a neutral background for the pursuit of life. In San Francisco, the environment itself has intrinsic value, like some good luck charm. Certainly San Franciscans are among the most active of all Californians in attending to their own personal whims and pleasures, but they also spend considerable time in talking and reading about San Francisco. They never tire of new San Francisco books. They know about the Gold Rush, the Forty-Niners, the Vigilantes, the Barbary Coast, the railroad kings and bonanza kings, the champagne days before the 1906 fire, the fire itself. They have studied the history of Chinatown, the cable cars, the ferries, the two world fairs, the famous hotels. The scrap pile of San Francisco lore has been raked over with a repetition that would be insufferable in any other town. But the San Franciscans will buy every new San Francisco book on the chance that it might turn up some fresh and absolutely fascinating nuggets.

In few other cities of the world—certainly not in Los Angeles or other California towns—are the inhabitants such expert local historians. One gets the impression that most Angelenos think their city has no past—that it suddenly appeared full-blown out of a promoter's dream. Even if it had a past, it holds nothing for them. They came out to enjoy the present and seize the future. As for California history, they will leave that to the San Franciscans, who seem to have a corner on it, anyway.

However, San Franciscans are equally fascinated with the present scene. Their newspapers devote regular space to pure descriptions of local sights and oddities—most of them completely familiar to the reader. Besides seeing them himself, he has read a hundred times about the sea gulls at Ocean Beach, the ducks at Golden Gate Park, and the pigeons in Union Square. But he still delights to read more.

The point is that San Franciscans can't seem to get enough about their public environment—what everyone can see, hear, smell, and taste about San Francisco. There is not much interest in—at least there is not much written about—private lives in San Francisco. One wonders what is going on inside those white houses and apartments sprawling over the hills, and what it might have to do with the outward face of the city. It is almost as though San Franciscans have, or want to have, a corporate consciousness and a corporate memory. The things that happen around town are almost a personal experience to each of them, and they can remember all the way back to the Gold Rush.

Whether the San Franciscan's image of his city is more mythical than real is beside the point. He has it and cultivates it to a far greater degree than most other people. It is difficult to think of a city (perhaps Copenhagen or Vienna) where the inhabitant has such emotional identification with his physical environment, as though it were a part of his personality.

Why does San Francisco have this effect on its inhabitants?

To venture an analysis, one must begin with the setting. Surrounded by bay and hills, uptilted to afford a better view, San Francisco exposes its whole self to the newcomer with

13

a splendor that might only find comparison among some cities of the Mediterranean.

But beside its unabashed beauty, there is something elusive and unbelievable about its locale. Here it is, the nation's traditional jumping-off place to the Orient, yet it faces back upon the continent. It is, as the old saying goes and as the transcontinental railroad builders discovered, on the wrong side of the bay. Oakland should, by the logic of commerce, be the metropolis. It is far easier for vessels to sail a little farther to the East Bay than for railroaders to skirt around its long southern arm and up the peninsula.

Then there are the San Francisco hills. Probably no city of comparable size in the world so blithely combats the law of gravity. Not just the buildings, but the steep earth itself, make this a three-dimensional city and impart an exhilarating sense of physical freedom.

This is, in short, an improbable place for a city. It is not the inexorable laws of trade, but chance, that put San Francisco just here. And so there is a feeling that San Francisco, unlike most other cities, is not born of the marketplace alone. Somehow, in this gracious and delightfully unsensible setting, it may be mainly a city for living.

The very wonder of San Francisco, therefore, tends to remove the layers of practicality that have formed over one's soul and to release one's youthful fancies. Conjured once again is the sense of exploration, adventure, intrigue. Man's natural capacity to romanticize his life, if given half the chance, gets a whole chance in the narrow streets, long shadows, creeping fog, and above all the strange, three-dimensional world of San Francisco. One can believe the old tales of gold miners on a spree, sea captains shanghaiing their crews, the secret tunnels and iniquitous dens of Chinatown, the conspiracies of the Nob Hill nabobs. One can also believe that around the next corner or in the next booth waits another chapter in one's private *Arabian Nights*.

14

Thus, the image of San Francisco, be it myth or fact, keeps one's life from being ordinary. The monotony that the Angeleno breaks by fun in the sun, the San Franciscan breaks by participating in a grand and permanent adventure. Having made his environment into a legend, he then becomes a part of the environment and of the legend.

For years this legend has also been a siren call for thousands of young Easterners with an overly romantic view of their lives. Because San Francisco is no longer growing, it is assumed that all the California newcomers are going to the south. But the bachelor men and girls who live in those hillside apartments eventually get married; when they have children they move out of San Francisco to a tract home down the peninsula or across the bay, making room for more pilgrims to the shrine. Only 42 percent of San Franciscans are even native Californians; most are San Franciscans by choice and therefore by temperament.[1]

Because San Francisco has gathered to itself people who like to identify themselves with their environment, and who have chosen this particular environment, it tends to show more homogeneity, more distinct and recognizable traits among its inhabitants, than most other American cities. While Los Angeles obviously has a big proportion of newcomers, there is a difference. They have been attracted by only part of the environment (the climate), or else by the employment opportunities in a dynamic economy. The average Angeleno loves California but not necessarily Los Angeles; he lives there because that's where the jobs are, and if he could, he would move to a less crowded spot up or down the coast. But the San Franciscan is enchanted with his whole environment. He loves the crazy, mixed-up weather that rolls through the Golden Gate; but he also loves the physical city itself, from the little flower stands on the corners to the gilded elegance of the best hotels. And so there is a kind of

15

harmony between the personality of San Francisco and the personality of its people. The outside appearance is, after all, not very different from the inside.

2.

Such San Francisco characteristics are the more obvious because they are unique in the bay area. With the possible exception of Sausalito, which might be thought of as a tiny fragment of nineteenth-century San Francisco cast across the Golden Gate to preserve something from the fire, the rest of the bay is distinctly un-San Franciscan.

Right after World War II, Gertrude Atherton wrote: "In time, of course, San Francisco will grow down the peninsula; there is plenty of land." In the hectic years since then there has been so much growth down the peninsula that there is, indeed, very little land left. But this is not San Francisco. It has been confined in its place, not only by small city limits and a coincidence of county and municipal boundaries but also by a kind of stubborn identification with locality for its own sake. The opposite Los Angeles attitude, on the other hand, is shown in its remarkable expansion of municipal area. I have seen a Los Angeles city limits sign in one of the tunnels deep inside Hoover Dam, and have heard of one on a wall in Shanghai. But San Francisco is where it is simply because that's where it ought to be. If it is going to grow, it will grow upward.

The cities down the peninsula and across the bay are therefore not part of any "Greater San Francisco" in the sense that Pasadena and Santa Monica are part of "Greater Los Angeles," or Chula Vista and El Cajon are part of "Greater San Diego." They are not suburbs, but separate parts of the bay area. San Francisco is another part, and bay people all the way down to San Jose (population about 200,000) call it "the city." (In fact, I have heard San Francisco called "the

16

city" so far south that the uninitiated would assume that it meant Los Angeles.)

Most bay people have an attachment for San Francisco that is second only to that of the San Franciscans themselves. Many of them once lived in the city and many more work there (about one-third of the working people in San Mateo and Marin counties commute daily to jobs in San Francisco). Some of them even admit that if it weren't for their desire to provide play room for the children, they would rather live in San Francisco. Bay people look to San Francisco as their entertainment center, and if one is going out on the town the question is whether one will go to San Francisco or settle for an ordinary evening. Although there are outstanding intellectual strongholds around the campuses at Berkeley and Stanford, and also such worthy cross-bay institutions as the Oakland Art Museum, San Francisco remains the region's cultural vortex. Even society life in such fashionable communities as Atherton, Hillsborough, and Piedmont has a tenuous but essential tie with San Francisco as the source of its wealth and its cultural sophistication. In short, all bay people share with San Franciscans an affirmative identification with the city that is only blurred in proportion to their distance from it.

But beyond this somewhat vague frame of reference, the bay people outside San Francisco live in separate worlds.

As a settled locality, the East Bay is almost as old as San Francisco, but scarcely shares the same tradition. More than once Oakland has been chosen for various studies because it was known as the "average American city." Since World War II, it has lost population and has suffered some of the social blight that has characterized many other and usually larger American cities. Oakland is coming out of an apparent decline through energetic city administration, and the chief complaint is not that redevelopment is changing

17

the city's character (which merited some change) but that it was delayed so long.

As for the North Bay, it has always been more rural than urban; since World War II, only isolated fragments have become suburban. Due to the improvement of highways, the lovely Sonoma Valley (and to a lesser extent, Napa Valley) has been invaded by many of San Francisco's young marrieds. After all, what could be more chic than commuting in a sports car from the wine country?

Exquisite Marin County—to the San Franciscan always a kind of gentle frontier beyond the Golden Gate—nearly doubled in population during the 1950's, but it still has less than 150,000 people. Nowhere has an entire county more consistently fought to preserve its natural beauty and rustic simplicity. Marin is still a reluctant neighbor in the growing bay complex, and many of its commuters are grudging daytime San Franciscans. The Marin dweller identifies himself not so much with his particular residential community, whose very existence is a compromise with necessity, but with the captivating countryside of rolling slopes, scattered oaks, and fractured shorelines. He is one of the very few people anywhere who, when asked where he lives, will simply give the name of his county.

In the rest of the bay, the contrast with San Francisco takes on the added dimension of growth. South of Oakland and on the lower peninsula, the postwar boom has been at least as intense as Southern California's. Defense companies have contributed an economic base with new missile and electronic plants, which have brought with them their Los Angeles staffs (and the Los Angeles viewpoint). At the south end of the bay, Santa Clara County already has as many people as San Francisco.

Indeed, though its inhabitants might resist the comparison, one could well say that the lower peninsula has almost become a transplanted segment of Southern California. Here

18

are the familiar tracts bulging with children, homes filled with labor-saving gadgets, garages occupied by two cars and a power mower, backyards equipped with portable barbecue, flagstone patio, and often a swimming pool. On weekdays, those who commute to San Francisco on the Bayshore Highway are sitting in their cars with the same impassive expressions as those seen on the freeways of Los Angeles. At the office they carry on the same liar's contest on how quickly they make it in; those driving in from the upper peninsula even insist "you can get into San Francisco faster than you would if you lived in the city." On weekends, the freeways as well as the back roads are jammed with the same cars filled with families and an assortment of equipment, including skis, golf bags, motor scooters, swimfins, and paddleboards.

Like the Southern Californians, the lower peninsula people are mostly from somewhere else—a potpourri of Americans who have left their roots behind. Seventy percent of the homeowners have lived at their present address less than ten years, and 60 percent of the renters less than one year. Most of them are driven by the desire to move up into something like the "Executive Homes" advertised in a "prestige neighborhood" near San Mateo, or the "Junior Executive Homes" farther down near San Jose. In the process, they want to get "west of Camino" and eventually "in the hills." Those in the middle peninsula communities of Palo Alto, Woodside, and Los Altos look with some condescension on such "further down" communities as Sunnyvale and Santa Clara.

It is this massive flow of suburbia from the south, more than the vertical thrust of sterile San Francisco skyscrapers, that threatens to alter the character of the city itself. One new community apartment already exploits its Nob Hill address as "one of the most desirable and important in San Francisco," and sure to impart "solid prestige." It is not the new apartments, but the suburban mentality to which their developers frankly appeal, that can undermine the "old" San Francisco. Formidable indeed are the estimates that the peninsula population south of San Francisco will be between two and three million by 1980—shifting the whole social epicenter southward as that of Los Angeles has been shifted westward. Far from San Francisco growing down the peninsula, the stronger possibility is that the peninsula—or at least its philosophy—will some day overwhelm San Francisco.

All this is not yet apparent to the true San Franciscan, who lives in the city and has little reason or desire to look over the edge of the San Bruno Hills and discover the invading host. Instead, he is concerned with the obvious signs about him. He sees his magic environment fading before an onslaught of freeways, parking lots, and clinical skyscrapers, and he feels a twinge of panic. The San Francisco he clings to is the San Francisco of fable and intrigue, of startling contrast between the sublime and the sinister. The antiseptic surfaces of the new San Francisco seem to offer no crevice for the imagination. And the San Franciscan fears to find himself without his protective jungle, exposed as a chameleon that has lost its color.

Here, it would seem, is the root of the San Franciscan's peculiar ambivalence, or rather indecision, between the new and the old. Often, the San Franciscan who complains of the lethargy and backwardness at city hall is the same one who protests when the old landmarks are cleared for redevelopment. Without the old, he can see San Francisco's unique character sliding into the bay. But without the new, he fears that its quaintness may become the quaintness of decline.

The fact is that the San Franciscan, despite his claims to cosmopolitan sophistication, is militantly local in his loyalties. The quickest way to arouse a San Franciscan is to claim that his city is now second to Los Angeles as the cultural and gastronomical capital of the West. The San Franciscan, unlike other Californians, is supposed to be civilized enough to disdain quantity in favor of quality. Yet he will not hesitate to remind you that the Golden Gate bridge and the Oakland Bay bridge are the biggest of their types in the world; Chinatown is the biggest outside of the Orient; the city hall is higher than the capitol dome in Washington. As for California life outside San Francisco, he believes there is little worth having except perhaps a summer weekend at Monterey Bay or a winter ski outing at Squaw Valley. Even though San Francisco is more Eastern in flavor than most other Western cities, San Franciscans never tire of repeating —and believing—the quotation from O. Henry: "East is East and West is—San Francisco." Pursuing this theme, the *San Francisco Chronicle* coolly advertises, "The *Chronicle* Means the West." As a priceless twist on the tourist's cliché that Sausalito is "like a Mediterranean fishing village," the *Chronicle* travel section ran a short piece on the Greek city of Mykonos entitled "An Aegean Sausalito."

And so the San Franciscan's sentimentality does not blind him to the brassier superlatives. When the 1960 census revealed that San Francisco had lost 10,000 residents in ten years, a crisis atmosphere seized the city. Angrily, San Francisco demanded a recount. Everyone was exhorted, by loudspeakers at public events, by notices which school children carried home to their parents, to step forward and be counted. When the returns were in once again, San Francisco was found to have actually lost 60,000—a major embarrassment in a state that had gained 5,000,000. Mayor George Christopher was so rattled that he asked news photographers to wait until he had composed himself before snapping his picture. One Southern Californian, who was unlucky enough to be in San Francisco, later commented, "It was really no place for an Angeleno to be at the time."

Clearly, the San Franciscan will not, in the long run, clutch blindly to the past while his city becomes the world's most picturesque mausoleum. He will recognize that the new, though it smacks of Los Angeles and all that is crass and insubstantial, still has something to do with the vitality, energy, and plain verve that is also San Francisco. For whoever seeks adventure is a doer and a mover. He cannot see himself as a party to decay.

3.

All of which serves to explain some of the apparent paradoxes in the San Francisco character.

On the one hand, the San Franciscan tends to be fun-loving, extroverted, frankly attracted to pleasure. Not only the tourists and sailors, but the San Franciscans themselves, make every Saturday night a New Year's Eve. On New Year's Eve itself, beginning about 11 P.M., Market Street from Third to Eighth is barred to autos and reserved, as a newspaper story put it, for "revelers who can walk." In the quieter home parties on the big night, as one cultured hostess explained, "We serve fifths of champagne during the evening ... then open the jeroboam at midnight. . . ."

San Franciscans, in fact, have a liberal attitude toward drinking that is apparently handed down from the Gold Rush and reflects the town's prided reputation for lusty Western hospitality and big spending. Unlike other California towns, San Francisco places no social stigma on drinking as such. San Francisco socialites go to the ball game, according to one news report, with hampers of fried chicken and jugs of martinis. Photos of partying people with drinks in their hands are common in the society pages of San Francisco newspapers, but not the Los Angeles papers. This interesting difference in attitude was captured in a San Francisco society-page photo of three people at a party; two of them held drinks, and the one without a drink was from Pasadena.

22

There is, moreover, a more sophisticated attitude toward sex and the marital ties. Not that San Francisco is more wicked than other California towns, but there is a somewhat mellower approach to the boy-girl relationship. San Francisco has more than its share of young secretaries and sales-girls who came to the Coast for fun, adventure, and a husband. It also has plenty of hawk-eyed young bachelors among the accountants, lawyers, and brokers in the financial district. One of the socially acceptable ways for members of these two irresistible forces to meet each other is the pickup in a fashionable bar. There is little or no stigma attached to this if done in good taste, and the only people who are indignant are the B-girls who don't like amateur competition.

There are not, in fact, many cities in which infidelity is an occasional item of interest in the social columns. The "who's going with whom" emphasis is a little like that in the high school gossip column, except that the people are married (not to each other), and the identities are only hinted at. And while in Los Angeles, the social pages are usually careful to picture married couples together, this is almost never done in the San Francisco papers. Instead, people are shown dancing cheek-to-cheek, twisting, or drinking it up with other people's spouses. On a typical "Woman's World" page in the *Chronicle*, three out of four pictures were of mixed couples, and while the fourth showed a married pair, the caption took the curse of provincialism off the scene by explaining that they were estranged.

In addition, San Franciscans seem to regard vice, not as an absolute evil, but as a sort of safety valve, which, kept in its place, has a useful social function. Though the pattern varies, it may be said that burlesque and striptease acts in San Francisco are from time to time more daring (some-times downright vulgar) than in other American cities. One of my surprises while going to college in the bay area was the way burlesque shows were attended, not only by curious teenagers and lascivious old men, but also by San Francisco couples out on a date. The B-girl racket, complete with colored-water drinks for the little lady, flourishes with apparent impunity. As for prostitution, San Franciscans accept the philosophy that you can't stop it, you can just try to control it. The police make their raids and places are from time to time closed up. But almost any cop knows of places that, for the moment, aren't molested.

In fact, San Franciscans seem to regard the institution with a certain fascination, perhaps as a living connection with the old Barbary Coast. Just before the last war, several teen-age sons of some of San Francisco's leading families were caught by police in a famous bordello. At the time a friend of mine (a San Francisco native) explained that they were probably not paying customers but were hanging around out of curiosity and a sense of adventure. Dropping in at a call house was, he said, "just something to do after a show."

In short, compared to other Californians, San Franciscans tend to regard the weaknesses of the flesh as a natural part of the whole man. They have not made vice a virtue, but they have a broader interpretation of good, clean fun. One can do more things and feel less compunction and social disapproval in San Francisco than in almost any other American city.

This may also explain the San Franciscan's attitude toward the police. Contrary to most other Californians, who tend to think of a policeman as an opponent, San Franciscans call him by his first name and regard him as a sort of relative in uniform. This is apparently because he is not really out to arrest anybody, but is more like a citified constable who is trying to keep the place looking respectable.

Unfortunately, San Francisco's approach to the good life has its corollary in some seamy statistics. In alcoholism, suicide, divorce, homosexuality—most of the accepted barometers of social health—San Francisco often shows the highest incidence of any American city. Particularly in alcoholism and suicide, its supremacy is unchallenged.

For several years San Francisco has had the highest per capita alcohol consumption of any U.S. city, and more than 2.5 times higher than the rest of California.[2] Certainly this kind of statistic is inflated by the sailor trade and the convention trade; a lot of drinks going down the throats of tourists are being chalked up to residents. But other figures are not so easily dismissed. Every day an average of one person drinks himself to death in San Francisco. Approximately one person in six is in the "problem drinker" category.

It has been claimed that the suicide numbers are also padded by outsiders who are attracted by the Golden Gate bridge as a dramatic mode of exit. One enterprising suicide flew up from San Diego just to jump off the bridge. The jumping rate is, in fact, nearly one per month, and it is a measure of San Francisco tolerance that little has ever been done to halt the process. It is even said that some San Franciscans get up pools on the day and hour of the next jump.

Yet the bridge is by no means the main mode of departure. Jumping from high places is used by only 16 percent of San Francisco suicides, and in one typical year only about one-third of these used the bridge. It is hardly credible, then, that the San Francisco suicide rate is boosted appreciably by tourists. The annual rate is, in fact, remarkably high— approximately 25 per 100,000 of population, as compared to a national average of 10 per 100,000, and 16.4 in Miami, the next highest city.[3]

Are these sordid statistics on alcoholism and suicide related to San Francisco's generally breezy attitude toward sin? Certainly when the moral threshold is lowered for drinking or any vice, intemperance gains respectability. At least it can go longer without being recognized as a problem.

But there is a more subtle explanation for San Francisco's

share of inebriates. As one resident put it, "The alcoholics are the ones who came to San Francisco in pursuit of some wild dream of their own, couldn't make the grade, and took to drinking." The key point here is that they sought their dream in the city of San Francisco, which is hardly the most likely American city in which to seek one's fortune. But the San Francisco dream is not that prosaic. It is, rather, a more elementary, mystical, and childlike fantasy of adventure in far-off places. It is not San Francisco's fault that the dream never really comes true; it is the dreamers' fault for being so immature in the first place. Some of them grow up, others leave town, cursing it as a phony; still others, for whom San Francisco is the last resort in the dream-quest, become a statistic.

Yet even the dream theory is not the ultimate explanation. Still more basic is the San Franciscan's affirmative zest for life. He has fewer fears, inhibitions, or misgivings to hold him back. Committing himself farther, he risks more. And some of those who are hurt badly enough will take it hard. Even this is not necessarily a reproach to San Francisco. For, as the San Franciscan apparently believes, he who is only half living is already half dead.

Remarkably enough, while showing an ample capacity for personal indulgence, San Franciscans also show an intellectual awareness, a social concern, and an aesthetic sensitivity that are almost European. Traditionally priding itself as the cultural capital of the West, San Francisco has patronized every art form and invented new ones of its own. This interest has been neither superficial nor uncomprehending. That San Franciscans generally have good taste is revealed in their flare for interior decoration, and in the quality of art objects marketed in their stores and displayed in their homes. Standing at a gateway for the Far East trade, San Franciscans have always brought to their homes the most exquisite examples of Oriental craftsmanship, and no matter how monotonous the exterior of their apartments, they have made a showplace of the interiors. What the garden is to the Southern Californian, the inside decoration is to the San Franciscan.

Moreover, San Francisco's approach to the arts has generally been fresh and innovative. In the visual arts, it evokes talent that is experimental, courageous, and in many cases so unaffected by contemporary trends as to be both distinctive and distinctively Californian. In a time when poetry has lost much of its market and hence much of its influence, the bay area continues to produce poets of quality and stature. It has been and still is one of the boiling pots of social protest; such protest has found new media in the nightclub comic's monologue and the beatnik's conspicuous nonconformity. For it was in San Francisco that the "shock tactic" and "sick humor" monologists first found responsive audiences that were both acutely informed and socially sensitive; and it was in San Francisco that the Beat Generation found a climate relatively uncensored by moral and ideological pressure.

In other words, the San Franciscan tends to be more aware than most Californians of the social and political conflicts of his time. It could be argued that he simply wants to be intellectually "hip," and that his main concern is not to be considered narrow or provincial. He has been accused of being a phony egghead—"glib in the patois of the intellectual but less dedicated to his truths than to his technique."

Probably San Francisco has its share of cocktail-party intellectuals who keep up with literature by reading book reviews, who will rave indiscriminately over every piece of abstract art, and who can respond as expected to every catchword by means of a kind of cerebral card file. But this diagnosis fails to account for the average San Franciscan's essential empathy with life about him, including a degree of human understanding that is more intuitive than acquired.

His mental penetration may not be so deep, but what can sympathy gain from logic?

4.

Turning to another extreme, the San Franciscan may be said to be a dedicated conformist in matters of dress and other marks of social grace. It has become commonplace to note that San Francisco men and women are well dressed in the Eastern sense. But they also tend to be devoted to the amenities and courtesies of life that are summed up in the term "etiquette." They know, for example, what wines to serve when and at what temperature.

All this is not because San Franciscans are more formal than Southern Californians, but because they put more emphasis on style. There is a dash of the boulevardier in the average San Francisco male, and of studied sophistication in the typical female. They both have a self-conscious pride in savoir-faire, whose first ingredient is conformity.

Yet except for such social conventions, your San Franciscan is more uninhibited, unpredictable, and plain nonconformist than your average Southern Californian. Despite San Francisco's frightening traffic, San Franciscans jaywalk without any warning, making their city a pedestrian's town and keeping its transportation pattern in wondrous confusion. One San Francisco nightclub specializing in the striptease offers amateur nights, which are seized upon by housewives and other nonprofessionals as an opportunity to peel off in public. Strangers talk to each other in public places without a second thought, apparently sharing some mysterious rapport that is unaccountable to the out-of-towner. Says one observer, "A ride in a cable car is not merely transportation, it is like a trip in a mobile public forum."

Indeed, nowhere outside the British Isles is there such a sense of family in so large a population—as though all were descended from mutual and not-too-distant ancestors. The newcomer tends to fall into this easygoing life quickly and thoroughly—a sort of galvanized San Franciscan who is almost indistinguishable from the original. But native or adopted, San Franciscans seem to draw from their city's wonderful improbability a certain release from inhibition.

A few other paradoxes are too provocative to overlook. On the one hand, the San Franciscan has a taste for rich things, an enjoyment of opulent surroundings, and a flare for living in what he likes to call "the grand manner." While high society in other cities is usually inclined to shun an overdisplay of wealth as frightfully bourgeois, San Francisco socialites are said to spread the most elegant tables and generally to make no apology for ostentation. San Franciscans, in fact, seem to accept social stratification as a part of life and are proud of San Francisco's wealthy families as bona fide exhibits of their city's gilded tradition. In Los Angeles, and indeed, most other large American cities, social standing has come to be identified with activity in cultural and charitable causes. While this is true to some degree of San Francisco, it also recognizes a social elite that is based simply on money.

Such frank delight in lavish consumption is, perhaps, a heritage of the earliest days when California miners descended each year from the mountains with their accumulated gold dust to winter in San Francisco's sumptuous luxuries. Probably it finds antecedents in the flamboyant tastes of the grocers and bartenders who achieved sudden wealth during the reckless exploitation of California and Nevada resources in the late nineteenth century. In fact, it might be said that San Franciscans, in their values and sensibilities if not in moral stricture, are Victorians at heart.

On the other hand, San Franciscans have a distaste for pure materialism. As Gertrude Atherton put it, "Money has never been all in San Francisco." Blatant commercialism is apparent in the cheap establishments on Market Street, the midway atmosphere of Fisherman's Wharf, and a number of "tourist trap" nightclubs. But these are no more San Francisco than Hollywood Boulevard is Los Angeles. One cannot avoid contrasting Ocean Beach, where the waves and the shore can be seen from the highway for miles at a stretch, with Los Angeles County's shoreline, which except for one section is hidden from view by rows of shacks that are a monument to promotional greed. Said a struggling novelist of San Francisco, "It is the best town in the world to be poor in—there are so many things to do that are free." Whether justified or not, the San Franciscan's chief complaint about Los Angeles is, as one Sausalito artist observed, "I think it is a town with a lot of phonies. . . . Down there I get the feeling all everybody wants is money."

Finally, it may be said that San Franciscans profess, and actually display, considerable tolerance and openmindedness. They generally take a mellow attitude toward offbeat ideas, and consider fanatical argumentation as immature. They are inclined to judge people less by their beliefs than their behavior, and in behavior there is plenty of latitude. In politics San Franciscans tend to distrust dogmatism in themselves and others. Dr. Fred Schwartz's Christian Anti-Communist Crusade, which makes its headquarters in Long Beach, finds an enthusiastic following in Southern California. But in carrying his crusade to the north his bay-area rally was poorly attended, and even received some public opposition from a large group of clergymen. When Khrushchev visited the United States, he got a chilly reception in Los Angeles, while San Francisco's welcome was effusive (to many observers, nauseating).

Such behavior has nothing to do with the political opinions of San Franciscans. They are simply too human to be stiff-necked over anything.

Despite all this, and despite San Francisco's reputation for cosmopolitanism, San Franciscans have not been especially progressive in social acceptance of minorities. True, more than in almost any American city, Jews have traditionally played a significant and respected role in San Francisco society. But though proud of their Chinatown, the San Franciscans still maintained strict racial covenants for many years in nearby property deeds, thus contributing to the appallingly crowded conditions in the prescribed Chinese ghetto. Since the Supreme Court ruling against such covenants in 1948, they have continued to maintain informal but nevertheless effective neighborhood segregation, both of Chinatown and of the Negro enclaves in the Mission and Fillmore districts.

Since the last war, in fact, the San Francisco Bay region has been the object of some of the nation's most unfavorable publicity in race relations. It was here that the star ballplayer, Willie Mays, was initially denied a home in a neighborhood of his choice. Most shameful of all such episodes outside the South was the case of Sing Sheng, a Chinese who tried to buy a home for his family in south San Francisco in 1952. When neighborhood opposition developed in the form of frenzied meetings and threatening telephone calls, Sheng showed enough faith in American fair play to suggest a community vote on the question. But the Shengs were rejected 174 to 28.

It is by no means clear that this particular neighborhood stands alone in bigotry. A survey made in Berkeley by the Japanese-American Citizens' League showed that approximately 75 percent of apartments were closed to nonwhite tenants; another in San Francisco indicated that one-third of rentals were barred to Orientals and two-thirds to Negroes.[4] It was, pointedly, a San Francisco case of housing discrimination that brought forth a State Supreme Court ruling in 1962 that enforced California fair housing legislation previously considered ineffectual. Reports the director of one antidiscrimination group, "We believe there is more racial segregation here than at any time in our history."

Nor does the bay region's record in fair employment offer much room for pride. A thorough study completed in 1956 showed that, although 74 percent of employers claimed to be nondiscriminatory, most of them employed no Negroes.[5] Moreover, some unions "practiced differential treatment in job referrals and assignments and tended to leave their non-white members in lower-graded categories." One young Negro professional man summed it up nicely. "San Francisco is funny; on the one hand I have found good acceptance on a social level. But when I looked for a job and a place to live, I ran head on into prejudice and discrimination."

In fairness it should be recognized that San Francisco was forward-looking enough to institute a fair employment ordinance in 1957—something that Los Angeles and most other California cities have never done. In fact, it may be said that since the late 1950's there has been notable progress in bay-area civil rights. Some companies and unions have implemented active programs against job discrimination. The San Francisco Realty Board has admitted a number of Negro members and appears to be the only integrated metropolitan realty board in the country. While racial exclusion is very strong down the peninsula, the San Jose Realty Board has taken the almost unheard-of step of going on record against discrimination. One large-scale bay-area developer, Joseph L. Eichler, is noted for his successful policy of nondiscriminatory home sales.

The changing climate has been particularly felt by Chinese and Japanese, who are more and more able to find jobs above menial or service positions. It is worth noting that stories and photographs of Chinese marriages are not uncommon on the society pages of San Francisco newspapers. It may be said, too, that it is easier for Chinese and Japanese than for Negroes to buy homes where they choose in the bay area.

Whether for good or bad from their own standpoint, second- and third-generation Orientals are, in the words of one observer, "up to their necks in Americanization." Many Chinese and Japanese employed in Chinatown live in another part of the bay, drive sports cars bought on time payments, and exhibit almost every other American characteristic in dress, cultural interests, values, and customs. Some of them, particularly among students and young intellectuals, are happily experiencing complete social acceptance. In short, there is a strong beginning for the genuine cosmopolitanism that up till now has been little more than a San Francisco myth.

6.

Granted, then, that San Franciscans exhibit a myriad of personality contradictions. They are fun-loving yet aesthetically sensitive and socially concerned; conformist in custom, nonconformist in behavior; impressed with wealth, yet scornful of materialism; broadminded and tolerant, yet comparatively indifferent to racial injustice. Are these paradoxes reconcilable in any reasonable composite, or are there two or more separate San Franciscos?

The answer, it seems, is that the San Franciscan is completely human. He has desires, and he also has a conscience. He likes comfort but hates pretense. He would abhor being thought a hick, but he will risk being called a ham. He is a whole man, with the whole man's vices and virtues, instincts and ideals, meanness and nobility. Life is for living, and the same person can feel, think, cry, laugh, and love.

And so if the San Franciscan is genuinely more tolerant than most Californians, this is chiefly because he instinctively regards issues, crusades, and rallying cries as transient phenomena. Such a many-dimensioned personality cannot really channel the necessary time, energy or singleminded interest into the solution of serious public problems. The well-rounded man is most at home in the well-rounded society; deep social issues tend to demand more attention than the San Franciscan is willing to commit. He may take pride in his forward-looking concern, but he seems to feel that his responsibility is discharged by contributing to public opinion. Even in San Francisco's avant-garde intellectualism, as a British observer wrote of the "sick humorists," "There is the danger that tough frankness can become a cannibalistic indulgence, a charade of atonement and a substitute for action . . ."

This is the key point, then, that qualifies the San Franciscan as a modern Californian, first class. For although he is emotionally committed to the community, it is an unresponsible commitment in which the expected benefit is all one way. The San Franciscan embraces his city because of what it does for him. It offers just the instrument on which to play his lusty song of life. It does not really occur to him that he is part of a society that demands something. He is aware of the principle of self-government in an intellectual way, but like the European, he is more aware of other and older human values. He will, in short, accept his environment if it suits him. San Francisco suits him because it appeals to the whole-souled zest and sense of excitement with which he approaches life. Little wonder, then, that while he panics at the gradual alteration of *his* San Francisco, he is frustratingly helpless by training and temperament to do much about it.

CHAPTER III

The Sun Worshipers

1.

In 1874, a Los Angeles stage driver reported on the progress of a new suburban community.

"When I drove out in the morning," he said, "there was nothing there. When I went out in the afternoon they had a house up and selling whiskey in it—which I think is tol'able good."

This is really the story of Southern Calfornia ever since— not about the whiskey, but the house. Change is normal and headlong. You cannot talk about what Southern California is—only what it is becoming. It will not sit still for its portrait.

In the stage driver's day, Southern California had about twenty thousand people. But all this was changed by climate, railroads, the chamber of commerce, oranges, oil, the chamber of commerce, movies, airplanes, and the chamber of commerce. Today Southern California has approximately ten million people, and is adding another thousand every day. To keep up with this growth, most large Southern California cities require new telephone books every few months, and there is nothing more worthless than last year's phone book.

San Francisco—and even San Francisco Bay—may be said

to have a certain identifiable character. Southern California will, almost overnight, jump out of any character that someone tries to give it. Los Angeles used to have a hick-town spirit of the sort that drove Sinclair Lewis to write *Main Street*. Today it is becoming big town, with every example of sophistication that goes with it. San Diego used to be a modest city that had been shunted off the main California highway, content with the navy in its harbor and its face in the sun. It looked like Davenport, Iowa, with sailors. Today it is heading for a skyscraper look, and its people toward the harassed, furtive look of the big-city commuter.

Up and down the coast and inland along what was once called the Orange Belt, smaller cities that had separate (and insular) identities have been engulfed by a flood of people and tract homes. During the 1950's, Orange County grew in population by 226 percent and changed completely from a rural to a suburban character. Beverly Hills, Santa Monica, La Jolla, and other quiet residential communities are fighting a rearguard action to preserve privacy against a tide of outside traffic. Pasadena, once the pinnacle of comfort and respectability, is battling the blight of smog from millions of other people's automobiles.

The old saw that Los Angeles is a collection of suburbs in search of a city is no longer valid. It is a collection of cities that have grown together to make one big metropolis. Until recently this was a two-dimensional city—that is, the surplus of flat land made it unnecessary to build skyward. Los Angeles became the prime example of what William H. Whyte has called "urban sprawl." As Wilfred Owen put it in *Cities in the Motor Age,* "In Southern California the only two things that keep us from completely filling in the open spaces are golf courses and military reservations." This broad, thin slice of megalopolis has escaped from the "human filing cabinet" concept, but it has its own deficiencies. It lacks order, cohesion, manageability. The individual is trapped in a two-dimensional world without wings. The frustration in trying to drive anywhere to do anything is the chief blight upon Southern California life. As one newcomer said, "To be a successful city, Los Angeles needs to get smaller, not bigger."

But the city's greatest problem is not its peculiar shape—rather, the failure to recognize this uniqueness and make the most of it. For it is impossible to put Los Angeles into the conventional concept of a city—that is, a large industrial and commercial nucleus surrounded by residential suburbs. Its traditional nucleus is surprisingly small. Except for half-a-dozen impressive new buildings, downtown Los Angeles looks about like Portland, Oregon; yet it is supposed to be the nucleus for a metropolis of 7,000,000 people. Its planners still regard it in this traditional sense, as witness the convergence of nearly all freeways into the downtown area (no matter where you want to go, you usually have to drive through central Los Angeles).

But in fact this has long been something other than a nuclear city. It is instead a suburban ocean with islands of business centers. Most of the larger centers are self-sufficient communities with their own business, financial, cultural, and even governmental structure. Within this grand compass, Los Angeles has all the attributes of a great city; it just happens to have them in two dimensions rather than three, as though its whole entity was a mass of water seeking its own level.

Nor is it true any longer to say that Los Angeles lacks the cuisine, the culture, the metropolitan polish of San Francisco, Chicago, or New York. Partly due to continued prosperity, partly to its status as a resort and convention center, and partly to a general maturing process, Los Angeles has developed a cuisine equal to that of any American city. It is also showing a new cultural interest; its great lack—proper display facilities—is being solved with the construction of an art museum and a music center of metropolitan stature. And

37

as for general sophistication—if this is a desirable attribute—sections of Wilshire Boulevard display an architectural splendor and a smartness of personal dress that will compare with any city in the world.

The difference is that in Los Angeles you have to search for these things. They are not stacked neatly in one place. Because of the inconvenience of urban sprawl, the newcomer takes longer to discover such things—to "learn the city"—than in almost any other metropolis. And so the out-of-town reporter who drops in for a few weeks tends to write an article on the barbarity of Los Angeles. Indeed, it has traditionally been as chic to knock Los Angeles as it has been to praise San Francisco. One San Franciscan woman left a will specifying that she be buried "anyplace but L.A." Even the *New York Times* editorializes, "If dreams counted for anything, we wish we could be more like San Francisco and less like Los Angeles." Yet it is to Los Angeles that the people keep coming—proving that it is possible to be popular without being loved, or even respected.

2.

Los Angeles is only the most conspicuous example of Southern California's change. The relentless advance of population continues to be Southern California's biggest economic and social fact. Not aircraft, not oil, not movies and TV, but the lavalike inpouring of humanity is Southern California's biggest commodity. For it is the constantly renewing demand for more space that raises the price of land, and in Southern California the price of land is the hook upon which all else hangs.

Formerly subject to real estate booms and busts that corresponded roughly to national economic conditions, Southern California has, since the last war, enjoyed what might almost be called a permanent boom. With minor fluctuations, the price of land keeps rising; there is no such thing as actual depreciation of real property in Southern California. Its value keeps rising because the value of the lot increases at a faster rate than the physical depreciation of the house. One of the reasons Californians move so often is that there is no financial penalty involved. On the contrary, they can count on making at least some profit, which they will put into the down payment on a better house. The home is, to them, a financial investment and a mode of enforced saving. Prime considerations in building or buying a house are the resale features; the idea is to broaden the appeal to the widest proportion of customers (a two-bedroom, one-bath house is bad from the resale standpoint, since its appeal is limited to small families).

Actually, Southern Californians have become so conscious of real estate values that, as the family expands, they prefer not to build a new room or a new wing, since the house will then be overbuilt for the neighborhood, and they will not get full value for the improvement at the time they might sell. So instead they move to a larger house in a neighborhood of larger homes. In fact, the ideal arrangement from the resale viewpoint is to have the smallest house in the neighborhood.

Along the Southern California coast, houses take on another dimension of value for the income they bring as rentals. Many families in the beach communities rent a room or a wing to vacationers, and sometimes even move temporarily to cheaper rentals so they can let out their houses to summer tourists. One Coronado boy was going to visit his grandmother in Missouri but changed his mind at the airport.

"But you have to go," cried his mother. "We've already rented your room."

Throughout Southern California, real estate consciousness and rising property value tend to force continual change. The appetite for land is so great that slums are generally self-liquidating. That is, when land becomes more valuable than the houses, the area is bought up by a large developer or a public agency and cleared for a new project. At Bunker Hill in downtown Los Angeles, at Ocean Park in Santa Monica, old and blighted communities are being leveled and replaced with some of the most desirable apartments and offices in Southern California. Largely because it was bisected by the prestige boulevards of Wilshire and San Vicente, the run-down community of Westgate is now becoming a modern business center with what is, for a time at least, the highest skyscraper in Los Angeles. At the other extreme, huge private estates developed in an era of lower land and construction costs often become literally too valuable to maintain, and are forced by high taxes into sale and subdivision. Even industry is sometimes engulfed by the demand for living space. Most of the old Twentieth Century-Fox studio near Beverly Hills is being transformed into a massive $500 million apartment, shopping, and hotel center—largest of its kind in the West.

Up and down the coast, the same lust for land is now turning the last of the great California ranchos into resorts, subdivisions, and retirement communities. Biggest by far is the development of the 93,000-acre Irvine Ranch as the largest planned community in California. San Diego is carrying out massive improvements to make Mission Bay the finest individual recreation center in California.

Other established Southern California communities have been altered just as drastically. As the orange trees were hacked down to make way for the tract homes, the citrus-grower was driven into isolated strongholds in Ventura, Riverside, and San Bernardino counties. His retreat marked a social revolution of the first order, for he had typified the prewar Southern California mentality. A classic description of the orange grower was written by historian Robert G. Cleland in his *California in Our Time:*

Those in southern California read the *Los Angeles Times,* or its equivalent (if there is such a paper); regard a high protective tariff as the keystone of American prosperity; send their children to college;

give liberally to churches, charities, and every other good cause; support women's clubs, lectures, and concerts; build and maintain the best schools; look with suspicion upon Wall Street and even upon their Republican brethren among Eastern manufacturers and bankers; show genuine and intelligent concern for the welfare of their employees, but decry labor unions and all forms of farm-labor organizations; regard socialism, communism, and the New Deal as synonymous; and condemn all forms of federal aid to the individual—except when such aid is needed by the citrus industry itself.[1]

Today this is Southern California's vanishing breed. They have sold out to the subdividers and retired to a home or apartment near the coast. They get their exercise puttering around the garden and clipping coupons. Southern California's once dominant citrus industry has shrunk to the point where much of the frozen orange juice carried home by the California housewife bears the Florida label. And in the foothills of the San Gabriels, on the plains stretching across Orange County to the sea, there is entrenched a new breed— the California suburbanite. Butt of a thousand cartoons on commuting, gardening, and barbecuing, this postwar California type is not as ridiculous as he has been painted, but neither is he as staunch as the country gentleman he replaced.

3.

Pure growth—the relentless avalanche of people—is only the most superficial aspect of Southern California's change. Before the war, Los Angeles was perhaps 80 percent Midwest in population origin. It was more Midwestern in character than Chicago, and proved conclusively that a large collection of small towns does not make a big town. Despite the influence of Hollywood, it was the most righteous metropolis in the country, and still retains a circumspect veneer.

Since the last war, however, Los Angeles has undergone a striking shift of personality. The mass of servicemen who passed through on their way to and from the Pacific Theater, plus the other mass of war workers who came out to the aircraft plants, hailed from the whole United States. After the war they stayed or came back, brought their relatives, and told their friends.

No longer Midwestern, Los Angeles today is, as one sociologist says, "the most American city in the United States." By the time people move to California they are at least second-generation Americans, and are not anxious to concentrate in a "Little Italy" or "Little Poland." As one former Chicagoan describes it, "Living in California is like living everywhere." One result is that you can't drop a Californian into a religious or ethnic category simply by the sound of his last name. When a friend of mine named O'Callaghan was in the hospital, a visiting priest making pastoral calls naturally stopped and sat by his bed to talk. Said my friend, "I should tell you, Father, I'm a Congregationalist." If it is possible to distill an American ethos, the laboratory is Southern California.

Enriching this compound is the nation's most diverse representation of minorities. Los Angeles is second only to New York in the size of its Jewish community. It has more people of Mexican descent than any metropolis outside Mexico City, and more Japanese-Americans than any other city in the United States. It also has a sizable representation of Filipinos, Chinese, and American Indians. Since World War I, it has had a growing Negro population, and since World War II, it has received most of a statewide Negro in-migration that has led the nation.

Los Angeles is going through one of the most exciting and momentous labors in United States social history; it is facing up to racial assimilation, and the outcome is by no means certain. The thrust in this movement comes from a new militancy and final loss of patience in a Negro community that, up to the early 1950's, had borne its indignities without much protest.

42

From the mounting number of racial incidents in Los Angeles, one might conclude that it is a hotbed of bigotry. But the real reason is that the Negro is daring to assert his rights more than in most other cities. Trouble is therefore inevitable, and it might be said that in other areas where such incidents are few the Negro is not pushing hard enough.

In a sense, some of the trail has been broken for the Los Angeles Negro by other minorities. It was the Mexican-Americans who took the brunt of the wartime zoot-suit riots that spurred Los Angeles churches, labor unions, and other opinion-molding groups into action against prejudice. It may be said that the basis for the concentration of the Mexican-Americans in east Los Angeles and a few other pockets is first, socioeconomic, and second, discriminatory. The large influx of population from Mexico since 1950 has been chiefly from the regions of low education, low income, and limited skills. While the median number of years in school for all Californians is twelve, the median for the Mexican-Americans is eight.[2] The comparative few who are able to afford more expensive homes in nonminority neighborhoods have generally encountered less resistance than that exhibited toward Negroes. Of ninety-five racial housing incidents recorded by the Urban League between 1950 and 1959, only six concerned Mexican-Americans. Moreover, the situation apparently improved in this period, with no incidents involving Mexican-Americans in the last five years.

Probably more dramatic progress has been made by the Japanese, who have quietly but firmly entered all realms of social and economic activity and made themselves welcome. Not only in Los Angeles but throughout the state, second- and third-generation Japanese have striven so mightily to absorb the American culture that the loss of their uniqueness is bemoaned by sociologists. Complains one white observer, "When I go to the Zenshu temple in San Francisco—what do I see? A sea of white faces." While second-generation Japa-

43

nese (Nisei) can generally speak Japanese as well as English, the third generation (Sansei) usually speak only English; many are almost noncommunicative with their grandparents. One of the latter complained to his son-in-law, "You will some day be learning Japanese from Caucasian teachers." Even some of the first generation (Issei) step boldly across cultural lines. According to one expert, the best tamales in California are made in San Jose at "Bee's Hot Tamale Shop," operated by a seventy-five-year-old Issei lady named Bee Okahara.

For their part, the California Caucasians seem to have been charmed since the last war by the Oriental influence. Since the ranch-style house passed its peak of popularity around 1953, its place has been taken by Hawaiian, Japanese, and Chinese modern architecture. Japanese art, fashion, cuisine, and other cultural aspects have clearly influenced California styles. When a Japanese-owned department store opened on Wilshire Boulevard, it was so crowded on the first day that one friend of mine found herself swept by the mob into one door, through the aisles, and out another door before she could stop.

The fascination with things Oriental has also included Oriental Americans. It is not uncommon for a Japanese couple to be among Caucasians at a Los Angeles party. In the audience of some of the avant-garde little theaters about town, it is not unusual to see a young Caucasian escorting a Japanese girl. The Laguna Beach Country Club has gone out of its way to invite Japanese-Americans to join. So far as neighborhood integration is concerned, Orientals are still excluded from some tracts by a policy of the developers against any minorities. But these cases—a relic of the prewar Los Angeles mentality—are diminishing.

In short, the temper of the Southern California mind today provides a favorable climate for racial integration. There are, to be sure, pockets of violent hatred within the fanatical fringe that still inhabits Los Angeles, and there is a much larger body of plain, dull prejudice. But the circles are widening in which these attitudes are unpopular. Among educated young people, social disapproval of racial bias is so ascendant that the future seems obvious.

It is tempting to agree with the statement of Theodore H. White: "Los Angeles is that city in the United States where the Negro probably receives the most decent treatment and has the best opportunity for decent housing." But while this might be a possibility, it is not a fact. There are, to be sure, a few areas in which some degree of integration is apparent; but the mixed neighborhood is usually in transition between all-white and all-colored occupancy. One Negro columnist in the *Los Angeles Sentinel* is specific. "Los Angeles is three times more segregated than Atlanta and Houston, five times more segregated than New Orleans and ten times more segregated than Memphis." Thus, there is the peculiar situation in which those of Oriental and Mexican extraction are making gains, while the Negro is almost as segregated as ever.

The main reasons for this anomaly are the dominant place of land value in the Southern California economy and the general belief that Negro occupancy depresses land value. The veneration of real estate prices is so widespread that it simply overrides the public conscience. The phenomenon is most noticeable among Caucasians with a social-climbing mentality, who have bought what they believe to be a fashionable address, and who fear that their newly won prestige will be shattered by a Negro neighbor.

Thus, the real estate fraternity is permitted to perpetuate residential segregation. The very growth of Los Angeles and San Diego, creating a state of population flux, has caused real estate agents to tighten their control until, even more than in most American cities, they are what one report calls "the managers of Jim Crow in housing." In San Diego, which is showing considerable improvement in fair employment and other areas except housing, a survey showed that 100 percent of real estate agents would not be a party to locating a Negro family in a white neighborhood. As one tract builder in Tujunga put it, "If you sold to minorities, you'd be ostracized from the business."

The chance of reforms through the local governmental process is slim indeed, since Los Angeles politics are still heavily influenced by propertied groups exhibiting the prewar outlook on race relations. Meanwhile, like most Californians, the minorities have not been sufficiently interested in government processes and are still not asserting all of their growing political strength.

Yet the climate for change was never brighter. As in the South, young Negro students are showing their elders how to force and win issues. They are also drawing successfully on the reservoir of decency, fair play, sympathy for the underdog, and respect for courage that is more native to the American character than bigotry. When a Negro family was excluded by developers from a Monterey Highlands subdivision, young members of the Congress of Racial Equality staged a "sleep-in" at the tract office and won support from white residents in the form of blankets, food, and verbal encouragement. Apparently for the first time, white homeowners were organized more strongly in favor of integration than against it.

Thus, while Los Angeles is in no sense the one city "where the Negro receives the most decent treatment," that opportunity is becoming ripe for the seizing. It could be that Southern California's refreshing heterogeneity will not really stop at the color line.

4.

Still another dimension of population change has been the age level. Up to the last war, Southern California had a disproportion of older folks who came out for their health or to retire. Since the war, chiefly because so many saw California as soldiers or defense workers, the younger people have led this migration. Some large communities have an unusually high proportion of young people. The median age of San Diegans is 27.7 years, as against a national median of 30 years. More than ever, Southern California has an air of youthful exuberance, independence, and impatience.

The jobs these people have stepped into are in manufacturing—aircraft, missiles, electronics, and spacecraft. Factories and laboratories are still sprouting, while the farms, which once made Los Angeles County the first agricultural county in the nation, are disappearing. All of this is changing the socioeconomic color of Southern California. Always known for its wealthy and upper-middle-class residents, Southern California used to exhibit a serious gulf between them and the lower class of unskilled laborers. Today this gap is filled with skilled workers, technicians, young engineers, and a complete range of educational and income levels. Southern California now has a well-rounded society rather than one of isolated segments.

Further, the now-infinite number of segments is thrown together in healthy abandon, as contrasted to the once tight little colonies of film people in Hollywood, oil workers in south Los Angeles, gentlemen farmers in the Orange Belt, retired Navy officers on the San Diego heights and Coronado Island, well-to-do merchants and retired people in Brentwood, Pasadena, and San Marino. Thanks to the FHA and the GI Loan, tract subdivisions threw open all of Southern California to quick settlement on low down payments and easy terms. People landed helter-skelter all over the landscape, regardless of economic orientation. A typical block in a tract development will have two or three breadwinners in defense companies, two or three in television, one in the oil business, one in contracting or the building trades, and one

47

in the automobile business. Their type of work will range from skilled house painter to salesman to engineer.

While Southern Californians have never been especially neighborly, this homogenizing process at least works against class consciousness. Although the stratifying and separating process is commencing all over again, Southern California tract dwellers are still less status conscious than most other Americans at the same economic level. In fact, with most of its people at any one time hailing from somewhere else, all of Southern California has traditionally had little awareness of class. Many arrivals had left home primarily to escape social pressures, and are not interested in renewing them here. The place is so full of newcomers that few people know who it is they're supposed to envy. Nowhere are the social elite more ignored than in Los Angeles, where they must battle against eclipse by the film colony on the one hand and the social ignorance of the public on the other.

Besides, in Southern California there are so few ways in which the elite can enjoy a better life than anyone else. So much that is good in life—the sun, the sea, the mountains—is free to all. In most California homes, the abundance of mechanical servants—from the garbage disposal to the clothes dryer—do more work than a flesh-and-blood servant. Many a working mother employs a day-housekeeper and baby-sitter who is really an untitled governess. And whereas the automobile is a sign of wealth in most countries, nearly all Southern California families have at least one and often two cars; due to the remarkable auto financing system, many employees drive a better car than their bosses.

With so little real difference between the material life of the various income groups, the dedicated status seeker is frustrated in Southern California. Perhaps this is one reason for the appearance here of different and often bizarre symbols that speak of other attributes besides wealth as such.

48

Thus, the sports car, whose acknowledged capital is Southern California, says that its driver is debonair, adventurous, discriminating. When the sports car first appeared in Southern California in the 1940's, it spawned its own fraternity. The countersign was a wave of the arm as you passed one another—not an excited wave, but a slow, deliberate elevation of the arm, which might be mistaken for a right-turn signal, accompanied by a serious expression of face signifying a deep bond of understanding. Nowadays Southern California is so full of sports cars that the wave is only exchanged between drivers of the same make of car. There are at least eighty Southern California clubs for sports-car owners, divided according to make or specialized interest, from cross-country excursions to track racing. Two locally edited magazines, a weekly newspaper, two restaurants, a bookstore, and one or two TV and radio shows all cater to the sports car crowd. Indeed, the sports car infection has spread to Northern California. At the Berkeley campus of the University of California special parking spaces are set aside for sports cars; and it was in Marysville that a sports car suffered the ultimate indignity: a truck ran completely over it, with only slight damage.

The most distinguishing characteristic about the sports car driver is his feeling of superiority over other drivers. To him the big car owner is a hopeless square and a crude displayer of wealth to no good purpose, since everybody knows it's more fun to drive a sports car. When Los Angeles autos began to appear with window stickers saying "Help Stamp Out Sports Cars," the latter blossomed with counter-stickers: "Help Stamp Out Cadillacs."

Equally shunned is the driver of the purely practical foreign car with small engine and low gas mileage. A Triumph-owning friend of mine who sometimes found himself racing with other Triumph drivers on the freeway once asked me, "Are there any penny-ante races between Volkswagens?"

Of course, the foreign-economy-car folks just can't muster enough dignity chugging along in things that look like toys, bugs, or bathyspheres on wheels. Besides, they get themselves in the crudest predicaments. Late one night, the driver of an Isetta, with the lone door opening in the front, pulled up to a wall in a downtown San Diego parking lot. Failing to get the door open against the wall, he tried to back up but the engine wouldn't start. There he sat. It was two-and-a-half hours before someone answered his cries of distress and pulled him back from the wall.

Another conveyor of Southern California status is physical accomplishment, particularly among young people. With every possible recreational facility at hand, Southern California turns out more than its share of champions in every conceivable sport. When I went to high school and college, the boy who didn't go out for any varsity sport was suspected of being unmanly or good-for-nothing. Today the ultimate professionalization of student sports has removed this stigma, but more than ever, outdoor sports from surfing to skiing carry real status overtones and have their own status standards. To be a "snow bunny" (nonskier or beginning skier at a ski resort) is as bad as being a "hodad" (nonsurfer at a surfing beach).

It is not simply that these sports require relatively expensive equipment and therefore signify money status. To attach this outworn yardstick to Southern California's sport consciousness is not to understand it. Physical prowess is actually the main idea. Probably in no adult society outside of primitive cultures is so much status accorded to physical condition and athletic achievement.

Not without reason has Southern California become the world's fashion center (ahead of New York and Paris) for swimsuits, beach attire, and sportswear. In the famed informality of Southern California dress, physical fitness is the underlying ingredient. It is not so much that Californians, with their loud shirts and abbreviated shorts, deliberately choose to look sloppy. They simply must give the impression that they are ready at any time for a round of golf or a jaunt to the beach. In many towns, particularly in San Fernando Valley and the beach communities, businessmen mind their stores in sport shirts. In most of San Fernando Valley, men may be expected to wear a sport shirt and slacks to a summer party, and the one who shows up with coat and tie risks being labeled a square.

In La Jolla, shoppers with overtime on their parking meters were regularly warned by friends on the approach of a policeman; when the city put a plainclothesman on the beat, he was naturally attired in a sport shirt and Bermuda shorts.

In San Bernardino, the city had to order taxi drivers to get some type of uniform. Said the mayor, "As it is now, when a man rolls up in front of your house dressed in a T-shirt you don't know whether he's a cab driver or not."

I have seen men in short-sleeved, open shirts attending church, and on one occasion two barefoot teenage boys clad in nothing but shorts parading through the leading department store in Pasadena. And although California law requires people drawing unemployment checks to be ready for a possible job interview, the lineup at the Department of Employment office in Los Angeles on a summer day has included barefoot men in bathing trunks, women in bare-midriff sunsuits and sandals.

All of this does not mean the California men do not wear suits. But while most managerial and professional men in Southern California cities wear white shirt, tie, and coat to work, most of them do not own a tuxedo or other formal attire. When President Kennedy visited California in 1961, practically all the men attending the major social event honoring him in Los Angeles wore simple dark suits. Hats are, of course, as out of style as garters. In the early 1920's, according to a Long Beach hatter, nine out of ten men wore hats; today only three out of ten wear them, and these are confined chiefly to lawyers, a few doctors, and a scattering of self-conscious baldheads.

There is a slight reversal of the California sportswear tradition in a new trend toward elegance in women's evening styles. This is not of the mink-stole variety; actually, fur coats both artificial and real are so commonplace in Southern California that they have lost their status symbolism. Instead, California women are making a social virtue out of a tasteful and striking overall appearance. And the effect is beginning to rub off on their husbands, who will wear suit and tie to a party, even in the summer, and keep the coat on all evening.

The truth is that California dress is still in a state of confusion. The clash between Midwest propriety and resort-style laxity has left no set rule on dress for any occasion. Before a party, a guest may phone the host or hostess to inquire about dress, will often get no straight answer, and as often will arrive out-of-dress with the other guests.

About the only place where dress convention is strictly observed is in specialized recreations. At the beach you must not wear regular clothes, such as pants, skirts, or shoes. This sort of thing went out with bath houses and trolley excursions. To show up on the beach in your clothes is something like wearing shoes in a mosque; it is a sacrilege against the sun-god. Nor is it acceptable to punch an umbrella in the sand, unless you are one of the old folks. Beach umbrellas went out in the 1930's and are considered an obvious insult to the sun.

Yet while bathing suits are a social requirement, bikinis have never taken hold in California. For one thing, some large cities are located along the coast, including San Diego and Long Beach, usually with a strong Midwest element; if you decided to walk from the beach into one of these cities you could get away with it in a regular swimsuit but not quite in a bikini. The gross difference between the two is an accurate gauge of Southern California manners and morals.

There is, however, nothing confused about the California devotion to physical fitness. Health fads and health-food stores abound. It was in Santa Monica, California, that physical culturist Vic Tanny got his start before exporting muscles all over the world. While Californians didn't invent the beauty contest, they took up the institution early and carried it to its present absurdity. Californians sponsor more than 500 annual beauty and queen contests; every local festival (and every city with an ounce of promotional spirit has one) must have its reigning queen. In addition, every industry, profession, and special interest must have its yearly Miss—everything from Miss Tramp Steamer to Miss Correct Posture to Miss Muffin. In many of these so-called contests, the only judges are the press agent for the Hollywood starlet and the public relations director for the special interest involved. The whole shallow business goes far toward perpetuating the myth among California girls that the only attribute worth honoring is good looks.

6.

All of which helps to make Los Angeles the real headquarters for the cosmetics business, and its practitioners the avant-garde in the art of personal beauty. In the nation as a whole, barber shops outnumber beauty parlors, but in Los Angeles the latter outnumber the former by more than three to one.[3]

For several years hair-dyeing has been the new frontier in the beauticians' trade. The origin of this trend is in part the California sun, which has a tendency to bleach out the hair of the most avid sun worshipers. Until the late 1940's this was considered a detriment, since the bleached parts were often mere streaks. However, this particular "California look" became known throughout the country as a sign of robust outdoor life, suggesting that one had the leisure time to play in the sun. Streaked hair became a status symbol, opening up a whole new world in beauty culture. The rage has gone so far that natural sun streaks are unwanted because they spoil the pattern created in the beauty parlor; there is actually a hair spray on the market to "protect tinted, colored, or natural hair against fading, streaking, dulling effects of the sun."

Thus, the debut of hair-streaking helped to make the whole hair coloring field respectable. As late as 1952, only one California woman out of ten had her hair dyed or even tinted, and then it was an unspoken subject;[4] even her friends tried not to comment on the change, and pretended her hair had always been that way. By the 1960's, it is safe to say that nearly all Southern California women have experimented with at least some form of hair coloration, if only a rinse. They talk about it freely, and expect others to make favorable comment the same as if they had bought a new dress.

In the process, color has lost any connection with one's age or complexion. Gray hair is popular among very young California women, and I have seen more than one Negro woman with red hair. Coloring the hair has, in short, become a decorative device, like jewelry, and is almost as socially acceptable. When a woman prisoner in the San Diego jail was refused permission to use bleach to keep her hair properly colored, she got a court order permitting her to do so. At Oxnard more than 100 beauty-shop customers petitioned the city to increase the time allowance on adjacent parking meters from one hour to four hours, since it takes that long for a dye job. "It is our privilege and duty," they declared, "to look our best for our husbands, sweethearts, and friends, and we would like some cooperation from the City Council."

To the cult of body worship, Hollywood has, of course, made an imperishable contribution. Since the 1920's, the movie industry has been a magnet for thousands of pretty girls who came out to be discovered and remained to enter a beauty contest. By the 1940's, a girl's acting ability was definitely secondary to the measurement of her bustline—the idea being that she could always be taught to act. This value standard made Hollywood the nation's leading market for falsies. So much attention was focused on the mammary glands that breast cosmetic surgery (insertion of a plastic material for an enlargement effect) became a recognized form of plastic surgery. In the Hollywood area, it became a fad among well-endowed high school and college girls to buy pointed brassieres, cut off the points, and wear them under a sweater. While this disconcerting fad has mercifully run its course in Southern California, it is now popular in some quarters in San Joaquin Valley.

Nor is body worship confined to the female form. For years the city of Santa Monica provided weight-lifting equipment for some of the national and Olympic champions at Muscle Beach, in Ocean Park. Adagio dancing, muscle posing, and other exhibitions of male pulchritude were part of the program. Today the weights have been tossed out, and the center has a children's section. But on a summer weekend you can still get a free show of trapeze and tumbling acts at Muscle Beach.

At the same time, Hollywood continues to be the favorite locale for the nation's annual Mr. America Contest, chiefly because a big proportion of contestants live in Southern California. In this contest actual athletic achievement is nothing and pose (front, back, side, and optional) is everything. Said one wise contestant who had reoriented his life from weight lifting to muscle posing, "I have it all down to a science. I've about forty poses worked up for exhibition and I know just which ones to display for my best features." Another, of an even more philosophical turn of mind, observed, "Now, there is no future in weight lifting. Once you've set a world record lifting 500 pounds, then you gotta try for 550. You end up with a bent pelvic and sagging sacro-iliac. But if you win 'Mr. America,' you can go on and become 'Mr. World,' 'Mr. Universe,' and—who knows? Maybe some day 'Mr. Outer Space.'"

Such values are not altogether confined to extremists. It was Hollywood advertising men who first thought of exploiting the upper male torso in billboard and newspaper ads. The way some California women look at it, a man can be forgiven almost anything so long as he's well built. In Long Beach, a seventy-three-year-old bunco artist was jailed after marrying thirty women in the same number of years. When informed of the polygamous record of her spouse, his current wife said, "I hate to lose him. He was so kind—and he had the most beautiful body I've ever seen on a man."

Aside from the Hollywood influence, the main reason for this emphasis on physical appearance is that for decades Southern California as a place of settlement has meant health and physical comfort. People are still coming out here to escape the rigors of Eastern weather and to get their children out of crowded Eastern cities. Beauticians note that the California concept of beauty requires a wholesome "outdoor" look. The sun becomes the chief god in the California pantheon; Southern Californians have become the first organized sun worshipers since the Incas.

Not that anyone admits such paganism. But the reality is that you must exhibit some evidence of the outdoor life. Even though Southern California gets an average of fifteen inches of rain a year, many men do not own a raincoat, most do not have a pair of rubbers, and almost none would be caught with an umbrella. As summer approaches you must get yourself a suntan. Not only at the beach, but in your own community where you are apt to be wearing shorts and an open shirt, you are going to be showing a lot of skin. The men actually need a tan more than the women, since without it the male figure looks like nothing so much as a plucked turkey. Even if you aren't a beachgoer, the possibility of being invited over to a neighbor's pool is a powerful incentive to get a tan. Without one you are suspected of being the type who would show up on the beach with your shoes and stockings on and pantslegs rolled up. As one Southern Californian put it, "You don't want to look like you just got off the train."

This particular form of sun worship is almost universally practiced among younger people even though the doctors say that it is bad for the skin, increases the tendency to skin cancer, and ages the skin prematurely. Fortunately, this dilemma is now solved with the appearance of suntan lotions that promise a tan without the sun. Out of a little bottle you suddenly become a seasoned athlete, accepted and admired everywhere. This *reductio ad absurdum* will probably not drive the suntan out of popularity, because it is a wonderful excuse for lying still and doing nothing. Some years ago the women members of a Santa Monica club were sunbathing on the roof with little or nothing on when they were discovered by the pilots of the helicopter mail service, who made a point of detouring over the building while on their appointed rounds and even hovering for a while over the roof. Did this stop the good women of Santa Monica from sunbathing? They simply brought suit to restrain the U.S. mails from lingering overhead.

For the seductive influence of the California sun, consider the plight of the sixty-seven-year-old vacationer who drove out of Palm Springs and parked his car at the foot of the mountains. Hiking up the hillside, he was so captivated by the warm sun that he disrobed completely and lay down to soak in the vitamin D. Noticing an interesting rock formation nearby, he walked away from his clothes and then couldn't find them. Since they contained his car keys and money, he felt the search was doubly important. By sundown it was getting cold and he couldn't see too well. Finally, climbing down the mountainside, he presented himself at the nearest house on the edge of Palm Springs, where he discovered that he had gained very little status, and in fact had lost some, as a result of his suntan.

Indeed, the preoccupation with the body, the sun, and the outdoors has given some Californians an undisciplined attitude toward clothing. One large and fleshy woman in Sherman Oaks runs her morning errands, including regular appearances at the bank, in a nightgown. Among this group there is a willingness to take a chance on public exposure, particularly in the resort communities where bathing suits are normal attire.

In Manhattan Beach, a woman who thought she was alone in a laundromat was leaning over to put her washing in one of the machines, which placed her temporarily out of sight. As she stood up she saw a nude man running for one of the machines, apparently making a quick foray out of a dressing room. Emptying the machine, he dashed back to the room, and a few moments later emerged fully dressed and nonchalantly sauntered out.

A couple on a vacation with a house trailer were crossing the Mojave Desert in mid-summer heat; near Barstow the husband asked his wife to relieve him at the wheel while he tried to cool off in the trailer. There he completely disrobed and lay down on the bed while his wife drove. After a while, for some reason, she pulled over to the side and stopped. Wondering what was up, the husband opened the door, which was located at the rear of the trailer. At that moment his wife started up again with a lurch. He was thrown outside wearing nothing but a horrified expression, as she drove out of sight. Two hours later she pulled into her driveway and hurried into the house to answer the telephone.

"This is the Barstow police. Do you know where your husband is?"

"Why, he's out in the trailer, asleep."

"Better look again, lady."

7.

It is from the Southern Californian's basic love affair with the out-of-doors that most of his other distinguishing trademarks spring. A suburbanite rather than a city dweller, he insists on a piece of earth for his own slice of the great resort that is Southern California. The Californian's backyard is a sort of shrine to the sun-god, and the trappings of worship are the patio, the barbecue, and the swimming pool.

In fact, the story of Southern California's social transformation may be traced in the history of its front and back yards. Up till about 1920, the front yard was the focal point of social intercourse. On a summer evening, one sat on the front porch and talked with the neighbors as they passed by. Among older people in long established communities this custom persisted into the early 1930's. I can remember my grandmother (and two great-aunts, for that matter) sitting in the squeaky front-porch swing, fanning herself with a palm fan and exchanging pleasantries with neighbors within hearing distance. It was an affirmative acceptance of the community and the world at large.

Today, new California homes have no front porches and many of them no front yards. A few avant-garde homes even have a wall across the front screening the whole property from the street. The emphasis has shifted to the backyard, which is duly fenced and protected from the outside world. Social intercourse is strictly invitational, even among the children.

The personal-country-club nature of the backyard is obvious in its built-in facilities. First among these in point of time was the barbecue, which as a California institution goes back to Spanish rancho days. For more than a century the barbecue was a public affair; no new subdivision was properly opened without a free barbecue, consisting of charcoal-broiled beef, chile beans, buns, and perhaps a salad. As late as the 1930's, my great-uncle, who had a cattle ranch near Newhall, would butcher a steer at his spring roundup and serve a barbecue to as many as a hundred guests. The city of Santa Maria, California, still embraces the barbecue as a community affair. As the acknowledged "barbecue capital of the West Coast," Santa Maria maintains king-sized barbecue pits at the Veterans Memorial Hall, the Elks Lodge, the high school, and some of the elementary schools, where barbecuing accompanies almost all social functions.

While backyard barbecuing began in the 1930's, it was after World War II that it became a fixed social ritual. In this ceremony, the host becomes the central figure—apparently out of a shrewd design by the hostess to unload as much of the cooking burden as possible. Clad in huge white apron and chef's hat, wielding spatula and saltshaker with equal aplomb, the host presided over this brick-and-mortar console with the majesty of a hotel chef.

Gradually the size of one's barbecue became a measure of status, like the wheelbase of one's car. Barbecues became so monstrous that they required a major engineering effort and FHA financing, and so complete in their culinary facilities that they threatened to shift the family center of gravity from the kitchen to the backyard, with resultant loss of status and raison d'être of the female.

Too, it became apparent that not every Southern California male was a natural-born chef; in some prolonged cocktail periods, steaks sometimes became indistinguishable from the charcoal. In the reaction that followed, small portable barbecues on wheels and small Japanese hibachis have effectively demolished the brick version. Homes with built-in barbecues became as outmoded as tailfins on a car. Today the barbecue is once again a grill for broiling steaks, not an altar to the god of the outdoors.

Taking its place in the Southern California backyard is the swimming pool, a more permanent icon because it appeals to the whole family rather than simply exalting the father. While pools had always been a Southern California specialty, and a flight over Bel Air and Beverly Hills was like looking down on a hatful of sapphires, it was not until approximately 1952 that the real craze began. About that time the use of gunite concreting methods lowered the cost of construction to the point where, with long-term financing, the swimming pool could invade the whole middle-class market and compete with the second car, the pleasure boat, and the savings account. As late as 1955, there were only 4,700 pools in Southern California. In 1962, there were about 130,000—approximately one-third of the national total.[5] More than 100 pool contractors in Southern California are building thousands more per year at prices beginning at $1,995. Roughly 90 percent of these are sold with nothing down and five years to pay.

Though born of Southern California's backyard psychosis, the swimming pool has actually become a social center. Californians have gone past the time when pool owners complained of the high expense in food and drink for neighborhood drop-ins. In most neighborhoods, drop-ins are apt to bring their own refreshments; some pool owners announce standing rules to this effect. Many families have a carte-blanche invitation to use a neighbor's pool; others take turns lifeguarding, until the pools are almost a common facility. Some pool families post a flag at hours when neighborhood children are welcome. Whereas the pool-owning family used

61

to be the most popular in the neighborhood, the situation now is sometimes reversed. On some blocks there are so many pools that the housewife not owning a pool gets the most invitations for afternoon coffee. The other mothers are watching the kids and can't leave the pool. The women, in fact, become virtual mothers to every child in the neighborhood. Poolside manners (no running, no pushing) are a serious thing, and mothers become disciplinarians to the whole gang.

In such California backyards, the trend to a personal country club has defeated itself. One Hollywood druggist with four sons has gone the whole way by building a miniature drug store with soda fountain at the poolside. Says he, happily, "It's nothing for twenty kids to be here at one time, mixing malts, diving into both the pool and ice cream bins."

Most Southern Californians take this ultimate loss of privacy in limited doses—that is, by going to the beach instead of owning a pool. Today, traffic and parking jams plus the insufferable crowds on the beach itself have made a day at the shore a major agony which is only ventured out of an excess of enthusiasm over common sense. One means of enjoying both the beach and a degree of privacy is the beach club, which after a serious setback in the Depression, is flourishing again. Belonging to a beach club is nowhere near the social necessity it was in the 1920's, but to some members it is the main source of both entertainment and friendships. Between the pool, the bar, the paddle tennis court, and the bridge game on the sand, the art of aimless leisure is refined more thoroughly than it has been since the eighteenth-century French court. In the summer, as one female club member told me, "The wives and children are down here every day but Monday."

"Why not Monday?"

"It's closed Monday."

For all their love of outdoors and their unique values stemming from this source, Southern Californians are not immune to the more sophisticated measures of status. The newest trend in the Southern California lexicon of values is not the body, the clothes, or the car, but the home. No longer just a piece of real estate, it has also become the biggest of all status symbols. A society noted for athletic prowess, outdoor attachment, love of travel and physical freedom, is coming back to the home as the real center of its aspiration.

This is partly due to the rise of the backyard as the family's pleasure kingdom. Yet the Southern California family was never prosaic enough to be chained to one piece of ground.

The new attachment to the home is an outgrowth of a status consciousness that is not just Californian, but American. In true California fashion, it has been given a twist to meet local traditions. The style, size, and decoration of the California home are important, but the key issue is location. Most cities have unwritten but well-known prestige dividers. In San Fernando Valley you must live south of Ventura Boulevard; in Santa Monica, north of Wilshire and preferably north of Montana; in Brentwood, north of San Vicente and preferably north of Sunset.

Having a smart address can add considerably to the value of your home, even in comparison to homes across the street that might be in a different and less chic municipality. It is for this reason that one San Fernando Valley development was advertised as "just over the hills from Bel Air"; actually, with typical California disregard for distance, it was across an entire mountain range from that pinnacle of substance and respectability.

There is the case of Dr. Hubert Eaton, head of the Forest Lawn funeral empire. According to *Fortnight* magazine,

"[Quote] Dr. Eaton's residence was moved from L.A. to Beverly Hills by the simple expedient . . . of the L.A. City Council's giving the borderline block Eaton lived in to Beverly Hills."

Due to the demand for a prestige address, a community enjoying such a reputation will cause a rash of nearby developments hoping to reap reflected glory. The fame of Palm Springs brought a bevy of later developments, some of them advertised as "minutes from downtown Palm Springs," and others even borrowing the lustrous name itself with such titles as Palm Springs Panorama. Royal Oaks, one of the plush names in San Francisco Valley, was the source of inspiration for nearby Royal Woods, Royal Hills, and Royal Heights, while one enterpriser bought steep hills overlooking Royal Oaks and spent thousands of dollars per lot to build a geological monstrosity known locally as the pyramids of Egypt, but advertised happily as a part of Royal Oaks itself.

This brings up what has become the overriding gimmick in Southern California real estate—the hillside home. To get this in proper perspective you have to understand that in Southern California the most inconvenient, not to say dangerous, place to live is in the hills. Driving to a store and taking the kids to school is a major chore. The worst fires that have ravaged the Los Angeles area are in the hills, where the brush is like tinder and the blaze doesn't know where the brush leaves off and the homes begin. Often, a few days or weeks after a good fire, it rains heavily. Where the hills have been swept bare by the flames, the water runs off the surface and carries tons of earth with it. So if you aren't fighting fire with your garden hose you are apt to be shoveling mud and piling sandbags. As a consequence, you can't get insurance against flood or landslide if you live in Los Angeles, and the fire rates if you live in brush-lined canyons are almost prohibitive.

64

Against this background, the California desire to live in the hills is almost psychopathic. People will strain every financial effort to buy a hillside home, with payments and taxes that preclude much enjoyment of life beyond the picture-window view. One couple moving into Friendly Hills in Whittier had to use bed sheets for drapes and packing boxes for furniture. Some of the hill communities actually have poor reputations for financial credit. Certain flatland tradesmen are said to look dimly on extending credit to the inhabitants of nearby hillside estates. One man in the hills sold a tricycle to a neighbor for $5, hounded him several weeks for the money, and finally got paid out of the wife's grocery money. So voraciously do Southern Californians devour hillside homes that builders will try miraculous feats of engineering and earth-shaping to carve out hillside lots. Some families will do without a front or back yard in order to be in the hills. Others are known to use a climber's rope to weed their gardens.

Clearly, living in the hills is something special. It evokes deep associations going back to Medieval castles on mountain crags overlooking the village below. It recalls the small Eastern mill town where the owner and his family lived in a mansion on top of the highest hill. As the Southern California hill dweller looks down upon his precious view, there stirs inside a sense that it somehow all belongs to him. Still, the more basic reason is that, as one ad so delicately put it, "the family that's arrived has a home in the hills." Or as another subdivision "high in the hills" advertised less delicately, "Come where the status grows."

This capitulation to a status system based on wealth is the most disturbing glimmer on the California horizon. For years Southern California imported people and exported a way of life to the rest of the country—a life of things (barbecues, supermarkets, sport clothes), but also a life with a viewpoint (love of outdoors, zest for sports, insistence on informality, even a certain innocence of status). Has the tide of newcomers overwhelmed California to the point where it is a net importer, rather than an exporter, of ideas? California will be less than California if it loses its unique values, which, though they were not very mature, were always different and often refreshing.

CHAPTER IV

The Heartlanders

1.

Five days before Christmas, on a nationwide TV show, Santa Claus is being interviewed. Among other things, he advises the tots to put out plain cookies for his midnight snack, "I don't like raisins."

This might seem like an innocent remark. But out of California's Central Valley comes a whirlwind of indignation. The network headquarters, local stations, and valley newspapers are besieged with irate letters. Finally, the manager of the California Raisin Advisory Board settles the matter. "I'm sure this was just a slip on the part of someone taking Santa's place..." Santa does love raisins, and all's well in the California heartland.

The fact is that San Joaquin Valley grows 85 percent of the world's raisins, and Santa had better like 'em. For that matter, California's Coachella Valley produces almost 90 percent of the nation's dates, and Santa had better not leave them out of the fruit cake. And don't forget the brandy sauce; nearly 80 percent of the wine consumed in the United States is made in California.[1] Urbanization may be the big movement in California, but more than ever, this is the nation's Number One farm state.

Contrary to the general belief, California's population growth has not been confined to the climate-rich southern coast, but has been statewide. The desert, for example, is alive with a new energy and buoyancy reminiscent of the old Southern California booster spirit. Boosterism has, in fact, shifted from the southern coast to the Mojave Desert and the Salton Sea, where whole new cities have been born with little economic basis beyond the salesmanship of the developer. One ambitious community in the Mojave was launched from scratch with one of the largest incorporated city limits in the United States.

In short, the exuberance, exaggeration, and limitless imagination of the old-time Southern California real estate promoter has emigrated to the part of California that, up till now, has been the least developed and the most neglected. The free bus ride and free lunch of the pioneer developer operating from Los Angeles are still with us—except that now air-conditioned coaches take prospects 150 miles from Los Angeles to Salton Sea or Mojave Desert points. Free airplane rides take people over the subdivisions, and many a buyer picks out his lot from the air without ever setting foot on it. Still others of a more venturesome nature choose theirs sight unseen from the plat map in the developer's Los Angeles office.

Nor is the new boosterism confined to the sagebrush. San Joaquin cities are getting a fresh sense of destiny as the prosperous years pile one upon another. What were country towns before the war have become cities. And cities have become metropolitan areas complete with traffic, parking, smog, and redevelopment problems. A few—Bakersfield, Fresno, Stockton, and Sacramento—have sprouted tract subdivisions or retirement communities on the order of those in Southern California. There is a general feeling that, as the president of the Fresno Realty Board puts it, "Southern and Northern California are nearing the saturation point and future growth and expansion is bound to come to Central California . . ." Bakersfield goes even farther with the promotional slogan "The Market Center of 17 Million Sun-Loving Californians."

The heartlanders first began to feel this new surge from the coast in the early 1950's, when the tract houses were driving the citrus groves and truck farms out of Southern California. Since the last war, San Bernardino County has lost half its citrus acreage to factories and subdivisions. Most of the rich vegetable lands between Los Angeles and the coast have given way to suburbia. But Californians still had to be fed; as one Fresnan puts it, "Eating never will go out of style." Vegetable farmers moved to Imperial Valley. Orange growers moved to Coachella Valley and the San Joaquin. Although it took several years for the newly planted trees to begin bearing, California citrus production is now rising once again.

Thus, the increasing urbanization of California (now 86 percent of the population) [2] did not damage agriculture as the state's leading industry; it simply shifted the farming center of gravity more decisively to the interior. Imperial Valley has become the breadbasket of all Southern California. In the Central Valley, Fresno, Kern, and Tulare are the nation's first, second, and third counties in farm income.

2.

More than anything else, the direction of California agricultural wealth hinges on water. In the rich Salinas Valley, where the city of Salinas calls itself the "Lettuce Capital of the World" farming still depends on the vagaries of the Salinas River. Nowhere is the old Spanish proverb—"The rivers of California run bottom upward"—better illustrated than in the sands of the Salinas, where most of the flow is underground and the surface is dry most of the year. Though rich in beans, alfalfa, sugar beets, and lettuce, the region is still one where the term "bottom land" is fully as significant as in the agricultural South.

By contrast, Imperial Valley has had a sure supply of water since 1901, when reclamationist George Chaffey turned part of the Colorado River out of its ancient course and sent it flowing to this below-sea-level corner of the Colorado Desert. The pioneer farmers who settled on the new land have sometimes had much more water than they wanted, but never too little. Since completion of the northern branch of the All-American Canal in 1949, the same firm water supply was delivered to Coachella Valley, some 120 miles from its Colorado River source—a long way to bring irrigating water. Land prices soared, and Coachella joined Imperial in reaping the postwar agricultural boom.

Secure water came late to San Joaquin Valley. Though blessed with bountiful rivers flowing out of the Sierra, the valley farmers were still prisoners of California's drought and flood cycle. At first they responded with local projects, either cooperatively or privately owned, to store and distribute more water. By the 1950's, the massive, state-operated Central Valley Project provided the kind of water storage and regional regulation that promised a sure supply from year to year. Even then, marginal land on the valley's west side still suffered from low water tables and high pumping costs. Though price supports for barley and cotton have permitted some large operations on the west side, for many farmers there was little to choose between the parched California land and the drought-stricken prairies many of them had left behind in Oklahoma and Kansas.

For a few critical years, every drop of drinking water in the town of Coalinga was hauled in by tank car. One day a

70

grizzled farmer was filling his water cans at the town faucet when a stranger struck up a conversation.

"How far do you have to take that water?"

The man at the faucet straightened up and pointed a lean finger to a farmhouse on the horizon. The stranger's mouth dropped.

"That's a long way to haul water," he gasped. "Why don't you dig a well?"

"Hell!" snorted the farmer, heaving the can onto his truck. "It's the same distance either way."

Today the sprawling Feather River Project will send water 700 miles down the length of California, serving western San Joaquin Valley on the way. Already, Coalinga is booming with construction activity on the new canal that will carry irrigation water from nearby San Luis Dam.

The San Joaquin farmers are winning their water struggle, but this is only one of the battles that shook this valley. From the time Southern Pacific tracklayers first invaded its level vacuum in the 1870's and made settlement possible, pioneer wheat farmers fought the railroad, which controlled shipments, and the grain manipulators, who controlled the market. Nowhere was the nineteenth-century American farmer's war against monopoly more savage than in California. Nowhere was the Grange movement more fiercely embraced as a weapon against privilege. In 1880, the feud between farmers and railroaders erupted in a pitched battle at Mussel Slough, near Hanford, where seven men were killed. In the 1890's, a gang of bandits robbed Southern Pacific trains and enjoyed the cordial abetment of some San Joaquin farmers. It was the embattled California farmer who, more than any other California type, provided the moral spark for the state's great era of political and social reform at the turn of the century. Among the leaders of the movement to free state politics from the Southern Pacific Railroad was Chester Rowell, publisher of the *Fresno Republican.* Finally, the rise of cooperative marketing associations, from the Sunmaid raisin group in the San Joaquin to the Sunkist citrus organization in Southern California, had a social as well as an economic significance.

In Imperial Valley, the fight was different but no less heroic. Beginning in 1905, the Colorado River burst loose and sent its whole flow raging into the valley for nearly two years. While river channels widened and destroyed parts of valley towns, the Salton Sea was formed and soon threatened to engulf rich farmlands. Even after the break was closed and the valley saved by the Southern Pacific Railroad, the river continued to jump its bounds in subsequent years, sending the settlers to the canal banks with shovels and sandbags.

Nor was water the only enemy. Dust storms, scorching heat, and the appearance of alkali in some ill-drained land continued to remind the Imperial farmer that he was really a willful guest in an inhospitable desert.

Thus, the heritage of the California valleys is one of epic struggle, of heroic forebears who fought the elements, the land, the sun, the outside "interests." Little wonder that these vast flatlands, whose landscape was so plain and monotonous in the great era of settlement, reared such whole-souled men. For all of California's striking scenic backgrounds, it was this two-dimensional land that has produced California's epic novels: Norris' *The Octopus*, Wright's *The Winning of Barbara Worth*, Hobart's *The Cleft Rock*, Steinbeck's *The Grapes of Wrath*. Perhaps it is the very lack of setting that gave its characters such giant proportions.

In any case, it was this least typical California landscape that produced what may be called the one true indigenous California man. For if most Californians today are individualistic, self-oriented, grimly concerned with personal affairs, their prototype is the heartland farmer. The difference is that his individualism stems from raw necessity, theirs from a preoccupation with the good life.

Still further, of all California localities the heartland has the most cosmopolitan origins. While it is the American cities that have been the chief magnets for immigrant colonies, in California the phenomenon has been most pronounced in the San Joaquin Valley. Not even the farmlands of the north central states, with their Germans and Scandinavians, can match the variety of peoples in California's inland empire, with its Armenians, Germans, Hindus, Italians, Japanese, Portuguese, and Swedes. Although there has been some clannishness separating these nationalities, it has generally not been on the scale so representative of the foreign-language neighborhoods of many American cities. There has traditionally been less racial tension and more genuine racial assimilation than in California's metropolitan areas. In the Fresno region, which is especially rich in cultural diversity, the Japanese have become so active in service clubs and other community groups that one of them complained of "too much organizational work." It should be noted, too, that the first Hindu to serve in the United States Congress was elected from California's Imperial Valley.

There is, to be sure, a jagged social cleavage between the growers on the one hand and the Mexican-American and Negro farm laborers on the other. Yet this phenomenon is created first by economic distinctions, which are deep-rooted in the heartland consciousness, and only second by plain racial discrimination, which is not. There is, among those who joined in the common task of subduing an inhospitable land, a mutual respect that is often indifferent to race. As might be expected of Americans, business success has been a great ethnic solvent. The wives of Armenian raisin growers figure prominently in the Fresno society pages, and their sons show up no less prominently on the Stanford football team.

In fact, among the farmers who have won their battle with the California flatlands, there is something of the mutual

73

admiration of combat soldiers who find themselves among mere civilians. There is often a certain ostentation in the display of material things and material achievement. If anything, the spirit is reminiscent of that unwritten Calvinist doctrine that came out of Colonial New England and spread throughout nineteenth-century America—the belief that the men of economic achievement were already exhibiting the grace that had put them among the elect destined for heaven. In coastal California, the term "farmer" is sometimes used as an epithet hurled by one motorist at another. It would never be so used in the heartland, where the farmer is king. When El Centro's grand old Barbara Worth Hotel burned down in 1962, the man who had cleaned her rugs for twenty-five years recalled his horror at seeing a farmer fresh from the fields come clumping into the lobby, seat himself in a sofa, and deliberately scrape the mud from his boots on the carpet. "Even if they are farmers," the rugcleaner said respectfully, "they shouldn't do that."

All this is not to say that today's California farmer is simply living on prosperity earned by others. On the contrary, farming in California is still so charged with both risk and opportunity that there are few examples of a hereditary landed class. Nowhere has the proverb, "Three generations from shirt sleeves to shirt sleeves" been more valid than in the rough and uncertain arena of Central Valley agriculture. As one Fresno County observer puts it, "Almost all the families who were prominent and wealthy sixty years ago have faded from the scene in prominence and wealth. They have been replaced by former 'dust bowlers,' farm laborers, and others who, in a relatively short period, have become the leading and wealthier citizens of the area."

The first reason for this revolution in two generations is that the pioneer who knew how to battle the elements with his hands has often been helpless in the modern-day battle of finances. Average prices of California farmland are more

than three times those in the rest of the country, and as one
reporter puts it, "are climbing nearly out of sight." And
while California's food prices are comparatively high, the
farmer's share of them has decreased. From 1947 to 1962,
average crop prices dropped 12 percent while crop costs
went up 20 percent.[3]

Nor have government subsidies had as much impact in
California as elsewhere. Among the more than 200 different
California crops, only an average of seven have been under
federal price supports at any one time. True, these few (cotton and rice are by far the largest) are among the most important, and some regions depend strongly on subsidies for
their prosperity. Some large operators are actually in the
business chiefly to "farm the government," taking advantage
of every legal angle for subsidies and loans. But for the state
as a whole, supports have generally represented only about
one or two percent of annual farm income.[4]

It is therefore not surprising that the vagaries of agriculture have caused an exodus from the farm at least as pronounced as in the rest of the country. From 1952 to 1962,
39,000 California farmers left the land—many of them moving to the cities.[5]

Their places have been taken by a tough breed who regarded farming first as a business, and only secondly as a
way of life. Some were not even raised on the soil. One, the
son of a Sanger barber, came to California from New York
State at the age of sixteen, saved $2,000 working summers
in a fruit-packing shed, and on graduation from high school
in 1947 started out as a farmer by renting twenty acres of
grapes. He worked long hours, learned from other farmers,
kept up with new agricultural trends by reading farm publications, and as he puts it, "married a girl who knows how
to keep books . . ." By 1962, he owned 180 acres, was leasing
270 more, and was doing custom harvesting for neighbors
with his own combine.

Leasing has, in fact, been the favorite device of new farmers in beating the high cost of land. In 1951, a gas-station attendant in Merced bought a second-hand tractor, put headlights on it, and worked fifty acres of leased land after hours. Within a year he raised $2,600 cash by selling his home and borrowing on furniture and appliances, and went into farming full time. By 1962, at the age of thirty-two, he owned a thousand head of cattle and 700 acres of land, leased 7,000 additional acres, and operated machinery worth some $500,000. He and his wife also had a new home complete with swimming pool.

These success stories, earned by sheer initiative and hard work, have sharpened the farmer's tenacity in what may be his longest and bitterest battle of all—the farm labor issue.

3.

Curiously, the farm worker is in the worst need of unionization and has the strongest potential bargaining position of any type of California laborer. Yet he is the last to be unionized.

For many California farm crops—particularly the truck vegetables—there is a period of ten days or so between ripening and spoilage. For a few, twelve hours' time can make the difference in the harvesting process. Approximately one-half of California farmers employ additional help, and they need them at this critical harvest season. Failure to get the crop harvested could mean financial ruin. Yet farm labor in California—as in most of the country—has not been organized to make the most of this enormous leverage. Several times the state AFL-CIO has attempted to unionize farm laborers, but while it claims to have improved farm wages, it has generally failed to organize the workers.

The reason lies mainly within the farm worker himself— his attitude and his condition. Many are true farmers by in-

76

stinct, if not by status. Despite their complete economic dependence on their employers, they are still independent in spirit, and sometimes this individualism is all that is left of their self-respect. Some of them hail from small and rather remote communities in Missouri, Arkansas, Oklahoma, or Texas—communities provincial, insulated, and ingrown. They have a natural resistance to the outsider who comes among them with offers of help. Many are Mexican-Americans who pose a language barrier and may tend to distrust the English-speaking stranger.

Further, California migrant families live at a subsistence level that robs them of any bargaining advantage they might have. Average California farm-labor families have five to six members, live in a three-room house with a floor space of about 450 square feet, and earn a total of $2,200 a year. Unable to find year-round work in one place, they commute to various nearby counties for half the year and go "on the road" as migrants for another three months. Existence is strictly from hand to mouth. Thus, if the farmer cannot hold out for long in a labor dispute, neither can the migrant. In this vicious circle, he is not only unable to save enough to get out of the migrant life altogether, he cannot even get far enough ahead to apply pressure for better conditions.

Actually, farm laborers have sometimes appeared to be almost passive instruments in a conflict between more powerful interests—the growers, supported by the local business communities and often the local authorities, versus the labor unions, who command the sympathy of Democratic state and federal administrations.

This battle of the giants has not been a pretty affair. Strike activity has sometimes been met with mass arrest, including some savage brutality. As recent as the 1961 lettuce strike in Imperial Valley, the director of union activities charged that arrested strikers no sooner put up bail than they were arrested on other charges, with bail set still higher. Sheriff's deputies, he declared, threw several pickets into the irrigation canals and fired shots in the water near them. On the other hand, cases have been reported of union men attacking workers who try to replace strikers. There are other cases in which a single organizer unknown to the workers has picketed an orchard where no labor dispute previously existed, and by this act has secured the intervention of state officials, the withdrawal of the workers, and the loss of a crop.

To the growers, furthermore, the rising government restrictions on the use of Mexican nationals (*braceros*) as contract labor are framed for the benefit of organized labor, which has considered the *braceros* program to have a depressing effect on farm wages and even a strikebreaking effect on union activities. While the law requires growers to pay *braceros* the same wages they would pay domestic workers, the availability of Mexican nationals has in the past often worked against efforts for higher domestic wages. But tightening government regulations, plus the failure of some *bracero* groups to arrive in California when needed, are making contract labor more trouble than it is worth. From a high point of 100,000 in 1956, *braceros* are becoming so short in numbers that crops have already been lost for lack of hands.

In brief, the labor situation in the California farmlands has reached the same level of bitterness, high tension, and intermittent violence that surrounded American industrial labor up to the 1930's.

The failure of past organizing efforts is not measured simply in the continuing low level of farm wages. Though desperately low compared to other industries, California farm wages are the highest in the country, averaging $1.24 an hour. The real tragedy is the living conditions of migrant families, which is not always a function of wages. Where housing is provided to migrants by the growers, sanitary and hygienic conditions can be execrable. Privacy and human dignity are often the last consideration. True, many workers themselves are ignorant of sanitary habits, and as one San Joaquin observer puts it, "wouldn't know a flush toilet if they saw it." Yet this has been used to justify growers in permitting conditions ripe for disease; in at least one instance, an epidemic in a labor camp threatened to spread to a nearby town.

The social impact is still more devastating at longer range. Children start working in the field at an early age; though the state tries to provide mobile schools and other means of educating pupils on the move, their educational level is too low to offer much hope of escaping the migrant's life. In the winter months when work is scarce, some families come close to starvation. In the winter of 1962, permanent farm families near Heber in Imperial Valley were found in desperate need of food, with some children living on greens picked from the roadside. It could be said that, as United States citizens, many farm workers are worse off than the Mexican national contract laborers, whose conditions are regulated by international agreement.

In short, the migrant labor camps and the neighborhoods of many semimigrant families are the real slums of California. Though state agencies are making some headway at improving sanitation, these efforts are still in the nature of pilot projects. As one social worker said, "Things are just as hard for farm workers as in the Depression . . ."

To cries for reform, many farmers plead little responsibility. The cost-price squeeze is already paralyzing them. As though the problem can be driven away with mere words, some farm spokesmen condemn would-be reformers as "do-gooders"—apparently in the belief that doing good has gone out of style. To this extent the California farmer has come full circle. His grandfather called for social justice against the rugged individualism of the railroads and grain speculators. Today he calls for rugged individualism as a counter to demands for social justice. As a mass employer of agricultural workers and in many cases their landlord, he finds himself confronting rather than representing the little man. He is no longer the underdog, but the top dog.

4.

Thus, California exhibits another unique characteristic in that it is not the large cities, but rather the farm regions, that present the most explosive social conditions. In the grotesque contrast between the large and often elegant homes of the successful farm families and the squalid shacks of the farm workers, one sees a social polarization that is too brittle for comfort. In contrast to the large California cities, where the middle class is almost suffocatingly dominant, much of rural California is composed of the well-to-do and the poor, with a thin middle class made up largely of shopkeepers.

This is not true of the large valley cities, which are more than farm market centers. Sacramento gains much from the activities of state government. As California's unique inland port at the head of San Joaquin River navigation, Stockton has a rich and growing shipping trade. Fresno is attracting more and more industry not directly related to agriculture. Since the 1890's, Bakersfield has been a center of oil production, and although its biggest fields have long passed their prime, petroleum is still a dynamic factor throughout the southern San Joaquin. In these cities, society is the healthier for an abundance of white-collar and organized blue-collar workers.

But in the heartland's true farm communities, the gulf between the proprietary class and the working class is still unbridgeable. Social organization is dominated by the growers and the principal merchants. The service clubs and women's clubs are the chief wellsprings of community opinion, and the agricultural worker families are almost never represented in the membership. Stratification is furthered by church division, with certain traditional Protestant denominations supported almost exclusively by the substantial people in town, and the more evangelistic sects drawing the worker families. There is, in short, an automatic cleavage based on income and occupation. One observer says, "Social evaluations are made at such a social distance that symbols are used in the determination of social worth, rather than a true evaluation of the individual on the basis of personally known qualities."

It is impossible to believe that this anachronous condition will endure. On the contrary, as one critic observed, "California farming is about where the national coal industry was when John L. Lewis started to work on it." It is the very social imbalance that will bring change. The real question is not whether change will come, but whether it will be brought about primarily by unionization or by still another phenomenon now in full tide—the technical revolution in farming. For in their battle against the cost-price squeeze, California farmers have led the nation in the application of chemistry, mechanization, and advanced fiscal method to the business of farming. An owner of a large turkey ranch already has no place for unskilled labor. "I want the college-trained man, the dietary nutritionist, the agricultural engineer," he says. Nowhere has there been closer cooperation among the farmers, the state agricultural schools, and government agricultural services.

Mechanization came early to California farms, which are notably ahead of those in the other states. California's leading crop (one of forty in which it is first in the nation) is cotton, which has been picked by machinery for many years. Potatoes have long been harvested mechanically. Aerial crop-dusting spread early in California, whose 1,000 crop-dusting planes make up the largest fleet of its kind in the country.[6] Most California dairy cows are so used to milking machines that when one farmer's electrical power failed, they kicked lustily at hand-milking efforts. Said a helper, "By the time we had milked eight of them, we had the amount of milk that two usually give."

Today these are only the most elementary examples of mechanization. Prune picking is now aided by an "inertial shaker" or "bazooka gun" that strikes the limb with a pellet and jolts off the fruit. On the larger ranches, turkey raising is thoroughly automated, from the mechanical feeders to the electrocution chamber and hydraulic feather-picking room. Hog farming now includes automatic pen-cleaning and feeding devices. The cattle business has been revolutionized by the spread of central feedlots, where stock are fattened with scientific formulae mixed and truck-loaded by one man at a large control board that resembles the instrument panel of an airplane. Since the war, almond growing has been completely mechanized, so that a farmer and one helper can do the work of forty crewmen. Peaches and some other fruit trees are pruned by a motorized, mechanical topper.

More revolutionary from the social standpoint, the next wave of inventions will begin to displace the traditional "stoop labor" of the *bracero* and migrant worker. A tomato harvester has been developed at the University of California's agricultural college at Davis. A grape harvester is well on the way, and efforts are proceeding on a celery harvester and citrus picker.

California agriculture is, in other words, becoming a business, run by businessmen. The typical California farmer has dropped his hoe and does much of his farming with clipboard and pencil.

5.

Still, the cost of mechanized equipment is so great that it will generally not pay on a small farm. One agricultural economist has said, "Expensive machinery must be kept busy to make it pay. And to keep machinery busy means the cultivation of more acres."

Since the last war, small farmers are either selling out or buying more land. The average California farm as an operating unit is 371 acres, as compared to 302 acres for the country as a whole. In Kern County, the average operating unit size is 837 acres.[7] Though 86 percent of California's 99,000 farms are family owned and operated, farming has become not only a business, but big business. The national policy of preserving the small farm as a way of life is finding minimum application in California. Here the small farm is associated with drudgery and monotony of the sort that has sent farm boys to the city for generations. Today it is not farm unionization but the shift to large technically run farms that is shaping California agriculture. For though unionization will surely come, it will serve mainly to spur farmers to further mechanization and to still bigger farms. When this happens, as one Imperial Valley farmer declares, "Workers who then qualify for employment on California farms will be of superior ability and will receive total wages and working conditions better than comparable workers in industry."

Already the new shape of California agriculture is reversing the flight of farmers' sons to the city. Farming as a business has lost much of the misery and regained enough glamour to keep more boys on the farm. Vocational agriculture courses that were dropped by some high schools a few years ago are being reopened, and enrollment is reaching new highs each year. Many young people active in the Future Farmers of America are already operating big farm enterprises of their own. As a result, while unskilled farm workers will diminish, the level of skill and specialization of those on the farm will continue to rise. The disturbing polarization of society in the heartlands may be eased by the simple means of eliminating one of the poles.

Such a trend is already symbolized in the new term,

"agribusiness." And the time is not far off when the only difference between these agribusinessmen and their conventional counterparts in the coastal cities will be that the former wear wide-brimmed hats and do their commuting by plane.

It is hard to believe that such developments are bad for California. Many heartland communities are already losing the backward and bygone touch that separated them from the rest of California. As usual, prosperity has cultivated the soul as well as the bank account. Heartland California once had more than its share of crudities and its eyesores, as though the monotony of the landscape had dulled the senses. The atmosphere seemed dominated by the scrap heaps on the edge of town, the tobacco and medicinal ads painted on the barn roofs, the odor of cow manure from the feedlots. Wrote one Imperial Valley editor, "It smells like money, and Calexico is a wealthy town."

But today many of these crudities are disappearing. Spurred by chamber of commerce drives, many towns are sprucing up to attract settlers and customers. Redevelopment projects are under way in Sacramento, Stockton, and Fresno, while the latter is expected to be the first Northern California city to have a shopping mall in the downtown area. In most of the larger cities, the wives of agribusinessmen have the leisure time to patronize the arts. Sacramento, with its famed Crocker Art Gallery, its symphony orchestra, its theater and ballet groups, is one of the most active cultural centers of its size in the nation. A flourishing art rental service is conducted both by Sacramento's Crocker and the Fresno Arts Centers. And nearly all county fairs now include art shows among their events.

In brief, the California heartlands are emerging from a long era in which economics determined the whole shape of society, simply because the business of making a living was too demanding to admit of other interests. These regions are, instead, entering a new age in which their social structure will be, eventually, little different from coastal Southern California. For while the great movement in California since the last war has been the urbanization of the south, the next transformation will be the spread of this movement to the hinterland. In the process, the heartlanders will begin to have the time and the money to be, not just workingmen, but whole men. There are faint hints that they might also have the inclination.

CHAPTER V

The Rimlanders

1.

Shortly after Christmas at Carmel-by-the-Sea, the mayor was asked about his hopes for the city during the coming year. Of his four principal desires, as reported in the local newspaper, two were:

"No new building in Carmel in the coming year ... no improvements of any kind."

If this is unbelievable in California, you don't know Carmel. Neither, for that matter, do you know the whole hairpin-shaped mountain country of California that stretches from Santa Barbara up the coast, across the Oregon border, and back down the high ranges to Tehachapi Pass.

This is the great rimland of California. And while the differences among its inhabitants are vast—from the social elite of Santa Barbara to the cattle ranchers of Modoc County—they have one thing in common. They are off the beaten path of California growth, and, generally speaking, they like it.

That the mayor of Carmel could declare himself against any improvements and expect to be reelected is an extreme case. But the rimland communities may be classed in two categories: those that resist change and those that are not soon destined for change anyway.

The origins of this insularity are twofold: topography and climate. The rimland is so mountainous that much of it has never progressed from the pastoral to the agricultural stage of civilization. True, the basic occupation of stock raising has for generations been supplemented by the extractive industries: gold mining in the Sierra, oil in Santa Barbara County, and lumbering in the whole region. But these have built no big cities locally; rather, mining and lumbering have simply spurred the growth of California's chief financial center, San Francisco. The rimland largely remains serene, insular, and in some places, wonderfully primitive.

As for climate, the rimland is hardly the part of California that draws health-seekers and sun worshipers from the East. True, the Santa Barbara coast is delightful, and the worst that can be said for Carmel Bay is that it is often overcast. But the Redwood Coast is one of the world's rain forests, with as much as fifty inches a year. In the Klamath National Forest, electrical storms can put on a display of cosmic fury that might blanch the most hardened Midwesterner. Says one mountaintop firewatcher, "You wouldn't want to be up here when the lightning starts striking. At first, it's enough to raise your hair. But after a storm starts, I have my hands full reporting fires; so much work in sighting them that I don't have time to be scared."

In the lava country of the northeast corner, the thermometer can dip under 30 degrees below zero. If the schools are closed on such occasions, it's not to pamper the children, but because the school buses won't start. In the blizzard of 1949, the temperature dropped to 30 below every night for seven weeks, snow was four feet deep on level ground, and hay had to be air-dropped for the cattle.

In the High Sierra, snow will drift fifteen to twenty feet deep in the canyons. For nearly a century, transcontinental train service over the crest has been carrying on a battle against blizzards and avalanches; winter passage has only been assured by miles of snowsheds covering the tracks. In 1962, a succession of storms stalled the westbound "City of San Francisco" on Donner Pass, named for an early-day party of emigrants who had suffered unspeakable tragedy in attempting to cross the Sierra in winter. While more than 200 passengers and crewmen waited for snowplows to arrive over roads choked with snow, railroad section hands worked in the blizzard shoveling the drifts away from the train windows to keep the passengers from suffocating. As the breakdown stretched into days, food was rationed, heating equipment failed, and sleeping-car ladders were smashed to make fuel for cooking. It was four days before the blizzard let up and rescue parties arrived. As one reporter put it, "Had just one more storm flailed down from Alaska, prolonging the blizzard, the story of the ill-fated train, like that of the Donner Party, might have ended differently."

In short, ruggedness of terrain and weather make the rimland the backwater of California. It is an anomaly in a state known for dynamic growth. Indeed, the rimland would be the least "Californian" part of the state were it not for its scenic beauty. What, after all, is California without its rich diversity of landscape? The rimland—from the wave-assaulted cliffs of the coast to the glaciated Sierra crags—is the aesthetic soul of California. The variety of view—the charming oak-covered hills of the central coast and the Mother Lode; the holy grandeur of the redwood groves; the sheer power of a granite Sierra gorge—is probably unequaled in so short a compass anywhere on earth. The rimland is the first source of the native's sentimental attachment to his state; it causes the Southern Californian to love the north as much as the south; it is the chief inspiration for the wanderlust and nature-mindedness that embraces the true Californian, native or adopted. This unutterable lure is what made old

John Muir write seven books in eulogy of the California wild; caused him, as soon as the snow receded and the grass appeared each spring, to leap the fence at his foothill home and spend the summer months tramping alone in the High Sierra. And this is also what impelled Luther Burbank, on arriving in California, to write home, "I almost cry with joy when I look upon the lovely Santa Rosa Valley from the hillsides."

In this sense the rimland belongs to—at least is part of the personal heritage of—all Californians. Nearly all of the state parks and all four of California's national parks are in this superb horseshoe. It is California's year-round playground —a sort of safety valve for the pent-up tensions of urban life. The tourist trade must therefore be added to the region's cattle and extracting industries. To some rimlanders, outside visitors are welcomed as a kind of crop; you put so much money into local promotion and you get so many tourist dollars. When a San Francisco columnist praised the Mendocino Coast as "The fairest of them all," the Fort Bragg newspaper rejoiced that it "looks like money in the bank, to the tune of several thousand dollars."

Yet only in a few places has tourism captured the souls of the rimland inhabitants. They either haven't seen the economic benefits, or they deliberately cling to more precious values. Even in such areas as the Monterey Peninsula, where tourism has gained a foothold in the native consciousness, it is battling against a still stronger campaign to preserve local privacy.

2.

On various occasions throughout the year, the rimlanders find their retreat violated by the California masses. In summertime, the vacationers crowd into the national and state parks until privacy is something left at home. More than a million visitors jam into Yosemite Valley in the space of four months, creating traffic congestions in one of the most precious scenic spots on earth. Campers in Yosemite Valley are crammed so close together they can participate in each other's conversations. One Angeleno who swore never to visit Yosemite again clinched the point with, "If I want crowds I can go down to Seventh and Broadway."

The situation is little better in some of the state parks. As the season opens at certain coastal parks people will line up long before dawn to get in and secure a place. On a sunny Independence Day weekend, outsiders invaded Santa Barbara County with trailers and boats, filled every campsite, and camped along the highway by the hundreds in every possible spot. Despite such frustrations, the Californian's thirst for the outdoors is unquenchable. When our family took a four-day hiking trip in the High Sierra, one party on the trail included a two-year-old baby and a woman who was five-months pregnant.

In the hunting season, the mass of amateurs who invade the rimland from "down below" is an annual plague. Not only do they flood the mountains with more hunters than game, but they are abominably poor shots. In duck and geese hunting, it is these outlanders who shoot at every bird in sight, scaring them away before they can come within range. In deer hunting, these are the ones who shoot at sounds and movements in the brush, accounting for the several accidental hunter injuries and deaths in California every year.

Such antics are inexcusable to every rimlander, for whom hunting is a passion. In El Dorado County, one young Nimrod broke his leg on a deer hunting trip; six weeks later he was in the field again, walking on crutches with his leg in a cast while a friend served as his gun bearer.

Another army invades the rimland in fishing season, breaking all the rules of streamside etiquette that have been honored since Isaac Walton. They tramp in the water, talk along the bank, and drop their lines in a pool already preempted by another fisherman. Here again, the rimlander feels the pinch. To him fishing is not just a sport, but a state of mind. When the steelhead are running in the redwood country, there is no other topic of male conversation.

Not even the winter months offer a respite for the rimlanders, for then the roads are filled with the ski fraternity. Though Californians have been enthusiastic skiers since the 1920's, it has only been since the last war that they have become fanatics. By now every possible ski locality has been scouted and developed, for a total of sixty-seven sites.

Of this mass winter migration, the rimlanders themselves are a part, but they were skiing long before the lowlanders ever caught on. In fact, skiing as an organized sport appeared in California long before it was imported from Scandinavia to the northeast states. In Plumas County, miners of a hundred years ago used the bucket tow of the Plumas-Eureka Mine for a ski lift and then raced downhill for prize money. In such mountain communities today, almost every child learns to ski; in several counties, skiing is a classroom subject, with school buses taking the pupils to the hillsides.

And so the crowds from below are greeted with, to say the least, mixed emotions. True, the town merchant hails with equal enthusiasm the hunter, the fisherman, the camper, and the skier. But most rimlanders are charmingly oblivious to the tourist trade. In the northern counties, many of them would just as soon limit the number of outside deer hunters by lottery or better yet, marksmanship tests. In Santa Barbara County, the authorities are considering a higher boat fee for outsiders using Cachuma Reservoir. Santa Barbara's famed Spanish Fiesta in August draws people from all over the state, but as one native puts it, "That's when all the Santa Barbarans except the merchants take their vacations and get out of town." And in the Mother Lode, Highway 49 towns have made no attempt to preserve the original character of their picturesque old buildings for the benefit of the curious; instead they have covered them over with modern materials and cheap signs in an effort to make their town look like any other characterless community. While this represents a lack of true local values, it does illustrate the indifference of rimlanders to Californians as a whole.

Such an attitude is not born of innocence alone, but is part of the ingrown mentality of the hinterland. For while neighborly love in the Biblical sense is a way of life for the rimlanders, so is tribalism. One distrusts newcomers and outsiders until they prove themselves as neighbors. When an acquaintance of mine established a business in Healdsburg, Sonoma County, he and his wife found it took two years to begin breaking the ice socially. The resistance to outsiders is so pronounced that some Northern California communities have Newcomers Clubs for people who have been in town less than one-and-a-half to two years. Thus, they help each other to span what one observer calls "the waiting period in which 'new folks' move into neighbor status."

3.

Essentially, coolness to outsiders stems from the rimlander's chief characteristic—satisfaction with things as they are. And in resisting change, the rimlander resists what most other Californians affirmatively embrace as economic progress. In fact, the values of Californians as a whole are almost turned upside down by the rimlanders. Except in very recent years, Santa Barbara has been the fastest growing community in the rimland, yet it may be said to have grown in spite of itself. The strongest assets of Santa Barbara and its immediate neighbor, Montecito, have been their rustic residential settings and the geared-down tempo of life. After the 1925 earthquake, Santa Barbara seized the opportunity to rebuild with purpose and established architectural restrictions for new buildings. Using its lovely mission as a guide, it recreated a Spanish flavor that had been buried under three generations of frontier-type, false-front buildings. Today Santa Barbara is becoming a city of white walls and tile roofs, of patios and inner courts and offstreet shops. Santa Barbara has been called the most beautiful residential city in the United States. One local enthusiast says, "No reasonable person who can make a good living in Santa Barbara would voluntarily live anywhere else."

Feeling proud of this recaptured heritage, Santa Barbarans have been less than enthusiastic at the appearance of the postwar tract subdivisions. With more foresight and courage than other Southern California communities, Santa Barbara County has placed restrictions on them, including demands for "green belts" to preserve the region's prewar charm. Industry has been regarded as a greater plague; even research centers with no industrial nuisance factors and with personnel of high income and educational levels have sometimes been resisted as a threat to community character.

Not all of Santa Barbara County has fought the tide. When Vandenberg Air Force Base was established, the flower-raising communities of Santa Maria and Lompoc were suddenly smitten with new tracts and traffic. The flower fields, which formerly supplied approximately 60 percent of the nation's seed stock, were inundated by homes and supermarkets. Overnight the hometown flavor faded in a cloud of commuter exhausts. Wrote one observer of Santa Maria, "Neighbors didn't know one another's names anymore." But though both communities are still getting over the shock, they have been enchanted with the rise of land values and the increase in business. The abrupt and forcible switch from flowers to missiles is considered a stroke of good fortune.

With a few such exceptions, the rimlanders oppose the onslaught of what most other Californians would call civilization. Up the lovely central coastline, which is one of the least inhabited areas of California, settlers successfully fought a state-planned freeway that would have desecrated the mountainsides with ugly cuts and fills. In the Monterey Peninsula, vacationists were invading the forests with motor scooters, thus destroying the silence of wooded trails, until local residents rose in anger and got them banned.

But the citadel of resistance to mass invasion is Carmel, one of the most inviting planned communities in the United States. Unlike Santa Barbarans, Carmelites are wonderfully oblivious to California's Spanish tradition and instead maintain a town that, but for the profusion of pine trees, could have been lifted out of rural England. There is no question that Carmel caters to tourists; but more than this, it is a refuge for retired residents who want privacy, quiet, and low taxes. Yet the very charm that it has gathered to itself by stern architectural regulation has made it so desirable that it must put up defenses against being loved to death.

Perhaps more than any other Californians, the Carmelites fight to preserve a bygone way of life. Beset by traffic, they resist to the last the pressures to surface their winding residential streets. They oppose supermarkets, chain stores of any kind, and what one official derisively calls "mushrooming motel growth." Street trees are so highly valued that any request to cut even a limb is reviewed by the city councilmen when they take their monthly "Tree Tour." All that the rest of the state calls progress is fiercely resisted in Carmel; the result is so delightful that one can't help thinking that the Carmelites must be right and all the other Californians wrong.

Equally adamant are the inhabitants of nearby Big Sur, which is not so much a place as a way of life. The few artists and writers who largely make up the Big Sur community evidently chose this spot, not only for its wild scenic beauty, but because its topography almost defies progress. You can't build much of a town on the side of a cliff, and this suits the

Big Sur people fine. It is a vertical rather than a horizontal community. In fact, it isn't really a community at all. Driving through it on Highway 1, you keep wondering where Big Sur is, until you have gone past it. No locality has less reason to be given an actual name. There are fewer people in the Big Sur area today than there were at the turn of the century, and those who are there live in splendid isolation from each other. One artist resident declares, "There is the wonderful thing of not visiting." Perhaps it is this pure isolation that causes the Big Sur artist to regard his fellow craftsmen on the Monterey Peninsula as generally pedestrian and commercial. For though Monterey and Carmel are out-of-the-way, they are, after all, tainted with tourists. The hermitlike mentality of Big Sur people is best described by novelist Henry Miller, in a local descriptive booklet: "The advent of city folks with their cares and worries is a pure dissonance. They come like the lepers of old. And so it happens that whoever settles in this region tries to keep others from coming here."

4.

But for most of the rimland there is still little need to resist, for the tide of California's growth is not set in that direction. Unlike the rest of California, the northern counties remain almost static in population. In the latest five-year period, Mendocino County showed a 9 percent decrease in the number of business firms. Due to the rising use of other materials for building construction, the lumber industry has suffered an overall decline, some mills have shut down, and for several years employment in much of the redwood country has been "soft."

Nor is competition between merchants and between communities maintained at the regular California pace. Alarmed at a drop in membership, the manager of the Modoc Chamber of Commerce announced that "we don't have enough money to assure paying our rent from month to month." In one town on the Redwood Coast, a chamber of commerce directors' meeting revealed, first, that there was not enough money in the treasury to pay current bills, and second, that no business could be transacted for lack of a quorum. At a municipal election in the same town, there were only three names on the ballot for three city council offices and as the local editor wrote, "We're darned lucky to have that many. Two of the incumbents had to be talked into running again because no one else had filed for the nomination."

Most dramatic example of static life is the Mother Lode country, which is the cradle of American society in California and the center of population a century ago. Most of the mines have long since played out, and the region subsists on lumbering, fruit raising, and tourism. Today the Mother Lode is a vast outdoor museum for the California Gold Rush. And while the towns along Highway 49 have revived on the tourist trade, the old camps off the beaten path carry the nostalgia, flavor, and pace of life of another era. This is the country where folks can still be found doing nothing at all—a capability which Booth Tarkington mistakingly reserved for "small boys and colored people." On a summer day in Murphy's, in Volcano, in Chinese Camp, you can see people sitting in the shade of a giant cottonwood and—just sitting. In Angel's Camp, a public building used for meetings by the Lions Club, the Soroptimists, and the Red Cross was closed down for a considerable period because someone had lost the key to the front door. There is, in short, an air of gracious and pleasant timelessness that provides an almost unbelievable contrast to the headlong pace of modern California.

Indeed, as one enters the mountains of northern and eastern California, one moves not only geographically, but also backward in time. Social drop-in calls without invitation or warning are commonplace. You have a first-name acquaintanceship with almost everyone you see. The church is the center of social life and, to a large degree, the arbiter of moral conduct. This is still the country of the quilting bee, the cake social, the charivari. At local festivals you can still see logrolling, canoe-tilting, and axe-throwing contests. In the spring and fall, it is not uncommon for herds of sheep or cattle to fill a main street of a foothill town as they move to or from the mountain meadows. Until recently, it was entirely legal for residents of the northern counties to go out in the woods and cut their own Christmas tree, free of charge; one can still do so by purchasing a $1 tree tag—the floral equivalent of a hunting license. It is in the northern country that door-to-door Christmas caroling is still practiced, whereas in the larger cities a group brave enough to go caroling is ignored by two-thirds of the residents, who probably consider them some kind of fanatics.

Nor are the rimlanders, like most forest people, altogether immune to superstition. In the redwood country, there is a lingering acceptance in some quarters of the existence of the Sasquatch, or timber giant—a huge, hairy half-man, half-beast on the order of the abominable snowman. Not long ago a logger near Fort Bragg claimed to have encountered such a creature standing head and shoulders above a six-foot fence. When this story hit the settlements there was a rush of local reporters and amateur anthropologists to the scene; people began barring their doors at night; vague reports of new "sightings" poured in; children ran to their school buses rather than linger on the edge of the woods; and grown men tramped the forests with rifles at the ready.

When these Californians from another era are suddenly confronted with the new California, the results can be shattering. Says one resident of Point Arena on the Redwood Coast, "It's pretty hair-raising to get back out in civilization." In eastern California, the once isolated Owens Valley has for years been invaded by skiers in wintertime and outdoor vacationers in the summer. The main streets of Independence and Big Pine, which used to be quiet lanes for local travel, have been turned into speedways by weekenders rushing from Los Angeles to the Sierra. Older residents still going about their appointed rounds at the traditional pace do so at their peril. Once when I was staying at Independence, three of the five people I visited were recovering from auto accidents incurred while trying to cross the main street.

All this is not to say that the hinterland is backward in the horse-and-buggy sense. True, in many counties, about half the dwellings have no telephone (in Trinity County, only about two in five have a phone). But many families have two cars in the garage and some have two television sets in the house. Nor do the rimlanders look backward to better days. As one puts it, "I can remember my mother boiling clothes every Monday morning and taking them over to the tub and then rubbing her knuckles bare . . . we had oil lamps or candles for our evening meals and out in the barn . . . it took us all day to go twelve miles to town and back on roads that were hub deep in mud. No thanks, I'll take progress."

The point is that, despite material change, the rimland is still touched by the old customs and graced by the old virtues. Here the terms "neighbor" and "friend" are synonymous. You act decently toward each other because you want a respected place in the only community you will ever know. You don't put on airs because everybody knows all there is to know about you. (In one northern California weekly newspaper, the editor thought nothing of mentioning in an editorial that some of his checks had just bounced.) The excess energies that sophisticated city dwellers expend on status symbols are channeled into social activities in the small town. In Alturas, Modoc County, Parent-Teacher Association meetings are attended by as many as 90 percent of the parents. People have both the time and instinct for old-fashioned Christian charity. When a Shasta County family lost its home by fire, the local Grange held a benefit and the whole community devoted materials and labor to rebuilding the home. So many people volunteered that, in the words of the family's mother, "We had them walking all over each other." At the approach of winter a family of thirteen was stranded in Canby, Modoc County, without enough food and clothing. A local resident took all thirteen into his home, supplied their wants, solicited the community for additional help, and lent his truck so they could tow their car to the nearest garage.

In short, human compassion in California's rimland is not something that is deducted each week from the paycheck. On a busy Los Angeles corner, I have seen a uniformed Salvation Army worker approach, one by one, several well-dressed men and offer the outstretched tambourine. Each one looked quickly away, without a word, in the same way he might treat a panhandler. Neighborhood workers calling door to door for charitable causes report not a few cases of outright rudeness, as though they were a public nuisance. Nor is it easy to get volunteer workers. One Community Chest chairman in Sherman Oaks got only four workers out of thirty tries, and had to import a friend from Arcadia to help out.

Actually, most Californians are in such a hurry to keep an appointment or beat the boss to work that even if the opportunity offered, they wouldn't have time to be good Samaritans. Metropolitan society has become so complex, in fact, that it is not always possible to help someone in distress. If you see a woman with a stalled car along the freeway, you usually can't pull over to help without causing an accident. The ultimate absurdity was achieved in the 1962 Bel Air fire, when the Red Cross rushed to set up nearby emergency receiving stations only to find that fleeing refugees had already headed for the plush Beverly Hilton Hotel.

But the rimland has never fallen into this predicament.

Compassion is not organized out of existence. It is still a first-hand experience between flesh-and-blood people.

In brief, the rimland offers the main exception to the generalization that Californians are superindividualized. In their uncrowded retreat, the rimlanders generally enjoy a degree of privacy. They are only required to defend it against the seasonal forays of vacationers. Usually unharassed and unrushed, they have little impulse to recoil from society. Rather, they are committed to society and to human relationships as the essence of life. They enjoy community activity, provided it is primarily social rather than political or commercial. Like most Californians, they accept minimum responsibility in government at all levels. But unlike most Californians, they need less government because they accept more responsibility toward each other as human beings.

This mode of life still persists in a few other parts of California, principally in the heartlands, but even there it is not the dominant trend. The heartlanders have generally adopted the values of the city dwellers; there is a general belief that most problems are economic and regional, and a tendency to discount social problems as unimportant or nonexistent. There is an identifiable trend in some heartland areas toward personal and family diversion at the expense of community interest.

But the rimlander has generally not been driven to this point. He is apt to be a long-time inhabitant, not a refugee from hardship with a passion for fun in the sun. His community is still sufficiently apart from the mainstream of California life to retain native values and interests. He has a sense of personal worth as a recognized participant in the community. He has little reason to seek artificial worth through material display or to abandon worth as a motivation and concentrate on pleasure. In short, his individuality is exercised in association with others, not mirrored back upon itself in private pursuits.

If the rimlander's concerns are often provincial and sometimes petty, they are at least concerns of the here and now. He is preoccupied, not with future hopes, but with the present reality. In an environment that changes little, he acts as though he will live forever.

CHAPTER VI

The First Child-Centered Society

1.

One afternoon a young California mother fell and sprained her ankle while working in the kitchen. Her cries for help brought her young boy on the run.

"Go next door and get Grandma," gasped the mother, "so she can drive me to the doctor's!"

The little helper's response was automatic.

"Who's gonna cook my dinner?"

California children are not naturally more self-centered than others. They have just come to expect more. One of the most often heard declarations in California is, "The children come first." The unspoken corollary is: Adults come last.

Nor is there a larger proportion of children in California. It just seems that way. A big percentage are concentrated in the new suburban areas of Southern California and the San Francisco peninsula, which are chiefly populated by young families. An extreme is reached in the west end of San Fernando Valley, where the median age is twenty years.[1] These are among the world's great locations for pediatricians, whose office schedules are so tight that a house call is unheard-of.

Not only is the population influx composed more of young families since the last war, but the average size of California families has grown. One or at most two children was the accepted number in the 1920's; three is considered "normal" in the 1960's and five is not unusual. The large family was, in the sophisticated twenties, considered in many quarters to be somewhat boorish; now it is praised universally as a wonderful blessing. Having children is not only popular, it is almost an act of piety. Couples who don't have children are sometimes regarded with suspicion as poor sports who won't join the club—"After all, they could always adopt children if they really wanted them." A happy-looking infant will turn heads and evoke smiles in any public place and is almost a certain conversation-opener between strangers. In fact, nearly any adult antic is excused if it has something to do with enthusiasm for children. I recall an excited father shouting "It's a boy!" from the third floor window of the Santa Monica Hospital, followed by a noisy demonstration by relatives in the street below.

In California, this conspicuous devotion to children has almost reached the point of child worship. For if many Californians have no strong religious faith, and if they are ashamed to acknowledge their basic materialism, they can yet gain a wonderful sense of atonement and self-righteousness through an avowed love of children. The Californian may doubt other traditional values or be unable to make up his mind between alternate claims on his allegiance, but he can always cling to one sure rock of truth that no one doubts: the infinite worth of a child.

There are, perhaps, other reasons for the pedestal position of California youngsters. One could be the frontier tradition of virtual worship for women and children in what was, a century ago, a predominantly male society. Another is the continuing fractured state of California society, in which most people are newcomers uprooted from their native com-

103

munities. The continuity of generations has been broken, at least so far as individual families are concerned. The grandparents and other relatives have been left back East; or else, in the high rate of moving from one community to another within California, close relatives have been left too far away for frequent association. The family is no longer taken for granted, as it might be in a more stable and traditional community. The remaining group, torn loose from its moorings, becomes more precious to its members. Separated from their own parents, young couples turn more completely to their children.

Still another reason can be the submersion of the individual in the urban life of many Californians. In the major cities, the bigness of organization in the political and economic spheres offers little opportunity for personal recognition. If one cannot be important anywhere else, one turns more fully to that institution—the family—in which importance is assured. Dad might not be very big at the office, but he is pretty big at home.

2.

It would be wrong, however, to claim that children are universally loved in California. One needs only to note the high incidence of apartment-house signs specifying "No children" to realize that California is sharply divided between those who love kids and those who don't. California has, of course, a large number of retired people and many others determined to enjoy "resort living" who don't include children in their plans. One reason for the deliberate lack of sidewalks in many expensive neighborhoods is that this eliminates any local traffic on roller skates, kiddy cars, and scooters. As for rental units, as one real estate agent avows, "The first question we have to ask a rental client is whether he has committed the crime of producing children." I know of one father of five children who had to phone sixteen trailer courts before he found one that would take his family. The general attitude is that if you have kids you can go out in the tracts where everybody else has 'em.

One has the feeling, however, that the child haters would be less adamant if California youngsters were more controllable. But part of the special status of California children is a parental indulgence that creates an unusual proportion of intolerable monsters.

California youngsters have traditionally been given considerable freedom. Two generations ago, when California was predominantly rural, the kids were safer outside the house than inside. With due regard for their health, mother would send them out in the sun, not see them again until lunch, and not worry if they didn't show up until dinner. Even in my childhood before the tract era, subdividers sold the vacant land, houses were erected individually, and because of the speculation in real estate, every new community had a large surplus of empty lots. These served as baseball diamonds in summer and football fields in the fall, while in winter and spring they were high with weeds that afforded cover in various battles between opposing sides using grass clods, bean shooters, or rubber guns. For hours at a time, mother would have no idea where Junior was.

There is, then, a tradition of childhood freedom in California. But there is no longer much space in which to exercise it. The street, the sidewalk, and other people's lawns are all that remain; and while these were often used as playgrounds in former days, the frequency was less because so much other land was available. A generation ago the whole neighborhood, including everyone's backyard, was open to all the kids on the block. Today, precisely because the children have nowhere else to go, there tends to be resentment when they trespass. Freedom is no more nor less than it ever was, but lack of space is increasing the nuisance factor. The growing complexity of California society has made it easier for the free-moving California youngster to get into trouble. Even in an outlying part of Santa Barbara County, boys accidentally caught their kite on a high-tension wire, threw things to loosen it, and created a short that caused a power blackout in two communities.

But all this is only one reason for the conspicuous liberties of California youngsters. Another is that California parents are subject to less pressure in the proper upbringing of the kids. Grandparents and other relatives who have strong feelings on the subject are usually not around. Other influences are scattered in several directions; the children may live in one community, go to school in another, to Sunday school in another, and to scout meetings in still another. The impact of these institutions tends to be fractionated, not combined. One feels little responsibility to any community opinion for one's own actions, and still less for the children's.

Consequently, one is freer to follow one's own ideas, to adopt the advice of the child psychiatrists (Spock and Gesell are household words in California), or to practice no particular child-rearing plan at all. Unfortunately, some California parents are so busy enjoying life for themselves that their chief concern for the children is to keep them out of their own hair, even if this means putting them in everybody else's. One of the favorite games played by neighborhood mothers is to see who can send the kids over to the other's house first; it is an undeclared contest, carried on with subtle suggestions like: "Why don't you go over and play with Nancy today?" We once discovered that a child who came to our house often and stayed late actually couldn't go home ("Mommy's away!"), and that we were serving as free baby-sitters.

Mass baby-sitting by the movie houses on Saturday afternoon is so overdone that many of the kids are tired of it. They have to be talked into going and are ready to leave after the first feature.

106

Since the theater is full of kids who are either the products of irresponsible parents or who are unenthusiastic about the movie, the Saturday matinee is generally pure chaos. The adult who is unwary enough to enter this frightening realm of childhood orgy is reminded of a Roman bacchanalia, except that the pleasures are on a different level. The nostrils are affronted with a sickening mélange of odors from buttered popcorn, bubble gum, and licorice. The ears are bombarded with, not only an undertone of conversation that almost drowns the movie dialogue, but from time to time as the screen action warrants, a cacophony of screams that reveals that a good portion of the audience is, after all, paying attention to the picture. Through the dim light one's eyes can make out a writhing sea of small forms, like a herd of seals on a rock. The quieter ones are simply squirming in their seats; the normal ones are continuously running up and down the aisles.

At one matinee described by our eleven-year-old daughter, several girls with a transistor radio going at top volume were twisting in front of the screen. The scene continued for some time because the lone usher was busy disciplining another unruly group in the rear.

In fact, being an usher at a kid's matinee is one of the most underpaid jobs imaginable. If soldiers get a bonus for combat duty, it is only fair to grant bonuses to matinee ushers. During one matinee in Dunsmuir, Siskiyou County, an usher was bitten by a little girl and shot by a boy with a water pistol —all in the same afternoon. Said the theater manager, "These occupational hazards make it hard to get good ushers."

The trouble is that movie exhibitors are still thinking in traditional terms of ushers as ushers. But matinee ushers don't usher anybody. If they tried this, they might be trampled to death. Their function is to prevent mayhem, confiscate dangerous weapons, and administer first aid. The customary teen-age girl in the role of usher is as unsuited for the matinee crowd as she would be serving as a bouncer in a water-front dive. What are needed are large, muscular adults with experience as truant officers, top sergeants, or zoo keepers.

However, this would probably kill the chief function of the Saturday matinee, which is no longer to exhibit a movie, but to provide an arena for the release of pent-up childhood aggressions—three delicious hours of riot, gloriously free from adult supervision. With any serious measures to maintain order, how would parents get the kids out of the house on Saturday?

3.

It is in California, too, that baby-sitting as an institution reaches its zenith. The profusion of children, the scarcity of grandparents, the almost universal lack of older relatives living in the home, make baby-sitting a necessity among people who are so strenuously on the go. In fact, some dutiful grandparents will accept the children for an evening, then get a baby-sitter while they go out.

As soon as a family moves into a new community, one of the wife's primary duties is to start lining up a roster of baby-sitters. One can check the local baby-sitting agency, which may send out an older woman in a nurse's uniform who charges $1.00 an hour and has a keen sense of professional pride that will not let her do menial tasks like clearing off the children's dishes. There is, however, a general hesitancy in hiring baby-sitters through the yellow pages, like a plumber. Most baby-sitters are found by prying names out of neighboring mothers. This is not always easy; some folks regard their baby-sitter list as a family secret, like the savings account balance. There is an understandable fear that when they want to go out they will find that Suzie is booked. One of the social mores of California life is that one doesn't contact a neighbor's baby-sitter directly; one inquires from the neighbor whether she might be able to give a name or two.

Somehow, one manages to build a stockpile of baby-sitters. They consist of two general classes: teen-age girls who want to earn spending money; and older women—often widows— who supplement a fixed income with baby-sitting, and who enjoy children and a change of scenery. Rates start at 50 cents an hour, but are more likely to be 75 cents; some older women insist on fringe requirements such as a minimum of $3.00, a higher rate after midnight, an extra charge for each additional child, and a transportation fee if they have their own car.

Thus, operated as a business, baby-sitting can bring in some fair returns. One eighty-year-old lady in Los Angeles financed a trip around the world by baby-sitting. Another in her seventies took trips to Hawaii, Canada, Alaska, and Europe "via the diaper route."

From the baby-sitter's standpoint, the biggest problem is judging on the first night the level of discipline to which the children are accustomed, and then being careful not to exceed it. If this means letting the little darlings jump on the furniture and look at horror shows on TV—okay. Because it is the children, not the parents, she must please if she is going to be called on again. If the youngsters don't like the baby-sitter, they will say so, and the California parent is constitutionally incapable of leaving them in the care of someone they don't want. I know of one couple whose children scream and refuse to let them go out if they don't get one particular baby-sitter.

As a consequence, the youngsters get to thinking of the baby-sitter not as the one in charge, but as a sort of pal or playmate; whereas the baby-sitter may tend to regard herself as one who merely monitors the scene and phones for help in an emergency.

Considering the unrepressed nature of California kids, this concept can lead to some nightmarish scenes. One teen-age girl found herself used as a target by two little boys playing cowboy with plastic pellets in their guns. She tried to stop them but was only able to hold down one at a time. When she suggested something quiet like finger painting, they put a child's rocking chair on the tray of the baby's high chair and climbed on top. After the baby-sitter got them off she threw herself on the chairs and as she later reported, triumphantly, "They were unable to pry me loose."

Among such children, a baby-sitter's qualifications must include agility, physical strength, and an ability to sense what is coming next. In Los Angeles, a four-year-old, jokingly known as Teddy the Terror, jumped over the couch and landed on the baby-sitter, fracturing two vertebrae and bringing on a damage suit for $150,000. In Santa Monica, an eight-year-old girl grabbed her elderly baby-sitter by the arm, yanked her to the floor, jumped on her, and fractured her knee. Damages: $125,000. These are exceptional cases; but most baby-sitters can provide horror stories about some of their customers.

There are, of course, various efforts to upgrade the baby-sitter's lot with a show of professionalism. The city of Pasadena provides a baby-sitting class where the neophytes learn such things as first aid and antidotes for poison. Another course is held in San Fernando Valley, the undisputed capital of baby-sitting, where students learn do's and don't's resulting from years of experience: "Do not take the children out riding with friends," and "Don't turn up the television so loudly that you can't hear the children."

Despite these civilizing efforts, parents can sometimes come home to sheer anarchy. Two friends of ours came back to find the teen-age baby-sitter holding a platter party in the house. Said the father, "They were dancing clear out to the curb." Another teen-age baby-sitter decided to take the parents' other car for a spin—an adventure made doubly hazardous by the fact that she hadn't learned to drive. After plowing through the rear wall of the garage, the car crashed

110

into a hedge and a fence; it was teetering on a small embankment when the neighbors arrived. By the time the parents got home, the place was surrounded by police, a large crowd, and an ambulance.

Yet the teen-age baby-sitter is a firmly established institution in California. The only restriction as to age is that the girl not be so young that she is an embarrassment to the oldest child. One Santa Monica girl indignantly complained that a proposed baby-sitter was "in my class at school." And though the young mother using a teen-age baby-sitter might phone up once or twice in the evening to see how things are going, it is not many months before she is dashing off without even remembering to leave the phone number where she can be reached. One sometimes senses a growing belief that getting a baby-sitter is in itself an act of responsibility that absolves one from further concern till one returns. A Pasadena woman (admittedly, an extreme case) stayed away all night without notifying the baby-sitter, who took the children to the police next morning. At 11 A.M. the mother told the desk sergeant that she "became ill and decided to stay with a friend all night."

All this is not to say that California parents are neglectful of their children. On the contrary, most are doting enough to keep from going many places without the young ones, who will assuredly complain if they feel they are being left out of too much fun. Several times I have heard parents decline to do something because "we've been going out too much lately without the children." I have known one or two couples who refuse to get any baby-sitters and aren't sure about trusting the grandparents, either.

But these are considered extremists. The very fact that California is unusually endowed with children has brought ways and means for parents to make temporary and merciful escapes. Chief among these is the cooperative nursery, in which mothers take turns caring for a whole yardful; in

111

return, as one mother said almost gleefully, "You get four mornings a week to yourself." In some areas such as the San Francisco peninsula, Orange County, and San Fernando Valley, the whole pace of commercial life seems geared to children. Supermarkets provide shopping carts with seats for infants and comic-book racks to keep the older children busy while Mama shops undistracted. Some department stores provide strollers for the children; bowling centers and other places of business sometimes offer a nursery complete with toys, lollipops, and a registered nurse. During the Christmas season, Van Nuys merchants give the children free tickets to the weekend matinees so their mothers can shop undisturbed. For the same reason, San Francisco has offered mass baby-sitting in the form of a six-hour bus tour of the zoo, aquarium, and Chinatown, including lunch. There seems to be a mutual understanding in the adult community that some social devices must be established to keep the kids from taking over completely.

4.

The fact is that most California parents are remarkably active with their children. Weekends and holidays are assumed to be reserved for the whole family, with the youngsters carrying a large voice in determining whether the scene of operations will be the beach, the mountains, or the desert. Nowhere is the Californian's withdrawal to personal interests (rather than community interests) more apparent than in his devotion to youth groups. The organizations to which the parents are committed are generally concerned with children's activity—Boy and Girl Scouts, Little League baseball, YMCA, PTA. A generation ago only a few parents of scouts were active in the troop. Today all fathers are expected to participate, and those who don't are suspected of hating children. Others who haven't the time for active work show their

112

commitment in smaller ways; one mother who refuses to put bumper strips on her car for political or other causes will make one exception: Girl Scout cookies. In the YMCA Indian Guides, the fathers go with the boys to meetings and sit in a circle with the sons wearing Indian headdresses. When I observed to a friend that maybe the Indian Guide kids would sometimes like to be left alone and that the fathers might feel a little silly in those feathers, he drew back and growled, "You're talking to a chief."

Even in Parent-Teacher Associations, very little of the grass-roots work is concerned with curricula and studies. These policy matters are determined at the regional and state level. Most of Mommy's PTA activity is with the annual carnivals, popcorn sales, and puppet shows, where she is working with the children.

The ultimate togetherness in youth activities has been achieved in Little League baseball, where a guy can't play ball without his parents being in the stands and telling him whether to swing, bunt, or walk. Undoubtedly Little League is an outgrowth of the loss of sandlots in California subdivisions. Impromptu ball games are almost out of the question; the streets are dangerous because of the headlong California traffic that seeks even the side roads as avenues for commuting. Baseball and almost any other sport has to be carried on at public facilities beyond walking distance. In short, recreation has to be organized. As one suburban father said, "An unorganized child is almost impossible to find."

So while there is a real need for activities such as Little League, an accompanying result is that the child has lost the experience of doing something on his own with his peers. In Little League, the coach and the parents are in charge. The boys are helped by the elders, but one gets the feeling that they are smothered with help. In extreme cases they become a floor show for the adults, who all the while take great pride in supporting Junior. On one block in Palos

113

Verdes Estates, two fathers nearly came to blows over whose son would be pitcher. Playing well for one's own pride is submerged in the desire to play well for one's parents; and it may well be asked what happens to those who aren't athletic enough to make the team, but who nevertheless like to play baseball.

One wonders, too, what has become of spontaneous games such as cowboys and bandits (Western kids have always played this instead of cops and robbers), which once spurred in boys the enthusiasm for adventure and the sense of self-reliance. There is no place for such games in front and back yards that are show places and not to be trampled on. Children get all the equipment they need—slides, swings, pools—and all the help they need—organizations, transportation, uniforms. One gets the feeling that parents are trying to make up in these ways for what society has denied the children by failing to provide play room—if not vacant lots, then small parks within walking distance of any neighborhood. The wonderful spontaneity of play is gone, and parents are trying to compensate by organization.

In fact, participation in youth groups has become a social necessity. Pressure comes not only from other parents, but more especially from the children, who make the point that they would be dreadfully embarrassed if theirs were the only parents who didn't participate. As one suburbanite says, "There is almost no chance that you can avoid working with youth."

Thus, it is not at all clear that every parent approaches this duty in the right spirit. On one Girl Scout camping trip, the mothers got the girls into their sleeping bags and then broke out the vodka and orange juice. In one parents' meeting, which had been scheduled to end at 9:00 P.M., the chairman found himself only partway through the agenda by the appointed time. The members got up en masse and took their leave. They had performed their duty for the night.

In brief, "working with the kids" has become a social duty that impinges on every parent in the community; through it, one achieves the general approval and the kind of moral grace once associated with going to church. Actually, in a society where church affiliation is much lower than in the rest of the nation, youth activity might be said to be a kind of secondhand religious identification. There is the same tendency to equate participation with personal goodness; the same belief that the procedure somehow has a "cleansing" influence and makes one "a better person"; and there is the same assumption by the community that one will certainly take his part if he regards himself as a first-class human.

Little wonder that in this new religion of child worship, backsliders and hypocrites are as common as in any other religion. What is significant is that the desire to do good is not necessarily stripped away as people lose religious affiliation; on the contrary, cut loose from one rock, they will find another that still satisfies their hunger for self-esteem.

The main problem in the Californian's devotion to youth work is not that it is wrong in itself; it is actually one of the healthiest and most desirable aspects of California life. The difficulty is that it is becoming the be-all of personal participation in the community. Children's groups are coming to be equated with community activity, as though there is no other. Wrote one Little League president in his appeal for more active parents, "It is another opportunity to show youngsters the real need for adult participation in community affairs." Political, social, cultural, even religious activities tend to become eclipsed by the priority on people's time demanded by youth work.

In brief, the tendency of Californians to abdicate from society, to operate on one's own for one's self and family, is becoming institutionalized and morally justified by youth organization. The fact that adults are involved in the youth groups tends to conceal the fact that these are not really adult activities. And it is not at all clear that the children themselves want this level of parental togetherness. One of them, whose parents were devoting literally all their spare time to the children, asked innocently, "Do you ever do anything as grown-ups?"

5.

Actually, the California child is a kind of projection of the parents' own ambitions. They came to California to better themselves, and to do even better for their children. They are determined to give the youngsters the best possible "advantages," both for their present enjoyment and for their future advancement. Public schools have always received strong support in California, but there is a growing personal interest by parents in their children's progress—more discussions with the teachers, more complaints to the principal. In the past, California schools were often noted for an excess of frills: elaborate cafeterias, sports equipment, gymnasia, even swimming pools (one school in San Fernando Valley is completely air-conditioned). But there has come to be more emphasis on academic excellence as part of the preparation for the great contest of life. One subdivision, flying in the face of competition emphasizing status-type features, bases its ads on the superior schools in the district: "Assure the best education for your children . . ."

Yet there are other factors accounting for the unusual place of California youngsters. One is the California adult's easygoing approach to life. He was attracted to the Coast by its ease of living, informality, and the latitude it provides for personal pursuits. California is therefore not filled with disciplinarians or formalists. One might even say that the mass of Californians do not have the determination and the conviction to enforce consistent principles on their children. Because the father's time at home is often limited by overtime hours in defense plants and long commuting distances, the mother is the main source of family discipline. California mothers and fathers both tend to have a high threshold of tolerance for the antics of their children; to avoid the unpleasant scenes that are necessary to maintain an atmosphere of order; to allow the children to wheedle them into or out of anything; and in general to let nature take its course in the family relationships. They have a relaxed and permissive attitude around the home that opens the door to more and more self-assertion by the children.

Uninhibited by the parents, children become the loudest and most insistent element in a family discussion. And parents inclined to take the easy way out will submit in order to keep the peace. At one outdoor party, the children were doing something obnoxious and one father objected to making them stop. "We can bargain with 'em," he announced, and thereupon entered negotiations prepared to make some other concession.

Thus, decision by pressure rather than by logic is an affliction of many California homes. One mother told me without blinking that their reason for leaving one church and joining another was that "the children liked it." When elementary schoolchildren were divided into different classes according to their academic needs, one mother tried to get her girl switched to a different class because "all of her Brownie troop is in it."

This apparent inability of many California parents to challenge their children reaches its apogee when criticism comes from the outside. In San Diego, a teacher took a boy to the principal's office for making a noise in the hall, and for this she later received a slapping by the boy's mother. It is not by accident that California teachers are generally prohibited from spanking their pupils; proper discipline apparently isn't worth the uproar it brings from the parents. One Santa Monica teacher was kicked by two of the students, who got

117

off without punishment. When an amazed observer questioned the principal about this, she shrugged it off with, "It was a substitute teacher." A seven-year-old schoolboy who was forbidden to paint pictures while the rest of the class was doing arithmetic became so provoked that during the lunch period he stayed inside and painted the whole room; the amazing part is that his mother, who is otherwise quite sensible, laughs uproariously whenever she tells the story.

There is in this frame of mind a curious absence of right and wrong. One sticks up for one's children out of loyalty. The idea is that kids (especially one's own) are wonderful, and let 'em have fun.

Such an attitude leads to some extraordinary indulgences. When asked whether he discussed his work with his wife, a Daly City man admitted frankly that "at the table the kids dominate what you'll talk about." When the *New York Times* came to the Coast with its Western Edition, one subscriber also continued to take the *Los Angeles Times* because "the children wanted to read the comics." Children's pets are tolerated to the point where the home can become an amateur menagerie; one of our children's friends has no less than seventeen hamsters, in addition to a dog, cat, and goldfish. Much of mother's day, and part of father's evening, is spent chauffeuring the youngsters to meetings. I have seen mothers driving their sons around on their paper routes while the little darlings sit in the back seat throwing the papers out the window. Allowances have become so inflated that the kids make a custom out of throwing money away. When new seventh graders enter some junior high schools the other kids will throw pennies at their feet; the victim who is unsophisticated enough to reach for a penny is shamed with the epithet, "Chop," which is apparently the modern equivalent of "jerk." One teacher who waited until class was over gleaned more than a dollar's worth of pennies from the floor.

Christmas, which has a strangely unreal flavor in California due to the general absence of snow, is connected only occasionally with religion and has become a month-long festival for children. In Studio City, the annual Christmas parade carries a Western theme, with Santa riding in a stagecoach. In another local Christmas parade, religious carols were rendered by a school drum and bugle corps; "Adeste Fideles" was accompanied by drum majorettes and exhibitions of baton twirling. Some communities such as Santa Monica and Van Nuys make an exceptional effort to keep the Christmas meaning through pageants and parades depicting the life of Christ. But most California children have a vague impression that Christmas, as one seventh-grade girl described it, "is a time to be religious and have fun."

Halloween has passed from the era of mischief and has become a kind of wholesale grab bag for kids who wouldn't know how to inflict a trick if they were challenged to do so. Paper sacks in hand, the little goblins descend on the neighborhood as though the evening's loot is a constitutional right. One boy announced that he had collected four bagsful last year, and was going to set a record with six. Other kids are by no means backward in expressing disappointment at a meager haul. Said one of the more tactful ones, "Thanks. Are you running out?" I have heard youngsters make monetary estimates of value received on leaving the door, "Five cents worth of candy!" Some families commercialize the evening to the point of driving the kids to other neighborhoods after their own is worked out. One doorstep contributor had the last laugh when the little ones were back home sorting their evening's take on the living-room rug; there, amidst the candy, gum, and popcorn, was a dog biscuit.

Quick to realize their elevated status, California children have come to expect that everyone will watch out for them. While playing at another child's house, many feel free to ask the mother for something to eat and will even invite themselves to lunch. On North Island in San Diego, two little

119

girls going home from school made motorists wait while they turned cartwheels across the street. One day I was driving past several boys who had stopped with their bicycles along a busy thoroughfare; one of them stepped into the street, held up his hand, and displayed a most serious expression as though they were in trouble. When I slammed on the brakes, he walked up and inquired, "Which way to Westwood?"

For their part, California adults seem to have great faith in the ability of their children to do most anything. There is a growing fad among business executives to decorate their offices with the paintings of their children or grandchildren. I have heard visitors rave over this art until they were told proudly that it was the work of, say, a three-year-old. Most California zoos have a section where a child can get inside the enclosure, pick up an animal, and feed it—all on the sublime assumption that neither will bite the other. In San Francisco, the natural history museum even lends out animals, reptiles, and birds to the youngsters. In one coastal town a sixth-grade class launches its own rockets, recovering the nose cones complete with "moustronauts" by parachute. In Van Nuys, a fifth-grade class wrote and produced a forty-minute opera.

Encouraged by such freedom, California youngsters are apt to pull off some rather adult adventures. In North Hollywood, a twelve-year-old boy whose bicycle had been run over by a car took the grievance to the small claims court, pleaded his own case, and won a damage claim. In Solano County, a woman was wrapping a package to be sent to her brother in the Vacaville Prison Hospital. When she left the room a moment, her little boy slipped a cap pistol in the package, later causing a small panic when it was discovered by prison inspectors. In San Francisco, a storekeeper lent money to youngsters on condition that they spend it in his store; when arrested he had in his pocket a dozen IOU's in the handwriting of tots from eight to thirteen.

Since there is considered to be, after all, very little difference between adults and children, there is a noticeable trend among mothers to expect, even to encourage, their daughters to take an interest in the opposite sex at an age when they are still playing with dolls. Dancing classes, in which there is a distressing lack of interest by the boys, are commonly held for the sixth graders. One Pasadena class takes children as young as seven, and to boys who keep the girls at arm's length the instructor is merciless. "If I can see between you, you're too far apart." In the public school at Thousand Oaks, Ventura County, social dancing was part of the instruction for seventh and eighth graders until two ministers protested on moral grounds. Since then the footwork has been limited to folk dancing and square dancing as part of the social studies course.

Private parties of mixed boys and girls can begin at age ten, though many mothers think this a trifle early. Even before this, girls begin to spend fantastic periods of time in the bathroom fussing with their hair. Avant-garde hairdos begin to show up at ten and are universal at twelve. At eleven, a few girls begin wearing a trace of lipstick. By ten, girls are spending a lot of time talking about boys, though the accepted approach is to protest how desperately they hate them. By eleven, a girl may have what her chums recognize as a boy friend, though she is the first to deny it and the boy in question is oblivious to the whole matter.

The fact is that for all this undercover attention, the boys are exasperatingly unconcerned. As early as eleven, a particularly precocious boy might begin displaying an interest in a girl by such antics as riding by her house doing acrobatics on his bicycle. By twelve, he might take a more active role by hitting her on the arm, chasing her with lizards, or dropping books on her head. But the male Californian is primarily

121

interested in sports from the moment he is old enough to throw a ball; he generally puts off diverting attention to girls until they become a biological and psychological challenge that can no longer be ignored.

All of which makes the subteen period the one of sharpest contrast between California boys and girls. The girls are becoming little women. They have learned how to cook, though they seem to concentrate on cakes, pies, and cookies. They willingly help with the baby, which becomes far more than a real-life doll; one of our daughters admitted when she went to camp that she would miss her little brother most of all. They are conscious of appearance; at Halloween, while the boys masquerade as ghosts and other scary creatures, the girls seize the chance to dress as ballet dancers, flappers, or movie stars.

They become conscious of the role of money; when one girl asked her sister if she wanted to help make a scrap book, the reply was, "What will you pay me?" Once when I hired a teen-age boy to do some yard work, I discovered that he had, in turn, hired my eleven-year-old daughter to wash his car.

Finally, they become addicted to organized activity, which has a kind of small-fry social status. Doing what is fashionable becomes a prime rule of life, and if one's friends are joining the Bluebirds one wouldn't think of becoming a Brownie. The tyranny of fashion shows itself in more unexpected ways; one girl was determined to keep her notebook clean, but finally drew pictures all over it because all the other kids did.

Nowhere does the remarkable transformation of California girls show itself more than in their sudden attachment for horses. Beginning at the age of nine, they collect pictures of horses, put little statues of them on their dressers, watch "horsy" shows on TV, and start agitating to take riding lessons. In California, the riding academies, particularly those offering controlled riding and jumping lessons with English

122

saddles, are swamped with girls from age nine to fifteen. Some Girl Scout and Campfire Girl groups operate as mounted patrols, learning not only how to ride and jump, but how to shoe a horse. In Palos Verdes, the First Baptist minister noticed a sharp drop in female Sunday school attendance at the beginning of the riding season. He met the problem by instituting a "hunt breakfast" culminating in Sunday school services at the church. The former truants are now known as the "Riding Baptists."

Why girls in California become fascinated with horses is one of the many mysteries of womanhood. Says one riding master, "They like to mother horses." Yet they can mother other pets; the manifest power of the horse may be associated in some deep Freudian wellspring with the human male, particularly since the power is harnessed and controlled in true female fashion. Probably the little dears are also aware of the smart figure cut by the accomplished horsewoman. In any case, one is struck with the thought that the whole process has something to do with becoming a woman.

On the other hand, California boys are not little men, but a separate breed in a separate world. If they were not so blessedly unconscious of being different they might be considered something like half-pint beatniks. In contrast to the California girl, who is dressed as smartly as her mother, the boy has the appearance of a sawed-off derelict. He takes a kind of manly pride in looking like something washed up with the driftwood. Anyone wearing more than faded jeans and a T-shirt (with the tail out) is suspected either of putting on airs or being a "new kid" from back East.

In fact, the California boy displays a fine disdain for pretense and outward display that predates the beatniks. When I was a boy, my parents gave me a bicycle complete with all the extras—lamp, toolbox, and basket—but social pressures against such frills impelled me to take them off and hide them before the other kids could see them.

Provided he has a bicycle, the average California boy is as self-sufficient and as independent of material possession as Mahatma Gandhi. He goes a step beyond by not only ignoring the value of purchased things, but actively putting value on the valueless. That is, he attaches worth, not to that which is bought in a store, but to that which he finds in a neighbor's trash barrel.

If the California boy is different from the American boy, it is only that he has a little more room, considerably more parental latitude, and a lot more outdoor climate, to be himself. Out of such freedom he was unwittingly developed the original protest movement against the threadbare values of his time. Philosophically he lies somewhere between Henry David Thoreau and Jean Paul Sartre; he drifts through life with that precious aimlessness that lives spontaneously and makes no plans; his biggest problem, and the sum of his personal program, is the question of how to get to the beach this afternoon.

6.

This is not to say that California children are not influenced by the values of their parents. Girls and boys alike may put great store by the newness, bigness, or smartness of the family car; there is considerable awareness—and frank discussion—of comparative sizes of family swimming pools; the child with color TV in the house is not likely to keep it a secret.

But these are family icons. They seem to be tied in with the child's loyalties, rather than his scale of real worth; that is, he sounds off about the family car in the same way that he insists his grammar school is the best in town, or California is the greatest state in the Union. One cannot help suspecting that the viewpoint is indoctrinated, not spontaneous.

Yet this, in the last analysis, pinpoints the basic ingredient in the unusual relationship between California children and adults. There is really very little difference in the rights, the prerogatives, and the values of the two. It is as though the traditional Western equality between women and men is extended also to children. All are citizens of the family—all have an equal voice. And in a society that prizes action rather than thought, fun rather than duty, there is little to choose between the values of the young and the adults. The youngsters are anxious to appear "big," "smart," and "popular." Though the methods are different, so are their parents. Adults put undiluted emphasis on "having fun" in life, with work regarded only as a necessary means to that end. Correspondingly, the children universally profess to dislike school, since this is work. One of my daughters admitted privately that she liked school, "but I wouldn't tell that to the other kids." The children put their treasure in material goodies out of a lack of appreciation for the intangible values of life; the adults put their treasure in bigger homes and newer cars, which are, in a sense, simply grown-up toys.

The main difference is that the parents actually have responsibilities, while the children have almost none. To the youngster there appears no particular incentive to grow up; he is happy where he is, and if he has an ambition to be something else, it is a teen-ager, not an adult, and least of all a parent. Nowadays, preteen girls are less apt to play with baby dolls than with teen-age dolls, through which they act out the sophisticated apartment life of the young professional girl.

On the other hand, the average Californian tends to have a certain envy, even admiration, of children, who know what they want, generally get it, and pay for it with no compensating duties or problems. Such an idyllic existence the adult will never see again; the California native therefore tends to look back on childhood and youth as the happiest days of his life. Youth, in fact, becomes the prime of life; the adult not only wants to help assure this for his children, but subconsciously wants to share it with them by a kind of secondhand or permanent childhood.

Thus, permitting the children equality with adults also permits adults equality with children. In many cases, the family becomes a sort of corporate creature with the values of a child and the finances of an adult. The result is a near-complete dedication to fun in the obvious and material sense— outings, sports, shows, and things. The intellectual contribution that the adult can make to an adult-managed society is diverted into the aims of the family. The adult mind is, in short, reduced to child's play.

The result is that, in California, children have the best chance of growing up without the frustrations, inhibitions, and traumatic experiences customarily associated with problems of the human mind. In the period of life considered to be formative, Californians may be unusually well adjusted.

For this achievement many of them pay the price of growing up into an adulthood that, in terms of adult capabilities, can be almost meaningless. The well-adjusted personality graduating from childhood has no place to go. Adulthood therefore tends to look back to childhood for its significance. Many Californians are so occupied with children and with the values of childhood that there is no such thing as growing up. They have been so intent on raising well-adjusted children that they have never adjusted to adulthood. In contrast to other societies that have been centered around the church, the feudal lord, or the national state, California society is apparently becoming the first to be centered around children.

CHAPTER VII

The Alien World of Youth

1.

"Adolescence," according to a California junior high school newspaper, "is that period in a child's life when his parents become most difficult."

Fortunately, California teen-agers are tolerant. They realize the old folks are just going through a phase. And so the teen-agers solve this problem by giving their parents more freedom. Around fourteen for girls and fifteen for boys, they stop running the household. They leave the decisions to the parents. Mentally, if not physically, they leave home.

In many California homes, the stage has already been set for this schism by the children's freedom to come and go as they please. By the time they are old enough to fry an egg—say, at ten—some of them have been getting their own breakfasts, packing their lunches, and catching the school bus while Mama sleeps. For the teen-ager, it is an easy step to include dinner among the separate meals. In some households there are no set mealtimes, the youngsters pick up a sandwich for themselves and the traditional period for family discussion is gone.

"In too many homes today," says one Los Angeles marriage

counselor, "home is a hotel where the children check in for meals and then proceed to go about their business, coming and going at will—and so do their parents."

The truth is that teen-agers and adults tend to live in separate worlds in California—even more separate than in the rest of the country. And there is a serious question which world is dominant. All day long radio disc jockeys cater to the musical tastes of the teeners. Drive-ins, from restaurants to movies, are physically preempted by them until an adult feels like a spy from another camp. They dominate the beaches with an arrogance that springs from their obvious physical superiority. In any public focal point—libraries, restaurants, buses, Saturday night movies—the presence of teen-agers transforms the scene and dominates it with their noises and their antics. Said one elderly woman, "Whenever I have to go downtown on the bus, I try to make the trip there and back while school children are in class, because I am actually afraid to ride on the same bus with them."

Even when the youngsters are at home—certainly not a likely occurrence—the facilities are marshaled to their command. From the time the little ones are old enough to watch TV, the parents generally capitulate in any conflict over the choice of shows to watch. Little wonder that the isolation of the teeners is not always just their idea, but a mutual agreement with the parents. Behind closed doors, their record player is not quite shattering to the whole house. And their separately listed telephone mercifully leaves the other line open to the rest of the family. In Los Angeles, where the Federal District Court uses the phone directly for selecting jury panels, girls as young as thirteen are apt to receive a jury duty questionnaire.

Nowhere is the ascendancy of the teens more apparent than in the California language. It is the youngsters who continually recharge it both with new words and new definitions for old words. Probably quicker than in most other societies, California adults adopt teen slang as their own because it helps them retain a necessary sense of youth and awareness. Grown-ups who talked of "having a ball" switched easily, on cue from their children, to "having a blast." Most Californians, including adults, consider themselves "hip"; to them, nonconformist youth have become the norm of conformity. Knowing the futility of trying to lick 'em, the adults joined 'em. A good many Californians of any age have, or think they have, a teen-age heart.

2.

The key factor that has given the California youth his independent status is the automobile. Though local buses operate on some California streets, they offer no hope of keeping up with the breathless pace of California life. For anyone seriously participating in the California society, a personal car is imperative. Further, a California juvenile is eligible for a driver's license at sixteen, and if he has a certificate of family necessity, at fourteen. As a result of these combined facts, nearly all California youths sixteen or older have the use of a car. When one Sacramento girl reached sixteen and asked for driving lessons, the only way the father could put her off was to let her learn to fly an airplane. "Flying is so much safer than driving a car," he explained. Taking a girl out on a date by bus is absolutely unthinkable, and most girls wouldn't go out a second time with a boy who couldn't scrape up a car.

A generation ago this generally meant talking Dad into lending the family car for a date. A relatively small percentage of high school pioneers owned their own cars; needless to say, they began to supplant athletes as the school heroes. They were the ones who, at any moment, could take the gang down to the nearest malt shop, which was the predecessor of the drive-in restaurant as the favorite teen-age

129

hangout. They could get to the beach after school or on weekends without having to wait for the family auto. And they could line up a date without first having to line up a car.

Since then, the high school boy without his own car is almost an exception. One Southern California teen-ager estimates that 70 percent of his acquaintances seventeen or older own their own cars. The thing may be a crate of prewar vintage, but it is probably in better running order than the old man's. For many teen-agers, the mechanical operation of the automobile is still more important than the style. These kids not only tune the engine to perfection, but they are constantly experimenting with improvements, which, through some mysterious grapevine, sometimes find their way into Detroit's latest models. In fact, Detroit has learned so well that most means of putting more power under the hood can be purchased in production models. It's getting so the only way the self-respecting youngster can keep his fingernails greasy is to keep the engine tuned.

Moreover, the teen-ager's car is apt to be in better physical shape than his dad's. The chrome is shined to mirror finish, the upholstery smells new, and at the slightest excuse the body gets a new paint job. Nor is the thing covered with signs or pictures—an affectation that went out in the twenties. The teen-age car has gone respectable; it's no longer necessary to make a joke out of it.

To many California boys, devotion to the car is a combination hobby, sport, and religion. Southern California is the original home of the hot rod, which is simply a jalopy with power. The boy's object is to save money by using a cheap frame (vintage chassis all the way back to the Model A Ford) and then keep himself insolvent by pouring every dollar he can scrape up in the engine.

The whole process is based on competition, starting with the first time two teen-agers pulled up at a Wilshire Boulevard stop signal and one shouted to the other, "Beat you at the dig!" For two decades Southern California streets were given an extra measure of hazard by the impromptu drag races of the teeners. By the late 1940's, these had become so well organized that, in the wee hours of night, a paved riverbed or a lonely highway would be the rendezvous for dozens of hot rod racers. One of the more intriguing cat-and-mouse games was that carried on between the racers and the police, who might get a tip on a drag race in much the same manner that they would hear about a floating crap game. There are still occasional unauthorized drag races, even in broad daylight. One motorist came from a side street to Pacific Coast Highway, where he was stopped at a roadblock and politely informed by a youngster, "You can't come through here, sir." The highway had been set off as a racetrack, complete with automatic timers and a short wave radio to warn of police car calls. On a main uptown street in San Diego, dragsters took over several blocks for more than an hour while a crowd of 3,000 gathered to watch the races. When police arrived to halt the fun, the mob attacked them, stole their guns, tried to overturn their car, and was only dispersed with tear gas.

But since about 1950 hot rodding has generally been made respectable by two pioneering California institutions, the drag strip and the car club. The National Hot Rod Association, with headquarters in Los Angeles, began searching for off-street sites to hold drag races under controlled conditions. They were soon aided by local police departments, who decided that if they couldn't beat the dragsters, they would join 'em. Strips sprang up, first in Southern California and then throughout the nation; by the end of the fifties, it was almost considered amateurish to race on the streets. The whole sport has been refined with trial heats, electrical timing devices, and some sixty-seven separate classes for different chassis and engine types. In the old tradition of the digout

131

at the stop signal, each heat is generally conducted between two participants, and the object is to see how fast one is going at the end of a quarter-mile. The institution is actually in danger of being taken over by adults; the average age of dragsters is twenty-six. Some strips are operated not as a public service but as a commercial enterprise, and little effort is made to maintain the original intent.

Meanwhile, police departments and other civic groups were also sponsoring car clubs, which have become a way of life to some 40,000 teen-age members of some 3,000 clubs in Los Angeles County alone. By now the clubs are generally less interested in racing than in modifying cars, breathing and sleeping cars. From its inception in Southern California, the car club craze has spread throughout the country to include the more than 500,000 youngsters represented in the National Hod Rod Association.

What is the magic appeal of the hot rod and the car club? The first clue is the determined effort for recognition. Hot rodding is rooted in show-offmanship. But the kids not only show their personal prowess on the track—they also want everybody to know about their club. Evidence of car-clubbism is seen in the formal metal name plates hanging from the back of club member cars and in the club signs painted in gaudy letters on the sandstone cliffs facing major highways. Another clue is found in the names of clubs—The Rod-busters, the Avengers, etc. Like young blades everywhere, the California male teener pictures himself in the role of the gay, debonair adventurer. His car is his white charger. The horsemen of other years were happiest when they were thundering at full tilt, wheeling on a dime, and throwing dirt where the girls could see them. The teen drivers are in their element when they lurch out from a dead stop, turn a corner with tires squealing, and leave streaks of hot rubber in the street— also where the girls can see.

The showmanship element in California's car consciousness

132

is seen in another variation of the sport—the modification of cars simply for appearance sake. Cutting down the cab, dropping the front axle—these are only the most elementary of the ideas that have caught the fancy of the car kids. Engines are not only tinkered with incessantly, but are often kept in a chrome-plated, gleam-polished condition, which the owner displays by leaving off the hood. Such mechanical craftsmanship almost qualifies as a new art form. At customized car shows, appearance rather than performance is rated by the judges. In one show in Santa Ana, an eighteen-year-old girl who came in second made the comment, "The boy whose car won had his towed into the show. I drove mine in."

But whether show-offmanship or craftsmanship, hot rodding is a distinct and insistent mode of self-expression by young people who may otherwise have little means of being heard. Indeed, whether a boy owns a hot rod or a conventional car, it is often the locus of his consciousness. He not only spends endless boy-hours fussing with it, but he puts in still more time earning money to sink into it. In the city of Los Angeles alone, 10,000 school children work half-days through the week and 40,000 more work Saturdays and vacations. This includes boys working as supermarket packers or gas station attendants and girls as store clerks or cashier, but it by no mean includes the thousands of girl baby-sitters or boy odd jobbers. Many have businesses of their own, complete with bookkeeping records, business cards, and even payrolls to meet. Says one girl in the jewelry business, "I have trouble with product quality control. We have up to 40 percent inspector rejects on our earrings." A thirteen-year-old entrepreneur does all manner of odd jobs, from gardening and housework to—his oddest job—burying a dead cat. When phoned for an interview he replied, "Please hold the phone, I'll have to consult my calendar," then allowed that he would "squeeze it in at three o'clock."

According to a school survey, most of the girls are earning

money to buy clothes, the boys to support cars. A Redondo High School official said, "The student seems to have an intense need for money." Some are farsighted enough to invest part of it. The investment clubs that sprang up in the early 1960's included some exclusively for teen-agers. The Highland Park Teen-age Investment Club takes $5 per month from each member; in the first few months of operation, the market value of its securities increased nearly 20 percent.

So experienced are California youngsters in handling money that some stores are establishing teen-age charge accounts. One large San Diego department store has had such accounts for teen-agers since 1957 and reports, "They have set a substantially better payment record than adults." It is not unusual for teen-age boys to earn $1,500 in summer work, and then put it all on a down payment for an expensive car. In San Fernando Valley, where one auto assembly plant hires boys as young as sixteen, the youngsters are among the best customers for high-priced sports cars. Living with their parents and operating without overhead, they can put all their money into their white charger.

What happens to their studies is a subject of wide concern among high school principals. After making a survey to correlate grades with car ownership, one principal announced, "High school boys are joyriding right out of an education." Anaheim Union High School sends a form letter to parents of new students warning of the pitfalls for car owners: lower grades, antisocial attitude toward nonowners, and a high rate of school dropouts due to "excessive interest in and attempting to support a car." In a final triumph for the auto over rival interests, Whittier High School reported difficulty in getting boys to turn out for varsity sports because they were spending after-school hours providing for their cars.

Just as serious is the effect of teen car ownership on highway safety. The California boy is inclined to view his car, not only as transportation, but as an extension of his personality and an instrument of self-assertion. He is neither as rude as many adult drivers nor so much in a hurry. But he is more apt to show off—to bystanders, to passengers, and to himself.

This explains why auto insurance rates for people under twenty-five are staggering. Of all Los Angeles County drivers between sixteen and eighteen years of age, some two out of three get traffic citations each year; the rate for adults is about one out of five. That much of this is the result of male self-assertion is at least hinted by the fact that only 10 percent of teen-age violators are girls.

Thus, the special place of the auto in California life has manufactured a serious social problem—teen-age carmanship. The most obvious alternative—raising the age requirement to eighteen—would in turn bring a major social change. Education would go up and traffic accidents would go down, but the male teener would have lost a major symbol of his manhood. That he cannot vote is of little consequence to him; that he is prohibited from buying drinks is widely circumvented; but stripping him of his car would be an unbearable humiliation. What means would be left to play the dashing cavalier? In this predicament, the possible aberrations of California's energetic youth are frightening to imagine.

3.

In vindication of teen carsmanship, it must be said that California youth are generally happy. Mobile, reasonably well financed, and with few parental restraints, they have a premature taste of freedom. They are not required to pay for this pleasant state with any particular responsibilities. And they live in a part of the world where climate and geography combine to provide a year-round grab bag of diversions.

135

Though winter offers mountain skiing and desert excursions, it is the summer that brings the teener into his element. Certainly most of California has nowhere near the seasonal changes suffered by the rest of the country; in fact, Southern California originally attracted Eastern tourists for its mild winter season. But to the Californian—teen-ager and adult —summer is something special. Except where man has filled the air with smog, the skies are clear, the sun is out all day, the earth is warm, and the very atmosphere is redolent with magic. The Californian comes out of his cocoon in a kind of blissful animation that lasts, depending on the year's weather, from June to October. Each year, if it is overcast through June—as it often is—the Californian is surprised and disgruntled. He looks to the sky as his source of health and well-being; if it is hazy when it should be sunny, he is depressed and grumpy all day; but if the sun is out and the light glints off the chromium, he comes alive as if he had been wound up with a key.

Contrary to some critics, the California sun is not enervating—at least not on the coast where it is tempered by the ocean breeze. The Californian's happiness is not that of the lizard on the rock. It is as though the sunshine, through some strange osmosis, penetrates his system like a wonderful tonic. The heat and the light affect him as though he had just emerged, half frozen, from a meat locker and were suddenly thawed.

All of this is what happens—in exaggerated degree—to the California teen-ager. Officially, the season begins with spring vacation, when California's young people convince themselves that the weather is better than it really is. There is a thunderous migration of high school and college kids to the beach resorts—Santa Cruz and Carmel in the north, and Newport, Laguna, and Avalon in the south. This is not a haphazard operation, but a pilgrimage demanded by tradition. A generation ago the exodus converged on two points: Monterey Bay and Balboa. But measures for self-protection raised by these communities, plus the sheer growth in the teen population, have opened up other beach towns, as well as Palm Springs, to the annual invasion.

The procedure is for a group of girls or boys to rent a house—at rates running from $200 to $500 a week—with a chaperon as young and irresponsible as possible. During the day, the streets, beaches, lagoons, and surf are swarming with kids all anxious to get acquainted with each other in order to be invited to house parties at night. Each resort becomes a large arena for the boy-meets-girl process. And with a minimum of chaperonage, the possibilities are limitless.

So while the kids call it Big Week, the residents call it Hell Week. Throwing bottles, racing in the streets, playing bongo drums all night—these are among the more normal disturbances. One Newport woman claimed she and her husband got only one or two hours' sleep each night of the week. In Palm Springs, it is not unusual for the kids to take over Palm Canyon Drive, parade down the street hanging all over the outside of cars, and direct traffic at the corners while the police stand by in cool forbearance. During one riot in Palm Springs, the chief of police was so frantic he put in a long distance phone call to the chief of police at Carmel, which was known to have curbed the kids. Another police chief called his men "glorified baby-sitters."

Thus, as the first kids roar into town at the beginning of the week, the police put on extra men and call in sheriff's reserves. Some of the more experienced towns such as Carmel have battened things down with curfew laws and other restrictions. Avalon has an ordinance against renting rooms to minors under eighteen without an adult (over eighteen). Balboa has gone all-out in prohibiting anyone on the island except residents and long-term renters. Such an extremity was required when the island got so crowded it was impossible for ambulances or fire trucks to move in case of emergency.

But most communities, being as interested in the teen-age dollar as in any other dollar, confine themselves to a kind of controlled anarchy—simply preventing bloodshed and minimizing riot. With 30,000 kids invading Newport over Easter, the police consider it a quiet week if juvenile arrests (for vandalism, possession of alcohol, etc.) total less than, say, 180. Palm Springs normally gets around 1,000 juvenile arrests on traffic violations alone. As the battle subsides on Easter Sunday and the invaders surge out of town, the residents quietly pick up the streets, repair their damage, and talk firmly about how they are going to stop this thing next year.

After such an outburst of inhibitions bottled up through the winter, there is a period of rest until the summer season opens in earnest on Mother's Day. About then the beach clubs open their facilities on the sand, the counties and cities post their lifeguards, beach residents start moving inland to rent their homes for summer, and the sporting goods stores display surfboards, swimfins, and snorkels. Starting with Avalon's Buccaneer Days, the resort towns hold their summer festivals as a sort of echo to Easter Week. California beach life, which is the special province of young people and others with good figures, is now in full swing.

4.

The first fact about the beaches is that the age level has been gradually dropping. Up to World War I, the sand was occupied by adults, with a preponderance of the middle-aged, who were usually either tourists or recent settlers from the East. They wandered out on the piers and even onto the sand fully dressed, without even taking off shoes and stockings, or else they changed in a bath house (extinct institu-

138

tion!) and appeared in striped, one-piece suits complete with sleeves nearly to the elbow and drawers nearly to the knee. The youngsters, if they were along, were very much in the tow of their elders.

When the boom of the twenties brought people of all ages to California—thus ending the emphasis on the retired and the health-seekers—the beach scene changed accordingly. The nouveau riche of California's oil, movie, real estate, and transportation industries joined beach clubs; beach life was no longer a novelty, but a sign of success and leisure. It was discovered that the human body looked much better with a tan; looking better, more of it could be exposed with skimpier bathing suits. California became conscious of body appearance, and the beach was no longer a place for anyone embarrassed about his figure, or for the amateur toe-dipper who would appear once a year and go home with an agonizing sunburn. Beachgoing became a pastime for the truly dedicated; the old folks—the plump ladies with all their bulges showing in the wrong places, and the pleasant old men with straw hats—disappeared. Instead, they confined themselves to the front porches of the rentals along the strand.

The final phase began after World War II, when new waves of immigration made California's beaches so fearfully crowded that they became, not a place of relaxation, but a scene of human indignity. The club members retreated inside their enclosed walls and left the shoreline to the outsiders. Most other adults sought out distant and less accessible spots or built their own swimming pools at home. Except for a few obvious ones of any age, only the teen-agers were left; they loved crowds and had developed neither a sense of dignity nor a yearning for privacy.

Thus, the California beaches have become the great show window for American physical fitness. Anyone worried about the condition of his countrymen can, by a peep at the California sand on a summer day, be happily reassured. Most of the odd and formless shapes in California have been elbowed out and made to stay at home by the survival of the fittest. Indeed, partly because of their outdoor life, California youngsters tend to be an inch or so taller than their counterparts elsewhere, and taller than the previous generation of youth.[1]

A special variation of the teen-age beach crowd is a somewhat older and more sophisticated set—some single and some married—who live by the beach in happy little colonies at places like Malibu Beach. These are young nonconformists, but of a more healthy and unpretentious cast than the beatniks. They may reject the "normal" standards and values, but this is only a by-product of an affirmative and energetic practice of their own values that may be lumped into the single formula of enjoying life. There is no particular name for such a casual and elusive group, though one observer has called them "Kookies."

If this group can be linked to any patterns of behavior, these are enjoying outdoor sports, particularly surfing; sitting around drinking beer; arguing on an intellectual plane; listening to progressive jazz; plain loafing; and maintaining what is by other standards the most outrageously sloppy appearance. The typical girl, for example, is barefoot, with tight pants to the knees, a sweat shirt with a convertible hood, no makeup, and a hairdo that looks as though she just climbed out of the surf.

In short, the so-called Kookies are closer in behavior to the young nonconformists cavorting on the French Riviera than to the somewhat somber young intellectuals of New York's Greenwich Village. Nearer home, they may be linked with the young colonists of Sausalito and many of the young marrieds dwelling in the upper reaches of Benedict, Beverly Glen, and Laurel canyons in Los Angeles, but they have an

140

advantage in being able at any time to dive into the world's biggest swimming pool.

It is not at all clear how these young folks have solved the financial question that besets us all. Certainly their needs are few and their expenses small. Most of what they require to enjoy life is pounding and thundering night and day just outside their back door. But the rent and the groceries are not to be lightly ignored, and one suspects that the turnover rate is high in the Kookie colonies.

Though these young types are usually surfers, they are not to be confused with a far greater body of youngsters who have no geographic unity, but do share a deadly singleness of purpose—surfriding. These youngsters don't necessarily live near the beach. They will drive up to two hours from inland points when good surf is running. I have seen some as young as twelve bicycling to the beach, pulling a surfboard trailer or "rickshaw." Some even hitchhike with their board, which is eight-to-nine feet long and a major problem to load in a car without breaking a window.

Nor is surfing confined to Southern California. Beaches as far north as Santa Cruz draw surfers from the entire San Francisco Bay region. In such cold waters, surfers will wear rubber diving suits to keep warm. The California surfing locale extends southward from Monterey Bay to the border, with the best surf—waves sometimes ten to twelve feet high —at Rincon, Malibu, Laguna, Dana Point, San Onofre, and La Jolla. With the surfing crowds growing each year, many are exploring and finding new surf spots below the border in Lower California.

Contrary to the general belief, surfing is not just a postwar California phenomenon. Its original goes back to 1907 when the first surfboard was introduced to the Southern California coast from Hawaii; but the real beginning of popularity came around 1930 when some of the youngsters who could afford to buy a board began switching over from what is known as body surfing. The latter is simply surfing without a board; one catches the wave at the split second before it "feathers over" at the top. With a couple of swift strokes, if one's timing is right, the wave takes one aboard as it is crashing over. From then on the surfer can ride on its churning breast all the way to shore. For the moment, one gives up one's own bodily control to a monster whose headlong force carries one suspended, indifferent to gravity. The whole process appeals to man's peculiar penchant for making sport out of something frightening.

Catching a wave with a board requires equally precise timing. The trick comes in standing on the board and balancing on two feet while riding it in. If one is a master, one can move toward the front—the farther the more masterly—until in a supreme display one "hangs five," that is, five toes over the nose of the board.

For coordination, timing, balance, and sheer nerve, the sport is unsurpassed. But its magical appeal is none of these; it is that exhilarating sense of being carried along—contrary to the normal laws of nature—by some force stronger than one's self. The antics of the surfer on the board introduce some initiative on his part within the general framework of helplessness, but even these antics—by putting one's weight ahead of the wave—are simply calculated to heighten the defiance of gravity. The sport has been likened to downhill skiing, but in the latter one has more control. Surfing is something like jumping onto a merry-go-round and not being able to get off till the music stops.

Up to the war, surfboards were heavy wooden panels weighing perhaps 100 pounds. If you were "wiped out"—that is, sent head over teakettle—in the middle of a surfing run, you risked being knocked cold by your board or someone else's. Since the war, with the introduction of fiber glass and polyeurethane materials, the weight has been reduced to between fifteen and thirty-five pounds; while it is no fun to be hit by such a board, the danger of serious injury is much reduced. Out of this reduction in weight (but not in price, which can vary from $80 to $150), the California surfboard industry boomed. In Southern California alone, manufacturers are making about 5,000 boards a year. It's possible for any healthy youngster from twelve on up, with a reasonable sense of balance and an excess of bravado, to go surfing.

In fact, the sport has become such an institution in California that at least three general types of surfers are now discernible. One is the old pro (anywhere from twenty-five to forty) who is otherwise a responsible citizen but nurses the sport as a holdover from his youth. Some of this type belong to the San Onofre Surf Club, which has almost exclusive use of a section of coast below San Clemente with some of the best waves in California. While surfing is the raison d'être of the club, associated with it is a pleasant social life that includes lounging around the beach, holding luaus, and otherwise acting like Hawaiians. Members come from as far as Bakersfield when they get a phone call that "there are some real beauties running down here!"

A second type, and by far the most numerous, is the young devotee for whom surfing is life itself. Existence is divided into two compartments—the time at the beach, and the time one is obliged to spend away from the beach. Some of these fanatics surf the year round, at times when one gets a chill just watching them, through the gray mist, bobbing on the water. Through the summer those living near the beach will be out there at seven or eight in the morning, before the fog lifts. They live in a perpetual state of wetness, some not even taking a towel to dry off in the interim periods on the sand. Besides a magnificent tan and rippling muscles, these zealots develop other identifying features: a knot of callus or muscle on the instep, from kneeling on the board, and hair that is yellowed in streaks from a combination of salt water and sun.

143

Away from the beach, they are in a kind of uncommunicative limbo awaiting deliverance by the school bell; when they talk, the talk is of surfing. And the non-surfer who joins the discussion group is cut off from the conversation with a social cruelty unsurpassed in California. One mother complained that her sixteen-year-old thought and talked nothing but surfing, "He was living in the same house with us, but we were miles apart." Indeed, a number of boys have run away from home to be free of restraints on surfing.

All this is not to say that surfing has robbed California youth of ambition. On the contrary, they are determined to save enough money to visit Hawaii, where the waves are said to be two stories high and roll for a mile.

Surfing has already developed a kind of symbolism that gives it the character of a secret fraternity or a religious order. The identifying sign is a shark's tooth, St. Christopher medal, or Maltese cross hung loosely about one's neck; in fact, the religious materials stores have had a difficult time keeping in a stock of St. Christopher medals due to the demand by surfers, to whom the piece is not so much a religious object as a fad of unexplained origin. For a long time, the most accepted form of transportation has been a wood-panel Ford station wagon of ancient vintage. But any car will do so long as it can accommodate a surfboard, since the sole object worth considering is to get to the beach. In proof of the religious character of the society, I have seen neat decals in the rear windows exhorting others to "Pray for Surf." A final identifying mark is the hair, which is often worn comparatively long and combed with meticulous care for periods up to half-an-hour at a time. And since sun-bleached hair is part of the surfer's identification, many boys who simply can't get the sun to do its work will resort to peroxide—a perfectly legitimate and acceptable device in the surfing world.

A third type of surfer is perhaps less a surfer than a beach

144

bum, who is generally at least sixteen years old, travels in gangs, and often has a girl hanging onto his arm. While he usually has a board, he will spend a great deal of time out of the water drinking beer, talking surf language, and staging extraordinary love scenes with his girl in full view of sightseers. Some are suspected of not being surfers at all, in which case they are derisively dubbed "hodads" by the true believers.

It is the beach-bum type who makes a nuisance of himself and gives a bad name to all surfers. He throws beer cans into people's yards, hollers obscenities in public, and changes clothes with almost no attempt to shield himself from view.

Yet most surfers are too devoted to the sport to be either a public nuisance or a beachgoing Romeo. Girls are okay, but they are not allowed to interfere with serious surfing. As columnist Jim Murray put it, "A surfer's idea of a date is two tickets to a surfing film." They clash with the public at only two points. One is when they dash with boards under their arms across the ocean-front highways, their eyes fixed in anticipatory delight on the white waves rolling out there; at such times, passing motorists are expected to look out for themselves. The other occasion is the competition for the water itself, where nonsurfers had better be on the lookout for flashing boards piling in on the next wave. This conflict has caused state officials to mark off sections of beach "For Surfers Only," or to specify certain hours set aside for surfing —thus giving the same kind of recognition and status that local police forces have provided the hot rodders with their drag strips. If youth must be served, California youth is served at least its full share.

5.

In short, California young people are probably more free, and more carefree, than their counterparts in other regions.

145

They have in California the latitude, the setting, and the equipment to enjoy the fullest measure of the bloom of life. For as the California child is too often hemmed in by tract subdivisions and forced into organized play supervised by others, the teen-ager can escape to other scenes through the magic wings of the automobile. With all of the powers of an adult, he exists in a wonderful world between the limitations upon childhood and the duties of parenthood.

Such a measure of freedom helps to account for the rising incidence of trouble among California juveniles. Rights without duties make too rich a diet for many to handle; delinquency in California is not confined to the underprivileged but also involves what one police chief calls "overprivileged children." For a number of years juvenile crime in California has been increasing faster than the rise in population. Juvenile arrests in California rose 13.7 percent in 1960, compared to 9 percent in the United States, and a 1 percent national increase in adult arrests.[2]

Part of the reason for growing juvenile crime is an increase in gang activity, which has a long history in California. Some Los Angeles gangs, principally in the Mexican-American district of East Los Angeles, are now in their third generation; two six-year-old boys fighting with each other could give no reason other than their families belonging to rival gangs. In Los Angeles County, there are more than 330 identifiable gangs, of which nearly 150 are Mexican-American, more than 70 Negro, some 52 Caucasian, and the remainder of different or mixed races.[3]

As elsewhere, such gang activity is generally associated with blighted neighborhoods, underprivileged surroundings, and broken homes. But in California, it is given added effectiveness by the automobile, which enables juveniles to seek trouble outside their own neighborhoods where they are not identified and also helps them elude arrest. According to one Los Angeles County survey, cars are involved in 40 to 45 percent of gang incidents.

In San Fernando Valley, rival gangs from the towns of Pacoima and San Fernando used to be limited in their ability to battle each other by lack of transportation. But in 1945, about twenty Pacoimans rode in a truck to San Fernando and, armed with shovels and picks, fought it out with a local gang in front of city hall while the city council was in session. Since then the feud between the two towns has been given a new dimension by use of automobiles, which permit one gang to make a hit-and-run raid and then escape before the police can arrive.

Cars also aid in what is becoming a favorite juvenile sport —party-crashing. In the Wilshire District of Los Angeles, party-crashing became so commonplace that the officer heading the juvenile bureau publicly announced, "Anyone having a party is urged to notify police so protection can be arranged." And by 1961, the state legislature made it unlawful to crash a party.

Still another contributor to juvenile delinquency has been the accessibility of alcoholic drinks to underage users, who manage to steal it from their parents, buy it through falsification of driver's licenses, or get a friend who is twenty-one years old to buy it. When the state liquor director was interviewed on a Sacramento TV program, he discussed some of the methods high schoolers used to doctor their driver's license in order to buy liquor. Thus informed, other kids adopted the same devices. Grumbled the official, "I should have kept my mouth shut."

However, police experts are generally convinced that the chief cause of California delinquency is parental weakness. The head of the Los Angeles juvenile division observes that parents do not maintain authority over their children but rather have become their "playmates."

"Kids who get in trouble with the law are stronger than

147

their parents," he declares. "They wear their parents out with strategy and pressure to get what they want ... and they do."

One of the bright spots in California juvenile records has been the near lack of crime among youngsters of Chinese and Japanese families, where parental respect and fatherly authority are strong. Yet so thorough is the Americanization process that delinquency is increasing among Japanese youths; one authority estimates that it will catch up to the general rate by 1972.[4]

Lending support to claims of parental laxity is the number of acts in open defiance of authority. Attempted arrests of adolescents have led in a number of instances to wholesale attacks on the officers, followed by general riots as police reinforcements arrive. In a drive-in at Alhambra, two officers arrested a nineteen-year-old for stirring up a riot and precipitated a wholesale melee that involved 500 youths at drive-ins in a six-block area and required 150 officers from six cities, the sheriff's office, and the State Highway Patrol before it was quelled.

At Zuma Beach, north of Malibu, a radio station sponsored a teen-age party and drew an unexpected crowd of 25,000. When the entertainment was over at 11 P.M., it was too early to go home. Having time on their hands, part of the crowd set fires, turned over trash cans, ripped doors off storerooms and lifeguard towers, tried to overturn lifeguard jeeps, and fought among themselves. When more than fifty officers arrived, they were attacked with bottles and tin cans.

Part of the difficulty is the leniency of too many California courts in dealing with juveniles; like the rules against corporal punishment in California schools, this is also a function of the doting and permissive attitude toward children in California. The result is that serious offenders are turned loose to commit further crimes. In Hawthorne, some thirty youths raided the police station and assaulted the officers.

148

One eighteen-year-old who broke an officer's leg was placed on a year's probation and was arrested again the same night for being drunk on the street. Another youth involved in the raid was freed on bail and a few nights later was part of a gang that clubbed, kicked, stomped, and ran over a seventeen-year-old boy. In San Francisco, several juveniles were charged with conducting a month-long reign of intimidation and vandalism against a Jewish couple in the Sunset district; on the night of their release by the court, they staged a "victory celebration" by driving back and forth over their victims' lawn and resuming their reign of terror.

This kind of savage rebellion has shown itself in still other forms. According to police reports, there is an increase in juvenile crimes of senseless sadism. In Sacramento, four youths invaded the home of an eighty-year-old widow, molested and tormented her for two horror-stricken hours, wrecked the interior of her home, then left her lying helpless in the rubble. In San Francisco, four teen-agers stomped a teacher into insensibility and left him on the street-car tracks to be run over and killed. In San Diego, fourteen junior high kids, including three girls thirteen and fourteen years old, struck down and kicked a girl from another school. In Highland Park, near Los Angeles, three boys in a car came up behind an elderly couple in an electric cart and deliberately bumped them, keeping it up until the cart crashed into another car.

Still another California aberration is a serious narcotics problem. With as many as 20,000 addicts in addition to medically authorized users, California is second only to New York in narcotics offenders, while Los Angeles is second to New York City.[5] Bounded both by the Pacific Ocean and Mexico, populous California is a prize market for both the heroin exported by the government of Red China and for marijuana that is grown in large quantities in Mexico. Both types are brought into California chiefly from Mexico, which helps account for the fact that over 83 percent of narcotics arrests are in Southern California.[6]

While less than one-tenth of California narcotics offenders are juveniles, approximately one-half are twenty-five or younger, and only 8 percent are over forty.[7] The problem is essentially a youth problem, and the age level of offenders is, if anything, getting lower. Boys as young as fourteen have been discovered crossing the Mexican border with narcotics. Heroin has been involved in less than 10 percent of the juvenile narcotics arrests, while marijuana accounts for 56 percent and other drugs, such as barbiturates, the remainder.[8] But while the latter types are considered less dangerous, since they are not habit-forming in a physical sense, they tend to make the user psychologically dependent on narcotics as a crutch in facing life and can make him vulnerable to experimentation with the far more deadly heroin.

At the bottom of the California problem, besides the state's proximity to sources of narcotics, is the undisciplined and experimental attitude of California youth. At their age, they are not getting much advice from their parents and are not listening to what little they get. Instead, their main concern is to be one of the bunch, to be popular, and by all means, not an oddball. This means that where the use of drugs is considered smart, there will always be some youngsters who will join in to keep from being called "chicken."

Although tighter laws to control narcotics offenders were passed in 1961, there is still no organized program of school education on the effects and dangers of narcotics usage. In typical form, most Californians have not been concerned enough to demand such a program.

Considering mere numbers, neither crime nor violence, and certainly not narcotics, is widespread among California youth. Police authorities say that perhaps 5 percent are delinquent in any measurable form, and only 2 percent are "hard core" cases. By far the great proportion of California youth are healthy, both physically and emotionally. Their youthful energy is channeled into the greatest variety of athletic and social activities available to any young people anywhere. Their mischievous side is satisfied by pranks that are generally harmless.

6.

What is far more prevalent, in this observer's opinion, is a degree of sexual freedom—whetted by a fairly wide use of alcohol, facilitated by the automobile, and encouraged by minimum accountability to the parents. There is in California a remarkable absence of controls over the contacts between boys and girls. Chaperonage is limited to official school functions except at parties for the very young teens. Once the boy reaches driving age, and the girl reaches the dating age for boys who drive, they are essentially beyond the eyes of their parents. By means of the auto, youngsters can seek entertainment in other communities where they are not known and their behavior not reported.

The auto also provides for that great national institution, carried to its broadest usage in California, known as parking (or in the new parlance, "making out"). For though the tradition goes back to the "sparking" of horse-and-buggy days, there was never the same degree of privacy or singlemindedness. The male was at least aware of what the horse was doing or might do, and the buggy provided no closed sides that make the automobile a private room. In short, since the closed car came in during the 1920's, anything can happen in the back seat or even in the front seat of an automobile. Indeed, one of the serious questions most often facing the California youth is whether to suggest to his date that they get in the back seat, where progress will be unimpeded by the steering wheel. For at least a generation, the institution has been so widely accepted in California that parking on a double or even triple date is not unusual. This has its limitations, of course, for serious effort, when the problem becomes one of discreetly avoiding double dates. I knew one young fellow so deadly in the art of parking as to carry a mattress in his trunk, though I have since suspected that this was chiefly to impress his pals.

For the typical California boy, lovemaking in some other setting—such as the girl's living room after the folks have gone to bed—is a trifle gauche, not to say risky; it affords little of the privacy, and none of the opportunity for getaway, offered by his car, where he feels more comfortably in charge of the situation.

The result is that for long periods of time a young couple may be together in the dark, unobserved and blissfully alone. Says a Los Angeles psychologist, "I would say this is dangerous at fourteen, fifteen, and sixteen." I would add that this is even more dangerous at seventeen, eighteen, and nineteen, when the boy has overcome his awe of the opposite sex and has become a bolder and more experienced Lothario, when alcohol may enter the picture, and when the couple are more apt to be "going steady."

Indeed, the auto is only one factor in bringing California boys and girls in closer relationship than they enjoy in many other parts of the country and in Europe. Nor is this relationship necessarily bad; in many ways it tends to reduce extreme behavior. On some college campuses, sororities and fraternities are not geographically separated but may be mixed on the same street. Both at the Berkeley and Westwood campuses of the University of California there is a mixed dormitory with men on the lower floors and women on the upper floors. While the rules forbid visiting on the wrong floors, the students share a common dining room, lobby, and recreation area. Says one boy, "Under this system a fellow's got a chance to study women, to understand them . . ." Says a girl, "When you know men are around just for the asking, you don't waste so much time daydreaming."

As for dancing classes and mixed parties, these begin at an early age. There are few private schools (mostly military schools) separating the sexes. Private girls' colleges are exceptional and of these, some are established in connection with men's colleges or coeducational schools, such as the official association of Scripps College with the others at Claremont. Many if not most California churches appeal to the young people by providing mixed youth programs, including socials and dances on the church campus. These are some of the factors tending to remove the degree of mystery that prevails between boys and girls in Europe, and in some Eastern and Southern communities, where separate and private schools are prevalent and chaperonage is still widely practiced.

One result is that, as one of my friends puts it, the "level of intimacy" between boys and girls is higher. The couple going steady are with each other almost constantly—between classes, in the study hall, the cafeteria, the tennis court. As late as the early 1940's, a boy was embarrassed to be seen in the company of the same girl all day long; he would be thought by his friends to be "in tow"—a fellow destined for wifely domination. Girls were chiefly for ogling at during the day, and the serious activity was reserved for nighttime —a kind of divided schedule by which the male asserted his independence. Since then the situation has gradually been reversed until girls and boys are all pals, all part of the gang, throughout the day. And among those going steady the "level of intimacy" shows itself in unabashed public displays of affection. One can see some rather hot lovemaking at the beach in broad daylight. One-armed driving, which used to be reserved for nighttime and usually on the way home from the party, is now a common daytime sight. Walking about campus arm-in-arm is also taken for granted. There is an honest recognition that boys and girls are and should be attracted to each other.

All this does not necessarily mean a general rise in promiscuity—that is, indiscriminate sexual behavior. True, the signs are that at least some young people are becoming more promiscuous. From 1955 to 1960, the incidence of syphilis in California rose 300 percent, with a figure of 500 percent for San Fernando Valley. From 1957 to mid 1960, it increased over 400 percent in Oakland and Long Beach, as compared to 305 percent in New York City. The percentage of cases accounted for by teen-agers is relatively small (in Los Angeles, 13 percent) but the percentage is increasing. On the west side, the incidence among teen-agers increased 50 percent in 1960 alone. One sixteen-year-old boy was infected by a prostitute and passed it to a fifteen-year-old girl, who had relations with nineteen males in two nights and infected half of them.[9] A West Los Angeles health Officer declares, "Teen-agers are more promiscuous than they used to be."

Yet this factor represents only a small fraction of California youth, most of whom are not promiscuous in the accepted sense. Rather, they tend to become infatuated with one person at a time, with whom they may or may not have intimate relations, and to whom (in either case) they are likely to be faithful. In one representative group of twenty high school seniors, fifteen were going steady. As for college, though few girls would say so, it is generally considered what one mother calls "today's marriage market." One noted marriage counselor who was guest lecturer at a California college was approached by a group of a dozen girls who, in a serious discussion, told him, "We are all graduating at the end of this semester and not one of us is engaged or even pinned. We know we will never get married now and we want your advice to help us adjust to a life of being single."

The point is that school days, including senior high school days, are coming to be considered the time of courtship. All the other levels of boy-girl relationships, including dating and "going steady," are pushed back to earlier ages. The stage of increasing intimacy is reached before the children are intellectually or emotionally able to handle it. The results can be either moral breakdowns bringing personal disgrace or premature marriages involving gross mismatches and marital misery. While there are no statistics on California abortions, since they are illegal, their increase is generally acknowledged among social workers and has been alarming enough to cause one county grand jury to call for controlled legalized abortions for many juvenile girls. Also unavailable are statewide statistics on illegitimacy; a careful study of this subject in Alameda County showed the illegitimacy ratio for white births to be exactly the same (1.8 percent) as the national figure.[10] It is believed, however, that the California rate is rising. Says one veteran sociologist, "Our homes for unwed mothers are overflowing."

Moreover, while the median age of California brides and grooms is only slightly lower than the national average, earlier marriages are becoming more conspicuous. In San Gabriel Valley, one couple in the freshman and sophomore high school classes was married. In San Francisco, a fourteen-year-old married a seventeen-year-old. In Oxnard, a fourteen-year-old girl in the eighth grade married a sixteen-year-old boy. In Santa Paula, a thirteen-year-old girl was absent from school for two days and returned a bride. When asked how she liked married life she replied, "It's just fine. Much better than playing with dolls."

7.

Yet the freedom enjoyed by California youth is not universally abused. It also has the effect among many of building self-reliance at an early age and of intensifying the healthy sense of exuberance native to the youthful soul. In the immediate postwar years, the nation's youth were accused of being the "Silent Generation"—too absorbed in conformity to play their traditional role as society's militant idealists. An article in *Look* magazine applied this especially to California: "The kids are happy-go-lucky, big, bronzed, and beautiful. But like the cellophane-wrapped fruit, they seem to have no tang." In 1961, a survey by George Gallup condemned American youngsters as "bland." A California high schooler was quoted, "Goals? We've got no goals. Our parents have achieved them for us."

Such a state of mind, reflecting a bankruptcy of values and of energy, would be far more catastrophic than the more spectacular rise of delinquency. But in this observer's opinion the situation was never this bad, and in any case has begun to reverse itself. As to energy, California youth have always been among the most active in the world, simply because there were more things to do, more sunny days to do them, and better transportation available on demand to get to the scene of action.

Nor have California kids been backward in thinking up new outlets for energy. In the bizarre thirties, California collegiates were among the leading exponents of the goldfish-swallowing craze and the panty raids on girls' dormitories. More recently, youthful exuberance has been diverted into more competitive channels. Rivalry has developed between colleges as to the number of girls it is possible to cram into a Volkswagen. A record was set at Ventura College when nineteen coeds got into the little car; the feat was challenged by students at Long Beach College, where twenty-four got into the VW but couldn't close the door. When students at Texas Tech claimed a thirty-six-hour record for the nation's longest telephone call, nearly 100 boys and girls at California Polytechnic in San Luis Obispo took turns on a dorm-to-dorm phone call which lasted 504 hours. When a team at the University of British Columbia set a world's record by pushing a roller bed forty miles in eight hours, twenty-five minutes, a rival team at American River Junior College pushed a bed the forty miles from Marysville to Sacramento and beat the time by twenty minutes. When a pair of boys in Albuquerque set a world's record by tossing an ice cube back and forth between them 1,403 times before it melted, two California sixteen-year-olds tossed one 2,020 times (the mother of one kept score). And in 1962, the students of Orange County State College held the first Intercollegiate Elephant Race with a crowd of 10,000 and entries from as far as Harvard University. One Orange County professor, shaking his head in disapproval, pleaded to a reporter, "Say we teach Chaucer here."

Such hijinks are by no means the only measure of the energy in California kids. Partly because they assert their own independence at an early age, many exhibit a remarkable seriousness of purpose. The "rah-rah" spirit, which lasted up to World War II, has not only faded, but is considered juvenile and high schoolish. College still has its fun, but there is an earnestness on the part of many if not most students, who regard it as the passport to a successful career. The change began after the war with GI students, most of whom were several years older than their other classmates, and many of whom were married. They studied hard, brought up the grade averages, and made the rest realize why they were really going to college.

One of the most remarkable exhibits of this phenomenon is the altered attitude toward football and football heroes. The game still turns high schools into a frenzy. In San Diego, there were so many fights and small riots after night football games that they were all scheduled for daylight. Even the parents, worried about the nature of the kids' other extracurricular interests, go along with the high school football mania. In Tulare County, the parents of two boys who had both suffered broken legs in high school football declared, "We'd so much rather have them hurt in the line of sports than as a result of reckless driving."

But in college the situation is different. The varsity team is no longer the nexus of campus spirit. There is a frank recognition that the players are subsidized by athletic scholarships and part-time jobs, and there is a growing attitude that such favors should more justifiably be given to serious students. In the mid-fifties, when an attempt was made to clean up the subsidization of player and the commercialization of the sport in the Pacific Coast Conference, the outraged opposition to reform came from the sports writers and the old alums. Nobody asked the students what they thought about it. What they and many of the younger alumni think may be reflected in an undeniable decline in football attendance. In their heyday, California's major college games drew 70,000 to 80,000 rooters. Though some big games still bring huge crowds, many are drawing 30,000 to 40,000. In 1951, the College of the Pacific at Stockton drew 134,623 to seven home games; in 1960 it drew 54,500 to six home games.[11]

Even those who attend no longer have the same spirit. The procedure is almost like a ceremonial rite in which the participants simply go through the motions expected of them. They enjoy the game both as a spectator sport and as a social experience, but there is almost a tongue-in-cheek attitude toward the men on the field. From Saturday's heroes, they have become hired gladiators to delight the alumni and help solve the university's financial problems.

As the unkindest cut of all, the coeds no longer regard the football players as the big men on campus. A poll taken among thirty girls at four colleges in Sacramento Valley showed, to quote the pollster, "You've got to be a science major to get along with the beautiful girls." As for the stalwarts of the gridiron, according to one of the women, "You don't see them running off the field with girls chasing them. After a game they usually walk over and kiss their wives and children."

158

This sort of difference between high school and college attitudes is also seen in their relative interest in campus activities. Says the dean of instruction at Pierce College in San Fernando Valley, "In high school, activities were everything. But they come to college mostly to learn." In a survey of sixty-two students at Pierce, forty-two didn't know the name of the college president, fifty-nine had never attended a student council meeting, and forty-six had never voted in a student body election. Answered one student, "I do not participate or care about anything." Then, as though in explanation of his position, "I am a teen-ager."

The first source of this indifference to extracurricular interests is a new determination to make the most of college studies as a springboard to economic advancement. The remarkable growth of California public colleges, which have more than coped with the equally remarkable population influx, has brought higher education within the reach of any serious student regardless of finances. Today's average California college student is neither a varsity athlete nor the child of well-to-do parents. He is from a lower-middle-class family and is spurred by the desire to do better and enjoy more in life than his father. College is to him not so much a place of broad education to create better men, but a vocational training school.

This brings up still another remarkable transformation between high school and college. In the former, scholastic attainment is far down on the scale of goals, giving ground to such measurements as the number of names on one's dance card at the sophomore cotillion and the pitch of the tailpipe rumble on one's car. Possibly even more than most youngsters, California teen-agers are among the most hopeless conformists; the key dogma in their accepted creed is that everyone likes fun and hates work. Those who excel in dancing, sports, or other activities that youth claims as its special province are admired; but those who obviously strive for intellectual achievement are considered to have resigned from the club. The truth is that the serious student constitutes a reproach to the others, since he reminds them of the existence of responsibilities. They therefore treat him with the same disdain adults would direct against someone they believed was "putting on airs" or acting "holier than thou." As one Marin County student complains, you are "looked down upon if you excel academically. The better student you are, the greater your nonconformity. Since few of us wish to be nonconformists, most of us deemphasize learning."

Remarkably enough, this attitude prevails generally even though grades determine one's choice of colleges. With its extensive junior college, city college, and state college system, in addition to the various public and private universities, California enables students to indulge in the idea that there is a place for them somewhere. As a last resort, they can always go to a junior college the first two years.

This attitude seems to vanish miraculously when one actually enters college. There is a kind of acceptance that the great competition of life has begun. Unlike the prewar era, the students are no longer anxious to load up with "snap" courses. At the University of California campus in Berkeley, several students were injured when a mob of 650 made a rush to sign up for a physics course.

Not only the veterans, but the growing proportion of married students, have sobered the college spirit since the war. At USC nearly 36 percent of all day students are married —a figure comparing with an estimated range of from 10 to 25 percent throughout the country.[12] The reason for this high incidence of married students in California may perhaps be traced to the more informal and less traditional approach to life, including a view of marriage as simply the culmination of a romance and not necessarily coincident with earning a living and rearing a family. But the point here is that married students are generally serious students; by their example, they tend to make other students realize that perhaps there is some good reason to study hard. As one Berkeley professor observed, "I do not think there is the slightest doubt today's college student is a far more serious student than in the decades past."

Since about 1960 this earnestness has been sharpened with a zest born of the space age. The emerging job hunter no longer faces a routine future. As one educator put it, "After Sputnik they found that the frontiers were not gone. That the future was exciting, especially for educated, intelligent people."

In most cases this intensity of purpose is directed toward an economic goal. During Easter vacation, many students are forsaking the beach resorts and crowding into the college libraries. But in one of the annual contests at UCLA offering prizes for the best private book collections, there were only five entries out of an enrollment that is one of the largest in the country. Knowledge for its own sake, as an elevation of consciousness and an enrichment of life, is a concept not even grasped by the average student.

There is in these postwar students little of the Beat philosophy that has been attributed to them. While California was the spawning ground of those particular Bohemians known at beatniks, they constitute a tiny minority. The attempt to attribute the Beat viewpoint to an entire generation (the term Beat Generation was coined by novelist Jack Kerouac as early as 1948) is about as valid as the fable that in the 1930's all young students were Communists. There have at most been only a few hundred real beatniks in the strongholds of San Francisco and Los Angeles.

This is not to downgrade the significance of the Beat phenomenon. For while Beatism may not be especially potent in winning adherents, it is nevertheless important for what it says about the rest of society.

The term "Beat" originally meant "bushed" or "exhausted,"

as, after a stint of hard work, "I'm really beat." Applied in the term "Beat Generation," it pictured the disillusionment of American youth who had fought a global war only to face the appalling implications of a nuclear arms race. Such monumental folly was believed to be the last straw in discrediting a society that youth had distrusted since World War I. But whereas the writers of the so-called Lost Generation in the 1920's had hoped to influence the world about them through social protest, the Beat Generation had "had it." To them the impending bankruptcy of society was irreversible. Participation in the final dance of death was not only immoral, but insane. The only resort was to resign from the world.

While many thousands of young people had this impulse, only a relative few acted on it. And since it was impossible to resign while maintaining one's old associations, the only solution was to seek the company of likeminded people in the tradition haunts of the disassociated: New York's Greenwich Village, San Francisco's North Beach, and L.A.'s strange beach slums in parts of Venice and Ocean Park.

Writers living in these haunts and noticing this phenomenon assumed that the experience was universal—that all youth belonged to a "Beat Generation." Later they tried to give the movement a pious color by connecting "Beat" with "Beatitude." But to its actual participants it has always expressed the exhaustion of their illusions. They were fed up with society and they walked out. To emphasize their exile they threw over the whole bit—all the values of twentieth-century life. Moral codes governing personal behavior were considered part of an archaic and discredited religious structure. As for the vaunted U.S. standard of living, it was dismissed as a vicious circle of production and consumption in which the average man was not the beneficiary, but the faceless victim. The solution was clear: repudiate society, abandon the economic rat race, reject bourgeois morality, and follow one's own desires.

162

It is this deliberate abandonment of prevailing virtues in the belief that they had proved a failure that is the key to most beatnik behavior. It accounts for the Beat preoccupation with understanding one's self, for if all the old values are repudiated, one must find other values somewhere, and the only source one can really trust is inside the self. For the same reason it accounts for the devotion to art and music as avenues toward truth. It accounts for the adoption of beards by the men, the absence of makeup among the girls, and the insistence on the most austere and unconventional attire by both. This is what one Beat writer calls the "admission fee" to win acceptance as a true "hipster"; for it announced to the world, "I don't care if you think I'm a crackpot; I'm not interested in being promoted in my job and I am not even much interested in my job." Finally, it accounts for the open embrace of pleasures tabooed by the society left behind, particularly illicit sex and illegal drugs.

Herein lies the weakness in the Beat movement. While Beat behavior is understandable it cannot pass for Truth simply because it is different. The widespread use of marijuana is explained as a means of reaching "a higher level of awareness"; yet no deep insight is required to recognize it as a form of materialism more primitive and soul-searing than the materialism of the world at large.

The importance of Beatism lies not in its attempted solution, which is a dead end, but in the fact of its existence, which is a rebuke to society. It cannot therefore be said that the Beat movement has failed just because it has lost adherents since the heyday of the espresso coffee houses and the impromptu jam sessions of the late 1950's. Beatism is not really a movement at all, since the Beats are too individualistic to be organized for anything.

Yet it has something to say about the world. And to many young people it has tended to confirm their own apprehensions. It was not only the jam session and the coffee house

163

that became universally popular, but also the bull session and the public debate. Youth in general went further than the Beats by actively discussing social problems as though something could be done about them. The generation was not Beat, and it was not Silent, either.

9.

Thus, even though California youth are generally "square" in their values, particularly in their economic motivations, they have added a healthy sense of doubt and concern. While they are fun-loving in the true California spirit, collegiates are considerably more aware of the world about them than either contemporary high schoolers or yesterday's collegiates. Far from being taboo subjects, religion and politics are prime requirements for the young conversationalist. And in both these interests, young people tend to show considerably more imagination and vitality than their parents.

In religion, the representative California collegiate is frankly querulous. While most students have some denominational background, they are not churchgoers and approach religion with an open mind. Dr. John E. Cantelon, chaplain at the University of Southern California, states that most avowed Christians among the students reject the concept of Jesus as divine Savior. "They have no sense of needing to be saved from anything." A survey of fifteen hundred students at the Associated Colleges of Claremont showed that 90 percent believed in God; only 65 percent believed in "a God who is active in history"—that is, who intervenes in the affairs of men; and only 14 percent believed it necessary to attend church regularly to be a practicing religionist.[13]

On the other hand, only a relative few are dogmatic atheists—probably a smaller proportion than among Californians in their thirties and forties. The present generation is not so cocksure, either in belief or unbelief. While only a minority (a reported 20 percent at one large university) are intensely interested in religion, almost all students accept it as a subject open to infinite analysis, like philosophy. If there is any prevailing concept of God among students, it has been summed up neatly by Dr. Cantelon; most students, he says, "believe in an impersonal deity, having to do with order in the universe and . . . some type of ultimate meaning. But not a living Father who desires fellowship with man."

Thus, the California students exhibit a more advanced stage of the state's general religious condition. Faith, particularly in its dogmatic forms, is disintegrating. This in itself might not be alarming if another structure of thought were taking its place. But many California young people, just as much as their parents, are substantially without a point of view beyond expediency. At least they are aware of it, which is more than can be said of their elders. They are quietly searching, and they are in no hurry to seize on a new dispensation.

Considerably more active is the student's approach to politics. Almost every California college has a Democratic and Republican Club. National political figures lecturing on the campus are drawing overflow crowds; protest marches, picketing, and other public demonstrations in the student tradition are once again appearing.

Certainly the most obvious aspect of this political rebirth is the emergence of a vocal and militant right. This is not necessarily a rejuvenated Republicanism, but a Far Right outburst within the GOP. Young Republicans are fighting among themselves, throwing each other out of meetings, calling each other names—all antics previously monopolized by the Democrats. Indeed, the bitter struggle for control of the state Young Republicans continues to be the focal point of the overall intraparty feud in California.

Nor does this necessarily mean a general swing to conservatism among young people, as has been widely heralded by right-wing spokesmen. Democratic clubs are as active as ever; public demonstrations in liberal causes are just as conspicuous. The celebrated San Francisco riots protesting against the House Un-American Activities Committee were carried out chiefly by students; and public appearances of the President bring out competing lines of pickets. "Ban the Bomb" and "Abolish HUAC" placards are just as numerous as the "Resign from the UN" and "No Aid to Tito" signs. The difference is that since the late 1950's the student Right is finally heard from—and loudly. On the campus, at least, the Right is not forcing conformity, as has been charged, but is the product of rising nonconformity.

The truth is that the really active students of both Right and Left constitute a small percentage—1 to 2 percent, according to one estimate—of the campus population. This is higher than in the mid-fifties, and is symptomatic of a widespread rise in student awareness of public issues. There is a tendency, though by no means a pronounced trend, toward regarding international issues from a broad moral viewpoint rather than along strictly nationalistic lines. In keeping with the intellectual influence of the campus, students are apt to argue more from logic and justice and less from slogans and epithets than many of their elders.

Among the most clear-cut convictions of California students is the support of racial equality, stemming first from their basic sense of fair play, and second from an idealistic urge to be identified with what is perhaps the most critical social cause of our time. The phenomenon has shown itself in the election of Japanese-Americans as student body presidents in two San Joaquin Valley and Ventura County high schools, and the election on more than one occasion of Negroes as college student body presidents. It is manifested, too, in the volunteering of Freedom Riders for service in the South. So strong is youth's opinion on this subject that in conversations, slurs against races are practically unheard-of.

In short, the threat of McCarthyism and the specter of a nuclear holocaust, which have been cited as the chief factors inhibiting the so-called Silent Generation of the early and middle 1950's, have lost their power—at least over the California student. The fatalistic, cynical, no-values attitude said to have pervaded some campuses in the Northeast under the name of "Negoism" has never overtaken the California campuses. The whole thing smacks too much of a pseudointellectual pose for the practical California student. One of them voices the suspicion that it is "a kind of label people wear like a second hat."

Why have California youngsters emerged from the shade into the sunlight in the 1960's? The answer probably is that they are simply being themselves again. How long does one wait for the world to end? In California, there is too much life to be lived to sit around crying doom for long. If the threat of nuclear extermination has had a lasting effect on them, it is not one of chronic pessimism, but rather of shame at the kind of world mankind has brought itself to, and a conviction that the species must improve or die. They are the first generation to recognize this choice and to start acting on it.

Perhaps this accounts for what is probably the greatest enigma of all in the character of California youth—an ethical code that admits both expediency and responsibility. In matters concerning one's personal interests, many students can be downright dishonest without a shiver of conscience—particularly if the injured party is not another person but some impersonal institution like the school, the company, or the government. An anonymous poll of 1,174 children at a Los Angeles junior high school showed a sharp rise in the willingness to cheat when the students reached grades where marks counted for college admission. To the question of whether they would peek at answers to a forthcoming test if given the chance, 6 percent of first-semester seventh graders, and 41 percent of second-semester ninth graders, answered that they would.[14] Cheating in high school and college has become one of California's pressing educational issues. A girl at California Polytechnic Institute in San Luis Obispo estimated that 80 percent of students cheated (a statement that others said was exaggerated).[15] At a meeting called to discuss the cheating problem, a North Hollywood high schooler stated that "Cheating is so prevalent now, because it's more or less accepted. Even teachers give lighter punishment for it than they used to." Said another, "You have to cheat to get ahead yourself or the guy who cheats will beat you."

But though hardened in helping themselves, they are perhaps softer than their parents in helping others. Forty high school seniors from the Arcadia Presbyterian Club spent an Easter vacation in San Joaquin Valley building a recreation center and chapel for migrant workers. Members of Baptist and Methodist youth fellowships traveled to desert California and Arizona to do welfare work on Indian reservations. Nor are such incidents confined to church groups. California car clubs practice driver courtesy and roadside assistance as a major activity. One young driver found a man with a stalled car and an expectant wife on the way to the hospital; after fixing the engine, he got them to their destination just in time. Another who helped an elderly man get his car started refused payment of a ten-dollar bill, even though he had just two cents in his pocket—"I finally had to jump in my car and beat it because the guy insisted on giving me that sawbuck." In San Francisco, a Youth for Service organization was recruited from what was termed the "depressed housing and rock 'n' roll crowd" to do improvement work without pay on a California Indian reservation. Declared one, "This is the first time I ever felt needed in my life."

If there is a way of reconciling such seemingly contradictory behavior, one must begin by recognizing that California's young people are out of touch with the absolute ethics of the Judaeo-Christian tradition. Few of them, even including those attending Sunday school, could name even some of the Ten Commandments. They constitute the first California generation that is the product of a predominantly secular society. They do not believe in any cosmic retribution for wrongdoing, nor have they been exposed to the more rational motive of self-esteem. When they are inhibited from wrongdoing it is chiefly through fear of being caught.

At the same time their common decency and even human kindness toward others are not just legacies of a religion-based society. Many of them are more compassionate than their parents. This side of their nature, at least, offers one of the first empirical supports for Kant's theory that man, left to himself, will know right from wrong. As a minimum, it hints that the uninhibited or "natural" man can be good as well as bad.

All of which indicates that the unusual and sometimes shocking freedom accorded to California youngsters is not a one-sided catastrophe. Under such freedom they have done both the worst and the best. The latitudes of permission and the extremes of performance are both wider in California. Young people play hard and work hard; they are both self-seekers and do-gooders; most of them want to "get ahead," but many also want to "make a mark." As one senior high school girl puts it, "I just want to do something worthwhile, so that I can contribute my part to society, so that I am not just sitting around being a vegetable." This youthful combination of personal practicality and public idealism is not only puzzling, but is perhaps the most promising aspect of the California scene.

CHAPTER VIII

The Ascent of Woman

1.

Miss Isabel Ramirez was driving across a drawbridge from Wilmington to Terminal Island when she saw a crowd gathering along a jagged hole in the guard rail. When she stopped, they told her a car had gone into the water. As she watched, bubbles were still popping on the surface. Then a man appeared, obviously dazed, with blood from his face coloring the water. As Isabel later recalled, "There were many people standing around—including several men—but nobody did anything."

So she shed her coat and shoes, climbed down into the water, paddled out to the man, pulled him to a dry spot, and stayed with him until the rescue firemen arrived.

"I can't swim very well," she said, "and I can't dive."

While Isabel is an exceptional woman, she symbolizes the modern relationship between the sexes in California. Women are not only more equal than in most other places, but they are becoming at least as equal as the California men.

This is not to say that women anywhere have ever been subordinate. But they have at least been subtle enough to let the male think he is in charge. In California, the mask is dropped. With some important exceptions, the California male doesn't particularly want to be in charge of anything, so he doesn't have to be fooled. His abdication has in many cases forced women to an unnatural aggressiveness on behalf of themselves and the family. In the process, the female has shed the cloak of sweet helplessness that her grandmother wore so charmingly. She is independent, active, and—one might almost say—virile.

Thus, there is no longer much evidence that the California woman belongs to the weaker sex. In Del Mar, a bank robber was captured by two women who grabbed and subdued him as he fled out the door; one of the good ladies was so unruffled that she held on to her pet poodle through the whole tussle. In Watts, near Los Angeles, three young women were fighting each other on the street following an auto accident; when a motorcycle officer moved in to stop them they turned on him, knocked him down, and sent him to the hospital. In Van Nuys, a big policeman (six feet, two inches) gave a traffic ticket to a small woman driver (five feet, two inches) who was so angry she broke his finger.

Such strong-arm stuff may be unusual, but it is the product of a sharp assertiveness that is becoming normal for the California woman. The story of her social progress (if it is really progress) is at least a century old, for in California the female has always had a special role. In frontier times, she was in short supply, and hence was held in near reverence. The primitive Western conditions made her self-reliant, and the long distances made her a master first of the horse and then of the auto.

In much of the Far West, women gained political status earlier than their Eastern sisters, apparently as a kind of prize just for being around. The saying, "Out West, where men are men and women are governors," was never literally true in California, but it has long been normal for the ladies to hold elective county and city offices, particularly in the rural districts, and in many cases to dominate the county central committees of political parties. Women have almost exclusively occupied the local election boards, to the point where a male member would be considered an intruder. It is the women who are the organizers, the doorbell pushers, and the poll watchers in election campaigns. They are the hostesses in that peculiar and vital California political institution, the kaffeeklatsch—an informal neighborhood gathering in which the candidate talks with voters in a social setting. The candidate in suburbia should make five or six of these a day in order to have a chance of winning.

It may be said, in fact, that no candidate has a serious chance without a corps of women volunteers. A successful campaign is made up of near-equal parts of three ingredients: campaign money, newspaper endorsements, and female workers. The candidate's awareness of the ladies' importance is revealed in the persistent appearance of his wife during the campaign. He is so continuously accompanied by his wife that the voter believes they are being elected as a team—which is the intended impression.

Thus, while the percentage of California women who participate in politics is very small, they far outnumber the active males. In any mixed political discussion, the ladies are at least as vocal as the men. I have known a number of families in which the wife has the dominant political convictions. It is such women who make the phone calls and pound the pavements to deliver the votes. At a time when the newspaper publishers and the big campaign contributors seem to be controlling elections, there remains one effective element of grass-roots power. It is the California woman.

2.

The ascent of the female in a man's world was accelerated in World War II, when she went to work in the shipyards and aircraft plants of San Francisco and Southern California. The feel of money that was her own to spend without accounting to anyone had a lasting impact. Since then the proportion of California workingwomen has grown sharply. Of the total female population over fourteen years old, approximately one-third work; of the total labor force, approximately one-third are women.[1] Both these California proportions are higher than the national average.

As a result, the husband's exclusive function as the breadwinner, which has always been the source of his special importance, has been watered down. Marriage has become an equal partnership, not only domestically, but financially. Even when the wife's duties are confined to the household, the husband is coming to accept the argument that she works at least as hard as he does. Nor does her relative contribution diminish as the family goes up the economic scale. For the mistress of the larger household handles not only the children's affairs, but bosses a gardener and a cleaning woman.

Beyond this, in most cases, the wife handles family finances, including payment of bills; in some instances, she doesn't consult with her husband even on expensive items. According to the sales staff of a San Francisco car dealer, even the automobile is generally selected by the wife, which accounts for the pastel colors and elegant upholstery that have appeared since the war. The auto has become more than transportation; it is an item of fashion and adornment for the well-kept female. And as a final tribute to the economic power of woman, most TV and radio commercials are clearly aimed at her tastes. She is, after all, the one with the money.

Thus, in effect, the husband's solvency and credit rating are out of his control. He is head of the household in only one sense—legally. The general attitude of California society is that male and female have equal status and that the only difference between them is a mere biological technicality.

This final feminine triumph is not official. It is not chis-

173

eled in any preamble as the result of some hatchet-swinging crusade. It has arrived by silent evolution born of man's abdications and woman's necessity. Yet it is probably the major premise on which contemporary California society rests.

However, for all their strength, California women are not in danger of going masculine. Unlike the California described in a sixteenth-century Spanish novel—from which the locality drew its name—there is no race of Amazons here, nor any chance of one appearing. California women are not only as beautiful as any in the world, but also as feminine. The combination of being both equal and female is so irresistible as to tip the whole balance of California life.

In consequence, the concerns, the goals, and the values of California are becoming those of its women. Concerns for the children and for security; the goals of social recognition and respect; the values of love, beauty, family, home—these are the preoccupations of California males and females.

Most of these values are altogether worthy and desirable —representing the best side of human nature. The point here is that some other human preoccupations of other ages and places are seriously neglected. These include the quest for meaning in life, the improvement of political institutions, and the demand for justice. Such endeavors require participation in one's society and an affirmation of one's environment beyond the home and the neighborhood.

Precisely for this reason they are not of much interest to Californians, who have adopted the traditional feminine attitude that life's problems, duties, and joys are bounded by one's family and perhaps one's friends. If a society may be said to be male or female in character, then in frontier times California was decidedly male. It was fortunately tempered and polished by the coming of women, it developed an ease of living that dulled the manly virtues, and California is probably becoming female.

Yet California women do not show their femininity in

traditional ways. In the first place, they are hardly domestic in the sewing, baking, and handiwork sense of their mothers in the East. To many the home is more a base of operations than a place of confinement. A minister making continual home calls on a very large body of parishioners throughout the day in San Fernando Valley finds one-third away from home. A California company using an extensive telephone sales campaign reports that one-half of its calls are unanswered.

What are the ladies doing? They are not visiting each other, nor are they staying home gossiping in long phone conversations. Such casual indulgences went out in the thirties and are only practiced occasionally by a few women having nothing better to do. They are not out shopping; they generally get this over with in one big push at the supermarket once a week.

On the contrary, they are spending their time in some organized activity—either with the children in summertime, or without them the rest of the year. They are attending meetings—usually in child-oriented organizations such as the PTA. They are chauffering the kids to some doctor's appointment or to a meeting of their own. They are going with the children to the beach. Or they are going to school. California adult education classes are becoming more crowded every year; for many courses it is necessary to sign up weeks in advance. As for college adult courses, the University of California alone enrolls 150,000 a year—one quarter of all those in extension courses at public universities throughout the country.

Something in the modern California woman demands that she complete her education. One-third of the university extension students are women; among our friends are three mothers who went back to school to get their bachelor's degree, and one is going after her doctorate.

Part of this educational drive is for art's sake. Among its

many other booms, California is going through (pardon the expression) an Art Boom. For decades, San Francisco, and perhaps a few colonies on the central coast, were considered the be-all of California culture. Too absorbed in making a living, most Californians had little time for aesthetics.

Still, they were free spirits by nature and were actually nursing a creative urge which first showed itself in offbeat and unprofessional media. Fascinated with the possibilities in wet cement, husbands built outlandish fish ponds in the 1920's and equally outlandish barbecues in the 1940's. Inspired by the power of a little water and sunshine, Californians invented the year-round flower garden. Allied with this was the growth of cactus gardens and driftwood art. Californians made a custom of outdoor Christmas decoration; the family without holiday lights is suspected of being antisocial. Many neighborhood blocks adopt a theme (candy canes, bells, snowmen) with which each homeowner is expected to comply. By word-of-mouth these special displays become known throughout a city, and one of the rituals of the holiday season is to take the family for an evening drive to see the home decorations.

But California's artistic fire has also seized the classic forms. Night courses in painting, sculpture, ceramics, poetry, and drama were never more crowded; many have, according to one educator, "waiting lists we can't fill." In the large cities, private galleries are multiplying, while the one-man show—appealing essentially to a knowledgeable rather than a mildly curious following—is blossoming in surprising numbers. Traveling exhibits of art collections or archaeological treasures draw long waiting lines of visitors. In some communities, well-located vacant lots are taken over for displays by local artists. In Santa Monica, a laundromat doubles as an art gallery for paintings priced as high as $13,000. Even in medium-sized cities, the ballet and the concert are packed with patrons, and in many circles, a familiarity with great works is becoming a social necessity. Los Angeles has joined San Francisco as a major art center and is said to be the second (after New York) art market in the country.

In the prevailing enthusiasm for art, some observers have overstated the case. Says one art dealer, "If Los Angeles is second, it is a very poor second." Yet many young artists no longer feel they must go to New York or Paris for recognition. In California, partly because of the very lack of communication, they have more freedom for individual expression rather than being swept into the conformity of some particular school. As George D. Culler comments in *Art in America:* "The work here seems to me somehow more open, informal, outgoing than that of Eastern centers, and at the same time lacking in some of the nervous brilliance exhibited elsewhere."

Nor is California taste confined to traditional art. In a Butte County town, the Lions Club sponsored a Nickels for Culture campaign to finance an abstract ceramic mural for a public building. In architecture and interior design, California represents the avant-garde, partly because California customers are more inclined to give the professionals a free hand. The use of modern art in home decoration is becoming a new symbol of status—a status measured not in wealth but in taste, intellect, and savoir-faire. As one woman devotee puts it, "You're just not with it if you don't like art."

All of this activity—involving the children, education, and culture—reveals a sense of purpose in the way the California woman spends her time. Unplanned activity is considered a sign of aimless resignation to one's lot in life—something that might be considered characteristic of older generations or the foreign born.

Much of this activity is the product of the sometimes pathetic rootlessness that besets many Californians. Though happily released from the family and community pressures of their hometowns "back East," they have lost the security and the settled viewpoint of a traditional society. They are no longer in the paternal embrace of an established community that knows all the answers so well that it has forgotten the questions. They are thrust into a kaleidoscopic world of diverse ethnic, religious, political, and economic backgrounds. They have lost the comfort of corporate behavior and belief and are unequipped by experience to seek Truth alone. To borrow from David Riesman's idiom in *The Lonely Crowd,* other-directed people are suddenly required to be inner-directed, and they can't make the grade. The intense activity prevents them from being alone long enough to face the question of meaning in life.

3.

The most acute phase of this problem is in religion, to which women as a group have generally appeared to be more committed than men. While approximately two out of three Americans are church members, this is true of only about one in three Californians—a crucial statistic in explaining California life.[2] What this comparison means is that a large proportion who were church members in their former communities did not bother to renew their affiliation after arriving in California.

This in itself is an appalling commentary on the type of impact which American churches have on the personality, hinting strongly of the predominance of conformity over conviction. But the result in California is that the church has lost its position as the nexus of society. It might be said to be shoved aside by the headlong pace of California's secular life.

Symbolic of the situation is the case of the Village Church of Westwood, which was completely obscured from auto traffic by construction of an elevated freeway. Bravely the little church raised a new brick column above the freeway level to display its name. In another community, one congregation succumbed to the spirit of the times and called itself the Freeway Baptist Church.

In pioneer days when the young men came West in search of a quick fortune, many forgot their religious heritage. It was not until the women came that California communities began to blossom with churches.

But in our time, one is entitled to ask, what happened to California women? The traditional guardians of the family faith have not, it seems, taken their men to church.

One answer is that two of the age-long motivations for churchgoing—personal misery and social pressure—are largely lacking in California. It offers the good life; faith is not embraced as a solace. Nor do Californians judge the Sunday morning stay-at-home; indeed, there is sometimes a sense of embarrassment as the dressed-up, churchgoing family waves to the neighbor in shorts who is watering his lawn.

This does not mean that Californians are nonbelievers. On the contrary, a large majority had some childhood Sunday school experience, and some send their children to Sunday school ("It'll do 'em good") even though they themselves don't go to church. They believe in some kind of God; they have a vague assumption of immortality; they are generally conscious of right and wrong; and they are decent and considerate to others. The more thoughtful among them will tell you, often smugly, "I have my own religion."

California society is, in fact, a child of the Judaeo-Christian tradition that has run away from home. It no longer acknowledges its parents, but it bears the marks of their upbringing.

How long these marks will last is yet another question. Among the professional classes, and among intellectuals of all classes, there is a tendency for many nonreligionists to become nonbelievers. Up to the 1950's, the atheist was just as abhorred in California as elsewhere. He was more afraid to bare his breast than, say, the Socialist. I have had more than a few friends whom I felt, judging by their expressed opinions, were probably atheists. But they have never said so, and California etiquette does not encourage one to ask. Somehow it has been more acceptable to acknowledge being an agnostic, who does not believe but is willing to be shown. This is more in California's open-minded tradition.

But with the turn of the 1960's, atheism is no longer taboo. I was conversing earnestly about religion with a woman at a party when she stated flatly, "Of course I'm an atheist and so is my husband." At dinner I mentioned this as a rather interesting phenomenon to the couple across from us; both of them immediately stated that they, too, were atheists. An active adult leader in the Boy Scouts reports that an increasing number of parents signing up for leadership roles will refuse to answer "Yes" to the form question, "Do you believe in God?" Either California nonbelievers are increasing, or they are more willing to be counted because the stigma is diminishing. My own opinion is that for many years there have been more than would admit it, perhaps even to themselves.

Yet even atheists, who could be presumed to have cut themselves off from religion-born ethics, do not appear less moral than California churchgoers. They tend to be responsible, humane, just, and often more socially concerned than many scrupulous religionists. One does not detect any particular philosophical school among them, though one suspects that John Dewey's religion of Humanism has become, unofficially, more successful than its founder knew.

There is, indeed, less reason to worry about those who know what they don't believe in, than about the much larger number who never think about belief at all. What Socrates called the "unexamined life" is almost a California characteristic. Not that the Californian is apathetic; he is, if anything, superactive. But while he has many purposes, he

180

typically has no ultimate purpose. The widespread lack of viewpoint, and therefore direction in life, may be suspected of having some relationship to California's high rates of alcoholism, suicide, and divorce. Speaking of California's devotion to relaxation and diversion, author Irving Stone has said that "we are on the way to creating an anxiety-free people." But the effect of a people living by expediency rather than conviction may be just the opposite; and the grand quest for diversion may be less a cure than a symptom.

There is also room for serious concern over some of the organized religion that does exist in California. True, in outward appearance it is all healthy enough. Churches and denominations continue to grow; they could hardly help growing in California. The collection plates are piled high; Presbyterians and Episcopalians report that per capita contributions are higher in the Los Angeles area than in the rest of the country. The Methodists have cited an annual per capita average of $70.04 in Southern California against $43.82 nationally. Across suburbia new churches are rising; many of them show striking architectural imagination that reflects the tolerance of the congregation.

In addition, California churches are fairly vibrating with activity. A good part of the minister's time is occupied in attending meetings, of which there may be several in one evening. Indeed, the danger is that the church will become overorganized. I have seen two people being assigned to do the same job by different committees, and I have been asked to perform the same task by two different chairmen.

Suburban churches in new communities display the curious spectacle of young people in their thirties serving as deacons, elders, and trustees. The result is that in many churches there is little of the pressure on the minister to refrain from controversial subjects—a phenomenon often observable in older communities having more substantial church donors.

181

There is also a religious vitality implicit in the invention of new faiths, for which Los Angeles is still the world headquarters. And many California ministers are adept at promoting the Gospel in unusual ways. The community of Garden Grove has a drive-in church, or at least one that includes a drive-in section where the physically or emotionally handicapped may view the service through a large window and listen by high fidelity loudspeakers while remaining in the privacy of their cars. In Los Angeles and in Santa Monica, the local church federations operate mobile trailer chapels to reach schoolchildren during released-time periods. And the San Fernando Valley Horse Owners Association sponsors an annual Church on Horseback, in which the riders wear Western attire and contribute to the collection by riding by and dropping their money on an outstretched blanket.

But such Californiantics are not typical. Most churchgoers belong to the conventional denominations, in about the same proportion as in other regions. The major exception is that, because it is largely the Protestants who have abandoned their formal affiliations, more than half of California church members are Catholics; this is especially true in some northern counties, such as San Francisco and Sacramento, where approximately two-thirds of church members are Catholic. Yet even Catholic affiliation has not been universally binding in California. In a limited survey made near San Jose, more than half of those calling themselves Catholics said that they attended church either rarely or never.[3] Two Protestant ministers have told me that they regularly receive former Catholics into membership, and I have known several former Catholics who have no affiliation. Yet the Catholic record of backsliding in California is not as pronounced as that of the Protestants.

The end result is that these bodies exist in a milieu that is essentially secular. One cannot help noticing that many, if not most, heads remain unbowed during an invocation prayer

in any public gathering—not out of disrespect, but of ignorance. California could well be considered a mission field,
yet some leading denominations and churches do not exhibit
any particular missionary zeal. The Christianity preached in
some of these pulpits is not very demanding. Those in the
congregation are told, not what religion expects of them, but
what they can expect of religion. As a Hollywood minister
put it, "People did not come to church to learn of their responsibility to other people." Even the sermon emphasizing
Christian concern will often avoid specifics. Some churches
exhibit a very active Christian conscience, conducting social
work among migrants, Indians, and others in need. But only
a tiny fraction of California churchgoers participate in such
programs.

One reason is that, except for those of the Catholic and
Jewish faiths, Californians generally do not have a strong
personal attachment to their denomination. They readily
cross denominational lines to join another church that suits
them. One San Fernando Valley Congregational church, for
example, is composed 80 percent of former Methodists. If
the California minister demands too much sacrifice, there is
little to prevent a member from taking a walk to a church
that is more comforting.

One of the most devastating examples is the issue of civil
rights. While many churches in California support this cause
at denominational headquarters, there is only isolated effort
to challenge individual congregations. In 1956, the Methodist Church—one of the most progressive in this field—sent
questionnaires to churches in Southern California and Arizona. To the question, "Does your church welcome interra-
cial membership?" the answers were "Yes," 113; "No," 99.[4] A
survey of church members in the Wilshire District of Los
Angeles disclosed that 34 percent had varying degrees of
prejudice against admitting members of other races.[5] Though
the situation is improving, the churches are not only default-

ing on leadership in this moral issue, but many of them are among the worst offenders.

Nor is there much real enthusiasm among many churches in spreading the Gospel. In some parts of California, several of the principal Protestant denominations have a comity agreement in which they take turns opening churches in new areas, with a restriction against competing denominations within a mile of each other. The purpose is to prevent damaging rivalry and a profusion of small, struggling churches; the assumption is that one denomination is about the same as another, and any neighborhood Protestant—being a footloose Californian—will not hesitate to join the new church on doctrinal grounds. But the result is that the evangelistic and fundamentalist churches outside the comity agreement are the ones moving rapidly ahead in numbers. The Southern Baptist Convention—largest in the fundamentalist tradition—is expanding more rapidly in California than the more liberal denominations. With some exceptions, the most dynamic religious forces are those churches that summon people to specific articles of faith as a condition of salvation.

At the same time, the supposedly liberal bodies appear to be drawn in a direction curiously parallel to the fundamentalists. First of all, they have largely shed their identifying doctrines; the concepts of God's grace, of Christ's atonement, of salvation by faith—these are quaint notions found only in the hymnbooks. There is simply a general belief in a God who answers prayer, a divine Christ who preached a Gospel of love, and some kind of life after death (though not a specific heaven or hell). Christianity is not a question of salvation, but of duty—a development which one might think is at last equal to the challenge of our times.

Yet one senses in some of these churches a strange lack of Christian zeal. Among many women and a few men there is an air of sweet piety, as though they are clearly among the elect just to be going to church in a heathen country. But

184

they are not, in the favorite words of one Baptist minister, "on fire." They sing quietly in church, and the man who booms out is apt to embarrass his wife. They don't discuss the sermon after the service. And in the case of religious classes or lectures for adults, it is necessary to make an extraordinary effort to secure a respectable turnout. It might almost be said that committee meetings are so well attended that there is not much time for religion.

Since the late 1950's there has been a noticeable return to the specifics of belief in many of the major California bodies. This is largely implemented in the so-called Liturgical Movement, which had spread to the Coast from the East. There is more emphasis on the particulars of the worship service; more formality and color in the robes and vestments of worship; more lay participation by deacons and elders; much closer observation of previously slighted dates on the church calendar; and more frequent and elaborate observance of Communion.

While this change was instituted by the ministers, it was willingly accepted by the members. Church became more ceremonial, and equally important, more ecclesiastical. It was answering the same need that the fundamentalists had answered with salvation, but in a different way. For evidently the Californian who was inclined toward worship wanted more than a mere institutionalization of "my own religion." He wanted it to be an experience—an aesthetic or emotional experience—that had something to do with his belief in God. After all, he didn't have to go to church; there was little of the pressure from relatives or friends that produced churchgoers elsewhere. He was going out of conscience, because he needed church to make him "feel right." And so church ought to be something special. Liturgy filled the gap that zeal left empty.

The result is that many California churches, whether of the fundamentalist or modernist persuasion, are reaching the

185

point where the member is offered, not a challenge, but a gimmick. Faith and worship become his key to salvation or a salved conscience. His church is a self-sufficient, self-per-petuating community within a community, steering its own course, raising its funds and building its buildings, serving its own and making them feel good. It offers religious satis-faction without religious commitment. It is a larger version of the compartmented, insulated California family.

In sum, California provides an almost unique experiment as a society largely divorced from organized religious guid-ance. It is almost as secular as France, where only one-fourth of the people are church affiliated. This is all the more remark-able since the Californian is offered not just one faith, but the widest possible choice. Most people choose not only no church but no philosophy either, since none is available. California may therefore be the first civilization to be not only secular, but essentially without corporate purpose.

4.

The remarkable thing is that such a system works as well as it does. For though there are some cracks in the machin-ery, there is no serious breakdown. And one of the reasons is the extraordinary personality of the California woman. Even though she has not generally preserved the family's religious heritage, she has preserved and often strengthened the family ties. Indeed, she may be said to have adopted the "togetherness" movement as a new religion. The family does everything together (at least the parents and the preteeners) because this is somehow wholesome and right. The home is endowed with as much equipment as possible to provide for every interest and recreation, thus precluding the need of anyone going elsewhere except as a family.

Even within the California home, individual privacy is being restricted by the elimination of partitions. The dining room has become a dining area—simply one corner of the living room. Under a beam ceiling there may be just one great open space that houses, with only the flimsiest dividers, the kitchen, dining area, living room, and family room. Since the den became the "family room" about 1955, father gave up his last redoubt. With such vague boundaries for the kitchen, mother is even losing hers. We are, in short, gradually reverting to the togetherness of the one-room log cabin. Privacy has retreated to the bedroom and the bathroom, where hopefully it will survive.

In a still more subtle way, many California homes exhibit the near-religious character of togetherness. They are not so much to be lived in as to look at. The grounds are immaculately groomed; interiors are decorated with taste; the place has a general air of unreality, as though the family had put everything in place and gone away on a trip. In many cases the aim is to preserve the home for company, like the old-fashioned parlor. Yet I have been to at least one party in which the guests were carefully ushered to the backyard via the kitchen, and although they could see the living room as they passed by, they were literally prevented from entering it. On the other hand, tours of large homes are used by ladies' charitable groups as fund-raising events, the guests being motivated by the desire to get new decorating ideas.

Such showplaces, while not characteristic of California, are significant in that the goal of the typical California woman is to make her own home a showplace. As the symbol of togetherness, the home is in danger of being institutionalized to the point where its purpose is buried under its appearance. In many cases it is not so much a home as a shrine. And it is therefore possible to foresee the cult of togetherness eventually defeating itself.

Though the typical California woman has not gone this far, she is nevertheless one of the world's truly dedicated homemakers. And she is motivated in this not so much by the sense of duty that sustained her grandmother but by genuine personal zest for the job.

The normal mother in many contemporary American communities still shows that proud Victorian consciousness of her role as the keeper of the family's morals, manners, cultural interests, and domestic values. She passes to her daughters the womanly accomplishments—sewing and cooking—much as a craftsman hands down his trade to the apprentice.

But the California mother is not so interested in processes as in results. She takes less pride in herself as a specialized virtuoso than as the creator and manager of a total effect. She spends little time sewing and no time on such vanishing arts as crocheting or embroidery. She can go out and buy what she needs in this category. She does on occasion wield a paint brush or an upholstery hammer, but these are practical means to an immediate end—that of saving money in furnishings and decorations.

All of this helps explain why the California woman, for all the labor-saving devices in her suburban tract home, is busier than her grandmother. She is relieved of much household drudgery by automatic appliances and prepackaged foods. She is even saved from using a muscle in opening a can or stirring a cold drink. She doesn't toil long hours in needlework or pie cooking. She is spending her time, besides running errands and attending meetings for herself and the children, in improving the home. She has, in fact, been at least as important as other factors in elevating her home from working-class to middle-class status. Mass home construction, long-term financing, and the elevation of wages by union pressure, have all done their share to give the workingman the kind of house his boss used to occupy. But the little woman's contribution in decorating and improving it is at least comparable to the others, and she has made it at great sacrifice to herself as a woman.

Generally, the higher up the social scale she goes, the less time she spends in the company of other women. She hasn't the time, since she is busy making and keeping a home. For even though she may be preening her home chiefly for the benefit of company, she seldom has company. In a study of 100 families in a modest tract near San Jose, 84 percent reported that they attend parties "never or rarely." [6] While there is considerable informal "dropping in" among next-door neighbors in such tracts, the incidence of casual contacts drops off as families climb the economic scale. It may be said that, in California at least, the higher the income and/or educational level, the less neighborhood socializing and the more restriction of contact to friends of like interests regardless of geography. This in turn means a major effort in visiting people across town. In such circles, unannounced drop-ins are almost unknown. Even "coming over for the evening" without dinner is outmoded; the idea is that you don't ask people to dress up and drive at least half an hour through traffic to your house without making the party amount to something (i.e., dinner).

Yet such parties are expensive. And the housewife, even in the upper-middle-class circumstance, is spending so much money on her house that she can't afford to entertain very often. One might reasonably estimate that the average length of time such Californians take to return a dinner, even among close friends, is at least four months.

Thus, in many cases the intense effort to decorate and improve the house is defeating its underlying purpose, since it cuts seriously into the pace of entertaining. Often its chief effect is to elevate the morale of the housewife, who sees that she is better off than her mother was, or sister is back home. The interviewer in the San Jose tract was amused on two occasions when he asked the couple to what class they belonged; simultaneously, the husband replied "working class" and the wife said "middle class." She is achieving status, but most of the time she is the only one who knows it.

189

There is, in short, a loss of social proximity in California life. People are tending to keep each other at arm's length; close relationships are kept within the family.

As a result, people know less about each other. The home-town environment—in which every one knew your business, your approximate income level, your comings and goings, and the behavior of your children—is familiar to only a small fraction of Californians. Your social and business acquaintances, even your closest friends, don't know you too well.

The corollary to this California phenomenon has been a disturbing rise of pretense. Since people don't know much about you, they can be fooled. Status seeking, which if not impossible was at least amusingly transparent in the home-town environment, has become a major California sport.

5.

What is remarkable at the outset is that pretense is basically alien to the Western character. In the nineteenth century, the Westerner, including the Californian, was fiercely practical; his self-pride was in honest work, and the man or woman who "put on airs" was possibly more contemptible than, say, a road agent, who was at least forthright and courageous. Certain affectations, such as formal clothes, are still avoided by Californians. The top officers of very large California companies will generally forego chauffeurs and some even adopt the values of the younger set by driving sports cars. There is no widespread awe of colleges or prep schools with prestige names; there is, in fact, some tendency to suspect the graduate of an Ivy League school, or a well-known Eastern girl's college, as a potential snob. Californians seldom plaster their car windows with sightseeing stickers; this is regarded as a tourist's crude attempt to prove he has really been around.

But subtly, pretense crept into the California mind, particularly the Southern California mind, sometime during the boom of the 1920's. It showed itself in such measurements as the name of one's beach club and the make of one's automobile (Packard was then *the* prestige car; Santa Monica was known as a "Packard town"). But while the name of one's neighborhood was also a measure of status, the possibility of pretense was limited by the short terms of home loans (from three to five years). If you lived in Bel Air or Piedmont, chances were you belonged there.

Beginning in the 1930's, long-term credit payments opened the status race to all comers, and somewhere around 1950 they began to defeat status altogether in the automobile field. It was widely noted that in the country as a whole, 95 percent of Cadillacs were bought for cash, while in Beverly Hills, 95 percent were bought for credit. It got so the only place a dedicated status seeker could make good without annoyance from the amateurs was in the custom-built home. But even custom homes began to be mass produced; the word "tract" as a term of derision lost its meaning when the promoters put up rows of individualized $60,000 homes. And the efforts of banks to restrict such homes to those who could afford to keep up the payments was considered unsporting by many real estate agents. I have heard one San Fernando Valley broker urge his client to "overestimate your income and assets, underestimate your liabilities," in filling out a loan application. When challenged on the subject, he argued that the practice was widespread and boasted that he was so skilled in getting loans for his clients that he could get one for a fictitious name.

By such means did status invade the mass market. Among California promoters, at least, status seeking is no longer subtle. On the contrary, they rub people's noses in it with billboards and full-page ads headlined:

"A new prestige community for those of means."

"The sophisticated blending of distinguished homes and a prestige address."

"Where 'Total Luxury' speaks eloquently of success."

"An address that is one of the most desirable and important in San Francisco."

"Move up to exclusive Hillside living."

"Ultimate elegance in Exclusive North Tustin."

"Fashionable Homes—the Fashionable Address in Garden Grove."

"People on their way up are building their future at . . ."

"Let us show you how simple it is to trade your present home . . . for our new prestige home!"

"Your home at Troy Hills is visible proof of your high community standing . . . a constant source of pride when you entertain friends . . . relatives . . . clients!"

This viewpoint is eloquently displayed in the names of new communities: "Executive Homes," "Country Club Estates," and "Influential Homes." And as a final ad nauseam, one ad promises "Champagne living at Beer prices!"

In these promotions, no conceivable gimmick calculated to impart status is overlooked: A walled-in community, implying exclusiveness; homesites beside a golf course (great for collecting golf balls in the living room); and for the tract that can't quite claim an all-executive population, the next best thing is a heavy dose of "teachers, engineers, and members of other professions." You aren't going to be hobnobbing here with guys having dirt under their fingernails.

It must be said of most Californians, however, that they are not this blunt. They may be just as status conscious as many of the commuters living in the exurbanite counties around New York City, but they try hard not to let it show. Thus, status-manship is a parlor game requiring at least as much finesse as name-dropping and place-dropping. One doesn't announce that he has a gardener; one simply complains that crabgrass has been introduced to his lawn via the gardener's lawnmower. One doesn't say, "We keep horses." One talks about how one insists on the children keeping the stalls clean. One doesn't say, "We've got a swimming pool." One simply worries aloud about going away on a trip for fear some neighbor kid will sneak in the yard and fall in the pool.

One of the most difficult points to top is, of course, the personal catastrophe. The only status symbol higher than being burned out of your home by a brush fire, for example, is to have some paintings stolen.

All in all, a far cheaper and still subtle refinement to the game is the conversation about wildlife prowling about the house—implying, of course, that you live in the hills and possibly at the end of a private road. One subdivision in Marin County was frankly named "Wildlife Acres." Another developer in Orange County simply put a picture of a quail on his ad; without reference to the little critter, he had suggested a sylvan setting that smacked of whitewashed fences and station wagons. However, I would rate quail relatively low on the scale of prestige wildlife—say, one or two points. Squirrels are about in the same category, since they abound in the flatland of San Fernando Valley, where they make things tough for the phone company by chewing the insulation off the wires. Raccoons, opossums, and deer rate a score of perhaps four; above this the score rises with the relative ferocity of the animal, since this indicates that you are up against the mountains, not just the foothills. Coyotes ("We hear them howling every night") rate at least six points, while the ten strike is reserved for the mountain lion and the bear.

It should be noted that all the status symbols cited are concerned with the home, and particularly the location of the home. The California female, and almost to an equal degree the California male, are perhaps as status conscious about homes as any people anywhere. This is largely because the home, as opposed to the apartment, is more prevalent in

193

California (except San Francisco) than in other urban areas. Los Angeles still is a metropolis, not of cliff dwellers, but of homeowners. Since the boom of the 1880's the real estate fraternity has drilled into newcomers the moral necessity of buying a lot and building a house on it. Owning your own home has been promoted as a natural goal of marriage, like having children, while apartment dwelling is relegated to young marrieds saving up for a house, or for older couples whose children have left home. So while the Californian's almost uncontrollable attachment to the home as a status symbol is disturbing, it is also somewhat understandable.

Since pretense means appearing to be something one is not, its effect on personal credit in California may well be imagined. In Los Angeles County, the rate of foreclosures per 1,000 real estate loans rose from six in 1950 to twenty-two in 1961.[7] Indeed, mortgages are taken for granted in California, and cash for a home is unheard-of. Some 70 percent of California families are paying off mortgages or trust deeds. With some 9 percent of the national population, California has 15 percent of the Savings and Loan Association first mortgages. A large cash equity in the house is actually considered by many to be a disadvantage, since it would require a large down payment or a second trust deed in case of resale. Paying off the mortgage is not even a goal of most Californians, who expect that they will probably have moved long before the loan expires. The fact of a mortgage is no family secret but rather the object of general humor. In some rural neighborhoods, it is customary to give the estate a name and attach a sign to that effect at the entrance to the driveway; one such sign carries the name, "Mortgage Manor." At new houses under construction it is customary for the contractor and architect to put up signs: "Built by ———" or "Designed by ———." The ultimate loss of financial privacy is reached in the appearance of signs such as "Financed by Lytton Savings and Loan."

But the home is only the beginning for the California debtor. According to one report, the average California family is making payments on the house, car, TV set, and some of the furniture and appliances. A water softener sales manager who arrived from Chicago found he had to change his whole sales technique—adopting low down payment, high interest charges, and the "hidden-angle sell" in order to meet the competition. In Fresno, the average consumer indebtedness, in addition to the loan on the house, is $3,400.

The California appetite for things on credit is apparently insatiable; there appears to be a general belief that if you buy something on time you aren't really paying for it. There is a bit of this folklore in the clerk's innocent query, "Do you want to pay for it or charge it?" The Californian's naïve attitude toward credit has brought on a spate of charge account and credit card gimmicks that has almost made people ashamed to carry cash. It was California's Bank of America that conceived of the all-purpose, revolving loan perpetuated simply by flashing a Bankamericard. One credit outfit provides "one charge card for nearly every family need and emergency" in more than 16,000 California establishments, and suggests that "You could probably go from San Diego to San Francisco without touching money once—except perhaps 10 cents for a newspaper." A Northern California clothingstore boasts that it will open a charge account for you "in 3 minutes flat (go ahead—time us!)."

Such easy credit has, of course, undermined the whole budget process. After joining a credit card system, a San Francisco supper club reported a 40 percent leap in orders for champagne. Those who are financially disorganized once had an automatic cutoff on their spending when they reached the end of the paycheck. Now the cutoff comes when they reach the end of their credit, by which time they are in serious trouble. In San Gabriel Valley, according to a collection bureau, approximately 14 to 17 percent of people were delinquent in paying bills, while from 3 to 6 percent reneged altogether on medical bills. A San Francisco company specializing in straightening out people's finances reported a 14 percent increase in business during one year. Another collection agent reported that in San Fernando Valley, housewives alone wrote an average of $30,000 worth of bad checks per month. This was mostly due to bad management, rather than deliberate dishonesty—yet only from 10 to 15 percent of the debts were collectible. Over a ten-year period one San Jose woman accumulated debts of $86,279.50 on some 500 charge accounts.[8]

"Didn't it ever occur to you," asked the referee in bankruptcy, "that you were getting in over your head?"

The answer was "No."

All of which accounts for the more than 740 collection agencies doing business in California. For years, Los Angeles has been known, according to one bankruptcy court attorney, as "the bankruptcy capital of the United States." Of the ten circuits in the U.S. bankruptcy courts, the Southern California circuit accounts for more than 27 percent of all bankruptcy petitions filed—and most of these are individual rather than business bankruptcies.

Quite naturally, the Californian's passion for automobiles has invested them with a prestige often leading to financial trouble. The car is never considered mere transportation. Indeed, the worst slur one can attach to any automobile is the comment, "Well, it's transportation." The status role of the car, together with the high-pressure and hidden-angle tactics of some auto dealers, have made auto payment defaults a near-normal phenomenon in California and repossession of autos a major industry. In an average year, there are approximately 25,000 repossessions in Los Angeles County alone. Indeed, the Californian's devotion to his car is so strong that he will often use every subterfuge and even forcible resistance to keep it, and he can sometimes count on help from bystanders. In Puente, a woman who was pulled out of her car by two repossessors screamed for help; neighbors came running out of their houses and surrounded the culprits until she could have them arrested. During World War II, a man tried to repossess a car from another in the heart of downtown Long Beach. The ruckus drew a crowd estimated at 3,000 people, who booed the repossessor, took up a collection of $50 as a partial payment on the car, and were only dispersed by calling out the police reserves.

This prevailing idea that a man's car is his castle has forced California repossessors into a modus operandi that, as one observer said, "borders on grand theft." Since obtaining and serving a court order involves too much red tape, the whole operation is a kind of sub-rosa conspiracy carried out by professional strong-arm men. Hardened operators will not go through the formality of knocking on the front door and demanding the car key. Under cover of darkness they quietly roll the car out of the driveway (even out of the garage) and into the street, where they start it by crossing the ignition wires. Before the victim can recognize the roar of his own engine, they are off.

These tactics have led to some remarkable scenes that could only happen in California. In Hollywood, a woman who didn't know her husband had missed any payments was sitting in her car when two repossessors suddenly flung open the door, snatched at the keys in the switch, and jabbed her in the stomach. In Venice, a couple returned from an evening of shopping and momentarily left their three-year-old girl in the car while they carried the groceries into the house. On returning they found the car missing; after a wild search the police returned the girl but not the car, which was in the hands of a repossessor. In Los Angeles, a man who was ahead in his payments had his car repossessed by mistake. He got

197

the car back, but not the suitcases full of clothing and other property that had been inside it and was never reimbursed for the loss.

Some encounters have ended still less happily. In West Hollywood, two repossessors were driving off with a Cadillac when the owner ran after them, grabbed at the car, and caught his arm in the right rear window. Undaunted, the driver continued down the street dragging the man and trying to brush him loose by swerving close to parked autos. After weaving from side to side, the repossessors shook the owner off and sent him sprawling under a parked car.

When a Pasadenan saw repossessors hooking a tow chain to his car, he slipped inside it, locked the doors, rolled up the windows, and set the handbrake—apparently a favorite anti-repossession trick. But his tormentors simply broke a window with a wrench, released the brake, and hauled the car away to the nearest garage. There the garageman refused to accept the auto while it still had the owner inside. The safari then picked its way to the Pasadena police station, but the officers refused to act on the ground that the case was civil, not criminal. Threading back to the man's home, the repossessors took the spark plugs and distributor cap and left the owner fuming in his car. By this time he had worked up such a rage that he went back to the police station to bring charges against the finance men. But the officers had checked their records and found a warrant for his arrest on an old traffic citation. While the Pasadenan went to jail, the repossessors returned and took his car.

Such are the predicaments that a Californian can get into through the necessity of having a car, and the process of paying more for it than he can afford. Indeed, the entire time payment system reached such a state of disrepute that the state has taken measures to protect Californians from their own folly. In 1959, the governor established the office of Consumer Counsel to keep a sharp watch for credit abuses, while

198

the Legislature passed a law setting maximum interest rates and requiring sellers to reveal what had previously been the "hidden angles."

Even Californians themselves are becoming aware of their own weakness. In the San Francisco Bay area a group of women started an organization called Charge Accounts Anonymous—no doubt with the cordial encouragement of their husbands. Says one Californian, "I have torn up my credit cards." But beating the credit disease will never be easy for Californians, who tend to have a combination of highly susceptible traits, including acquisitiveness, disorganization, and chronic optimism. As the state Consumer Counsel sadly reports, credit buying ruins more families than alcohol or narcotics. This vital weakness may be summed up in the plight of the Millionaire Club, a Hollywood night spot dedicated to making every customer feel like a millionaire. It had to close due to the "backlog of unpaid charge accounts." Said one observer, "They'd do a tremendous business if everybody paid."

6.

It is only fair to point out, however, that financial pretense is not generally accompanied by other sins of pride. Except among some hard-core pioneer families, most California communities are not concerned with the prestige of family names. One does not hear of an eligible young man or woman being of "proper stock"; what counts is not so much whether the young man's family is well-to-do (though this is no handicap), but whether the young man shows spirit, gumption, and the foresight to study for a promising occupation. California is still a young and virile society, only two or three generations removed from the frontier, with few of the artificial affectations and discriminations cherished by so-called mature societies. California as a society has not stopped running long enough to develop a fixed leadership class. With its population in such growth and inner flux, it is doubtful that it will for many years. Meanwhile, the economy is so dynamic that the energetic young enterpriser with a new idea can still revolutionize an industry. Personal success (including being married to success) is still the first mark of respect in California.

Perhaps this is why the California woman appears to be more natural and unaffected than her counterpart in an Eastern exurbia. One of my friends claims to be able to identify a native Californian at the first meeting. "They're so offhanded—not overly polite, not trying to impress. They sort of take it for granted that you'll hit it off."

But this description generally goes for adopted Californians as well. Somehow they fall into the pattern, partly because they're delighted with it, partly because, as one San Rafael housewife puts it, "People tend to stare at you if you don't."

Actually, in this observer's opinion, there is not much difference between native and adopted Californians, except in superficialities such as one's accent. Nor are the natives as much of a rarity as is assumed. Even in Los Angeles, one-third of the annual population growth is now natural births. And except in outlying and relatively static communities, the natives are by no means clannish; being of an old family confers no class distinction, except as a curiosity.

Moreover, if conformity of thinking is an exurbanite characteristic, it is not especially noticeable in California. Particularly among younger people who achieved adulthood during or since the war, there is a willingness, sometimes even a determination, to argue about controversial issues. Some California women may refrain from the discussion, but this is not so much from fear of offending someone, but rather from lack of information. However, such a drawback rarely inhibits the opinions of California men.

In short, what has happened in California is that a relatively naïve and unaffected society, concerned with the elementary yet generally wholesome pursuits of working hard and playing hard, has become infected with a peculiar sophistication that might be called "home-ism." This phenomenon is due, first, to the elevation of the California woman to at least equal status with the man, and his adoption of her values and goals; second, to their joint devotion to child-rearing and homemaking at the expense of other interests, including religion; third, to the institutionalization of homemaking as a kind of substitute religion, of which the home is the symbol and the shrine; and finally, to the cultivation of this shrine as a certificate of personal worth.

This somewhat complex yet makeshift system actually holds California society together. It tends to make up for the organized religion that most California immigrants left behind them.

How long will it work? Specifically, will it sustain the institution of the family, which is supposedly at its core?

7.

It must be acknowledged at the outset that, statistically, there is less chance of a marriage succeeding in California than in most other states. The national figures are alarming enough: five divorces recorded per year for every twelve marriages. In California, the ratio has moved up to slightly more than one to two. This does not, of course, account for separations and annulments; it has been estimated that almost as many California women are separated as are divorced. In Los Angeles County, the ratio runs still higher (around ten divorces for every twelve marriages); yet it is not necessarily the headquarters for broken marriages. In Sacramento County, the annual court actions filed to end marriages (divorce, annulment, and separate maintenance) exceed the number of marriage licenses issued. The social and personal tragedy implicit in such facts is appalling. For a typical year, divorces in Los Angeles County alone affect 40,000 children.[9]

What happens to California marriages? A partial explanation is that many marriages are in trouble before the couples ever reach California. Often the people come West for the express purpose of getting rid of what they believed was a disturbing environment and starting life anew in a fresh one. Some of them find that the cause was not in the environment, but in themselves. In Los Angeles County, 56 percent of uncontested divorces were of marriages contracted outside California.[10] They bring their marriage problem with them and there is no place else to run, as one officer of the Los Angeles Conciliation Court explains, "so the marriage becomes still sicker here. And we bury it."

Yet the sad statistics cannot really be blamed on outsiders, for most Californians were once outsiders. When one asks "What kind of people are the Californians?" one is really asking, "What kind of people come to California?" One apparent characteristic is that they are somewhat more divorce-prone than others. Why?

A partial answer is that to many, the solemn and sacred character of the marriage institution is lacking; it is no coincidence that in 95 percent of divorce cases in Los Angeles County, one or both of the spouses was not a regular church-goer.[11] The secular view of life has resulted in a secular view of marriage. The wedding vows may be discounted precisely because they are couched in religious terms. Though there is nothing cynical about the romance leading to the marriage, the wedding itself is often considered a civil contract.

The cavalier regard for the marriage institution in some quarters is seen in the large number of elopements to Las Vegas and other Nevada points, where one gets married "under a neon sign" with about as much sentiment and ceremony as in getting an inoculation. Marriage becomes a legal certificate for living together, rather than a personal commitment.

As might be expected, California also displays more than its share of stunt weddings, in which the people get married on horseback, in bathing suits, in airplanes. At Ontario, one couple sentimentally insisted on being married on ice skates at the rink where they first met. Near Lake Tahoe, another couple was married on the side of Squaw Peak in a merciless snowstorm so cold the groom couldn't get the ring on the bride's finger.

Not the sensational wedding itself, but the state of mind that makes a joke of the ceremony, is a serious threat to matrimony in California. In some circles, divorce is considered not so much a personal tragedy as a simple change of environment. One neighborhood romance ended in two divorces, and when the couple involved married each other they threw a grand party for their neighbors to celebrate the event; almost needless to say, no one missed the event. A friend of mine writing an article on the ingredients of marital happiness got some excellent material in an interview with a Los Angeles psychiatrist. Not long after the article was published, quoting the expert, he was reported in the divorce court. In the town of Paradise, California, two couples decided to swap spouses, drove together to Tijuana, got divorced and remarried, and drove back together as a happy quartet.

Yet this does not imply that California is becoming immoral. Though the state has a disproportionate number of divorces, they do not spring primarily from infidelity. Dr. Paul Popenoe, whose Institute of Family Relations in Los Angeles is one of the outstanding marriage counseling services in the country, states that his group has helped about 25,000 couples in their marriage problems; his files indicate only about 5,000 cases in which infidelity was a known factor.

Actually, the Californian hates subterfuge. The man who covets his neighbor's wife still shrinks from all the sneaking and tippy-toeing involved. California affairs—if they are risked at all—tend to be an adventure, not a career. Californians are generally too pragmatic to let an emotional outbreak destroy the whole fabric of their lives. Besides, they are generally so committed to various activities that their time is too well accounted for. In a region of great distances, infidelity requires too much strategy. It is not easy for a couple to keep a clandestine rendezvous; as one San Fernando Valleyite said, "They'd get caught in a traffic jam."

Thus, even though religious influence is minimal in California, morality among married adults is saved by the cult of home-ism. The lack of individual privacy at least keeps people honest. Californians are generally too busy to be bad.

Even the Hollywood entertainment colony, which once had a reputation for high living, no longer exhibits the old signs of wickedness. Since the 1940's the extravagant and scandalous party has become obsolete. Instead, entertaining has become a matter of small dinner parties among close friends. One reason is the businesslike shooting schedule in the television business. Stars and technicians alike are up early, put in a full day's work, and are ready for relaxation at home in the evening. Gone is the old leisure "between pictures" that encouraged all manner of diversion in a town where sex appeal stood at the top of the value scale.

Further, Hollywood is made outwardly Puritanical by the morals clause in most talent contracts for TV series. The sponsor is not going to risk a scandal by the star who is associated with his product. Nothing has had such a wholesome effect on Hollywood as the contract provision calling for dismissal if one is involved in morals difficulties.

But the change goes deeper; since the last war the mood of Hollywood has changed. The sense of prowl, on the part of he-wolves and she-wolves alike, has diminished. In its

204

place has come a kind of conscious sentimentality in support of the homely virtues, as though these were in danger of losing out until Hollywood endorsed them. Characteristically, the film colony has carried this new fad to a sickening extreme; sincerity, neatly packaged with a capital S, has taken the place of rude flippancy. Public displays of friendship are carried to the ultimate in the practice of grown men blowing kisses to their television fans.

California home-ism has thus caught up with the movie people. As one star complains, "They want to be sedate and respected like average folks. . . . Hollywood is getting to be like Pasadena."

One must therefore look elsewhere for the cause of California's divorce rate. Actually, it is implicit in the California character and the California values. The Californian's first mistake is often made at the time of courtship, when preoccupation with sports, hobbies, and other diversions is at a peak. In the typical California outlook, the end of life is having a good time. So one should look for a mate who has the same interests—one who can be a pal in bowling, scuba diving, or listening to progressive jazz. I have known couples whose romance was born because they both loved golf. Another couple were attracted to each other because they were both parachute jumpers. Actually, such couples have no more chance of a happy marriage than, say, the following prize California examples:

Among the ads placed by a Modesto lonely hearts agency was: "Good-looking Portuguese rancher, 57, 5'9", 200 lbs., seeks woman, 150 lbs. or over."

In San Diego, a young couple met in the city jail; he was incarcerated on a robbery charge, she for auto theft. They met because his cell was directly over hers on the floor above. Though they couldn't see each other, they communicated by tapping on the water pipes and hollering into the wash basins. Despite rules against communication between men and women prisoners, he proposed via the pipeline, she accepted, and the judge permitted them to be married before she went to prison.

By the time Californians find there are some other factors in a successful marriage besides liking the same ways of having fun, it is too late. What makes this all the more critical is that Californians as a class are not especially endowed with the grace and sweet reasonableness necessary to make marriage work. In San Fernando Valley, the director of a family service agency states that the high incidence of marriage problems derives from "fixed ideas by husbands and wives and a refusal to discuss the other's point of view." In Sacramento, the county marriage counselor was asked about the most common causes of marital strife. "Number one," he replied, "is lack of communication. Couples know how to talk at each other but not with each other. Another is the difficulty some find in accepting different points of view." The favorite ground for divorce—"mental cruelty"—is an honest revelation of the California divorce problem. The testimony of women in divorce courts shows the pathetic selfishness on both sides:

"He said I was the best of his three wives, but he wanted to be a bachelor."

"He had a hostile attitude toward my mother."

"He said I should have been a scrubwoman—not an actress."

"He took five-hour walks."

In short, many Californians tend to be less disciplined and more self-oriented in their approach to life, including marriage. The concept of cooperation and compromise does not occur to them as a prerequisite in human relations.

Finally, not to be overlooked as a cause of California divorce is the lack of social pressure against it. In the settled communities of the East and South, where one has grown up with all of one's friends and relations, the admission that one

206

has failed in one's marriage is an embarrassment too great to endure. Inhibitions by one's lifelong church and by other social institutions commanding conformity are too massive to defy. But in California these elements are vastly weakened. In consequence the unhappy couple is more willing to choose divorce; and to this degree the California mode may have one beneficial effect, in that there are not as many people who have resigned themselves to a lifetime of marital misery.

8.

Yet under these circumstances, the wonder is that California society holds together as well as it does. Without any firm religious or moral direction, a collection of self-oriented individuals is strenuously pursuing separate lives in a crowded arena. What sustains order in this potential chaos is the wonderful California woman. If her nest-feathering instincts are a matter of glandular secretion, then hers runneth over. She has preserved family life, not because it is necessary for survival, as it was for primitive woman; not because it is divinely ordained, as it has been to most other civilized women; but simply because it is desirable and satisfying. Without much chance of keeping the California father home on the grounds of morals or duty, she has done so by convincing him that home is, of itself, good. She has, therefore, revealed what prior generations had piously declared but never altogether believed. Home, at least in California, is its own reward.

A society depending so heavily on this one institution is, of course, curiously lopsided. Has the California woman, in her preoccupation with the home, caused this imbalance? On the contrary, home-ism is not so much a cause of community default as a result. Retreating from society, individual Californians have pinned their sense of personal worth on their position in the family.

California life, therefore, has not disintegrated. The individual, not the family, is society's smallest denominator. The strengthening of the family represents a step up from ultimate fragmentation.

Thus, while California has shed itself of many commitments that have been essential to a healthy society, it cannot be said to be decadent in the classic sense. In their rejection of organized religion and of community duty, Californians could have gone down other aberrant roads leading to dead ends. But the family is not only wholesome, it is imperative. If California society is being remolded by the California woman, she is at least beginning at the beginning.

CHAPTER IX

The Disengaged Man

1.

In Glendale, a pedestrian was crossing an intersection when a station wagon came swerving around the corner—so close that he had to jump for the curb. At his shout of disapproval, the wagon slammed to a stop. The driver got out, took a .22 rifle from the back, shot the pedestrian, and drove off.

The point here is not that the Californian on foot is a second-class citizen, although he is. The point is that the Californian, afoot or behind the wheel, is a hangover from the old frontier. He acts on his own, not as a member of society.

The Glendale station-wagoner is, of course, an extremist. But consider the cement contractor who, feuding with his neighbor, backed his giant mixer alongside the other's car, inserted the outlet trough into a back window, and filled the interior with wet concrete. Or the fellow who, exasperated by the perpetual barking of his neighbor's dog, made a recording of it and then, with his speaker aimed out the window and operating at full volume, played it back.

While the Californians are probably as basically honest as any Americans, they are not much impressed with rules. "No Trespassing" signs are so generally ignored that property owners have to quote from the Civil Code and warn that "violators will be prosecuted to the full extent of the law." Private parking lots are posted with warnings that unauthorized cars will be towed away at the owner's expense. Though fireworks are forbidden in some cities, Californians think nothing of buying them across the city limits in order to celebrate the Fourth. The Griffith Park Zoo in Los Angeles is plastered with signs against feeding the animals, but everyone does so, and there is a run on peanuts and crackerjack at the refreshment stands for this very purpose. Squatterism has a long tradition in California and hundreds of squatters are located illegally on government land; the entire town of Hawkinsville, Siskiyou County, is situated unlawfully on public property.

Perhaps the most obvious example is California driving, which is considered a matter of hide-and-seek between the motorist and the motorcycle cop, with traffic laws as the rules of the game. Many commuters drive with one eye on the road ahead and one on the rear-view mirror. The state legislature does its best to maintain the sporting element in this game. Radar speed traps are carefully posted as such to give the driver fair warning. Every time a legislator proposes "plainclothes" police cars the idea is voted down—not so much on grounds of civil liberties as simply to preserve the motorists' sporting chance. It is unlawful for a motorcycle cop to hide behind a billboard, and my brother-in-law once stopped and bawled one out for doing so.

Defiance of police can sometimes take a morbid turn; I have heard a tableful of commuters laugh uproariously on hearing about two motorcycle cops, one of whom turned suddenly to chase a speeder and was run over by his buddy. There is an appalling increase in resistance to police. In Huntington Beach, an attempt of two policemen to arrest a man for drunkenness precipitated an hour-long riot, which was only halted by the police forces of eleven cities. In

Canoga Park, officers breaking up a sidewalk dice game brought on a riot of some 300 people. As a crowning instance of the spirit of the times, a policeman in Placer County had his wallet picked by one thief and shortly afterward had his officer's cap stolen from the squad car by another.

In short, to the Californian, government is a kind of adversary—or at least a nuisance. This represents no carefully conceived viewpoint, but rather a vague feeling, like a distrust of used-car dealers. Government interferes with doing what one wants to do, and after all, isn't that why one came to California? At its worst, this attitude lies behind the sickening fact that in one out of four California auto accidents, the party at fault drives away without stopping. An official of the National Safety Council reported that it was "difficult to reach Californians" on driver education. Most of them had displayed a "strong sense of individualism and independence" by moving to California in the first place. "They resent being told what to do."

This does not mean that the Californian is an individualist on all fronts. For example, although California is known for its religious, political, and economic crackpots, the average Californian could hardly be termed a nonconformist in this sense. He is not about to get out in front for some cause—unless it has a direct benefit to himself. His individualism is self-oriented, not public-spirited.

For instance, there has been an obvious decline in militant radicalism among Californians since the 1930's. Those who might otherwise be critical of the existing order are moving ahead in their jobs and are involved in large mortgages and other financial commitments. They have succumbed to the charms of California Living, and they have traded their militancy for comfort. If radical views are expressed at all outside the home they are reserved for the small dinner party, which has become a kind of secular confessional. If one is going to crusade about something, one is more apt to choose an innocuous cause, such as the clamor against all-digit tele-phone numbers, which is organized into a statewide Anti-Digit Dialing League. Otherwise the Californian is not going to make a big display out of his individualism because this would interfere with his primary goal of pursuing his own life unhampered by society.

This helps to account for what is perhaps the most dis-tinguishing characteristic of the California male; he is a nonparticipant. Generally, he does not take part in the gov-ernmental process, except perhaps to vote, which gives him an exhilarating sense of pride as though he had discharged all his duties as a citizen for the rest of the year. In a survey taken in a Northern California suburban neighborhood, 53 percent of the respondents said they had "hardly any interest at all" in politics. Turnout in local elections is almost always less than half of the registered voters, and in some precincts has been as low as 15 percent. One San Francisco matron had so little comprehension of the franchise privilege that she sent her maid to the polls to vote in her place. Getting out of jury duty is so common that anyone who accepts the re-sponsibility feels almost apologetic: "You have no idea how much I've learned!" There is slightly less resistance than for-merly, since many companies have adopted policies provid-ing leaves of absence without financial penalty. But most Californians consider it a nuisance; I know of one citizen who never votes because he is afraid of being picked from the registration rolls for a jury panel.

Thus, the average Californian thinks of himself as a sort of permanent tourist, with no real stake in political affairs or social problems. The protest groups who show up at city council or board of education meetings are a tiny minority, and many people hesitate to join them for fear of being con-sidered crackpots. When one Southern California resident was asked to join his neighbors in opposing an undesirable construction across the street, he simply replied, "I'll see how it works out and if necessary I'll move."

Neither is the Californian particularly active in the kind of social and fraternal organizations that he left behind in his Eastern hometown. A suburban survey showed that 70 percent of the husbands belonged to no organization except perhaps their labor unions, and only 8 percent belonged to more than one organization. Moreover, only a small fraction of those belonging to clubs attended meetings "often." [1]

Actually, there are three types of clubs that thrive in California: youth activity groups, manifesting the California penchant for togetherness; hobby and sports clubs, which are avenues by which the Californian expresses his individuality; and service clubs, which are supported by business and professional leaders of more than ordinary community consciousness.

As for union activity, attendance at meetings is generally low (in one union, 7 to 10 percent of membership). And the typical union hall holds only a small proportion of the total membership. Indeed, California workers as a whole are among the least militant of any Americans in their unionism. There are notable exceptions: San Francisco is a true union town in the Eastern sense. Throughout the state some unions (the Longshoremen, the Teamsters, the Building Trades, and the entertainment industry unions) have virtually complete control of the labor market in their fields. But Central and Southern California have a traditional opposition to the closed shop and even to the union shop.

Since the passage of the Wagner Act in 1934, the labor movement has made vast gains in Southern California; but Los Angeles is still only partially unionized, and San Diego is probably the least unionized of any American city its size outside the South. In a vote on the union shop issue in three aerospace companies (requiring 66⅔ percent majority for passage), 42 percent of the workers voted "No." At the Ryan plant in San Diego the "No" vote included nearly 25 percent of the union members.[2]

Actually, the technological direction of California industry, particularly defense and space activity, is tending to outmode the production worker; for several years prior to 1961, union membership in California had continued to rise, though not as fast as the population. But from a high of 1,755,700 members in 1960, the number declined by a small amount in 1961, when it constituted 34.8 percent of the labor force.[3] Attempts to reverse this trend by organizing new fields, such as the farm laborers and white-collar workers, have generally failed in the past. Once again, the unions have bumped into the Californian's pride in remaining unassociated, uncommitted.

2.

In brief, the Californian seems intent on disproving the statement that "No man is an island." To him the French ideal of *l'homme engagé* is not even translatable. He is a man disengaged from society. Indeed, the very concept of a society of mutually responsible, mutually involved citizens goes over his head. He lives not in a society, but in an environment, which he means to make the most of for his own purposes.

What has brought the California male to this condition? Part of the reason may be found in the state of California society—particularly the widespread loss of individual influence in public affairs. The very bigness of the state, both in size and population, has reduced the stature of the citizen. If one lives in Los Angeles, there is not even a local-type government in which the lone voice is heeded. For in a city of 2,500,000 people with the biggest municipal area in the world, the individual's contact with his government is one of colossal frustration. In the city of Los Angeles it takes at least four times as long to get city hall action on some matters than in some of the medium-sized neighbor cities, and in some cases action is delayed indefinitely. Some agencies are practically outside the effective reach of the citizen; they have their own sources of revenue and do not depend on the city budget. When they submit to a popular demand it is only at the request of the mayor or city council by a kind of official courtesy rather than through line authority.

Equally frustrating is the machinery of large city legislation, even for simple municipal services. For years San Fernando Valley, which constitutes nearly one-third of the total population of Los Angeles, tried to get the city council to provide adequate streets, sewers, storm drains, and other necessities. In a major effort, the valley chambers of commerce arranged for an official tour of their districts to show the fifteen councilmen the needs at first hand. Only two councilmen showed up, and these were two of the valley's own four councilmen. At this final rebuff, the chambers of commerce launched a movement to consider seceding from the city of Los Angeles. Due to the paralysis that afflicts Los Angeles government, even pulling out of it may not be politically feasible. Some 800,000 people are captives of a city hall twenty miles away.

As much might also be said of the judicial process. Though some of the California civil courts are said to be better than many in the country, the population growth continues to outstrip the processes for justice. In Los Angeles Superior Court, the backlog of cases jumped in six years from 6,300 to 14,700. This situation does not prevail in most smaller cities; the average delay in California municipal courts is four months, as against a national average of nine-and-a-half months. But civil court cases are delayed thirteen months in San Francisco, fifteen-and-a-half months in Los Angeles, and sixteen months in San Diego. In Los Angeles, the calendar is so crowded that in one case involving a judgment of $13, the judge simply wrote his own personal check to the plaintiff for that amount and cleared the docket for the next case.

Under these conditions, the citizen leans over backward to avoid litigation. If he gets a traffic ticket, he dutifully pays the bail and foregoes a trial, even though he is convinced he is right, because he would have to waste most of a day in travel, parking, and waiting in a crowded courtroom for his case to come up.

Thus, many areas of California law are alarming examples of the maxim that justice delayed is justice denied. "Today," as Chief Justice Earl Warren told a Los Angeles audience, "because the legal remedies of many of our people can be realized only after they have sallowed with the passage of time, they are mere forms of justice."

These are some of the reasons why California's 360 small-and medium-sized cities constitute the only hope of retaining at least one level of government in which the citizen can actually participate. Political scientists may shake their heads at the myriad small municipalities that merge on one another in much of Southern California and the San Francisco peninsula. They cite the wasteful duplication of service departments and call for consolidations into larger county governments. Such steps would have the merit of neatness but would have the far bigger disadvantage of further reducing the Californian from a citizen to a mere inhabitant.

Thus, the very bigness and growth of California have tended to turn its people away from public affairs. Yet the blame must be shared by the character of the Californians themselves; if they were not individualists, they would not have pulled up stakes in the East and gone West in the first place. They considered California an answer to their problems; once arrived, they are in no mood to become involved in California's problems. Indeed, among many intelligent Californians who pride themselves on being alert and informed, attention is focused on national and international

216

issues, to the exclusion of state and local problems. When the *New York Times*'s Western Edition was launched, several of my friends switched to it from a local paper, even though it carried no local news. When challenged, they freely acknowledged that they didn't care much what was going on locally, anyway.

Still another factor is California's pace of life that is generally too swift to permit the kind of personal discussion that can solidify public opinion. One has too many commitments to one's job and one's family to indulge in the luxury of casual conversation. The drive-in and the self-service counter have helped to abolish the focal points of neighborliness. Except in the rural communities, the cracker-barrel philosopher and the barbershop oracle are now extinct. The spectacle of idle old folks sitting around talking to the proprietor is but a memory; they would be suspected of being good-for-nothings, and besides, there would be no place for them to sit. At the supermarket they would be in danger of serious injury from the rush of shopping carts to the checkout counter.

As for the barbershop, one hasn't the time to wait very long for a haircut, and it is a rare shop with more than one person waiting for each chair. Even when several are waiting there is none of the old-time banter that once made the tonsorial parlor a kind of male clubhouse. The barbers are doing plenty of talking, but mostly with each other. The customers are in their own worlds, reading a comic book or worrying whether they will get back to work on time.

Actually, California's very distances work against social contacts. The sizable portion of the day spent in the automobile, whether commuting to work or running errands, narrows the latitude for casual talk. The person interested in prolonging a discussion is resented, not as a bore, but for imposing on one's time. Relaxation is at such a premium that one is not willing to waste it in a chance encounter; rather, it is something to be carefully planned for, and the average Californian finds himself hurrying in order to relax.

In short, much of California society has become so complex that one has little time to participate in it, and even if one did, one would have very little influence, anyway. The male, who is supposed to be a political animal, has largely evacuated the field.

3.

Even more significant, the typical Californian is not especially absorbed in his occupation. Among skilled workers, pride of craftsmanship is inhibited by the specialization that goes with mass production. The hope for promotion in the classic American tradition is by no means universal. According to a study among auto assembly workers in Northern California, 64 percent stated they did not want to become foremen: "They have to take too much." [4]

What makes this attitude more acceptable in California is that there is plenty of life to be lived outside of one's work. The job becomes a means of raising money for one's real life. And one's long-term goal is retirement—the earlier the better.

At the same time, the pace of competition at professional and executive levels is not as intense as in some Eastern centers. In the sales professions, such as real estate and the advertising media, the energy is still boundless in the old California tradition. Yet the California insurance man generally would not think of broaching the subject with his friends. Even though there is considerable entertaining of clients in the advertising business, such friendships are seldom rushed. I have known of a media man, fresh from New York, who invited an account executive to dinner and was considered some kind of a nut. Though the intriguing for clients among Los Angeles advertising agencies is almost as deadly as on Madison Avenue, this is an isolated case fired

218

by the big stakes associated with the television industry. In San Francisco, the pace is slower; there is less in-fighting for new accounts and less switching of influential personnel from one firm to another. It is not unusual to take the afternoon's business to the golf course, and when one leaves the office at five, one seldom carries away homework.

It was San Francisco, actually, that originated the businessman's luncheon in the plush restaurant, complete with low lights, elegant appointments, and most important, the fashion show. By the late 1950's, the institution had appeared in Los Angeles, which naturally gave it an extra fillip by the modeling of negligees, nighties, and bathing suits, including semi-bikinis. One restaurant has a fashion show every weekday, and Wednesday is "nightie day." In manufacturing areas, which would otherwise have little demand for them, posh restaurants have sprung up with maximum competition in gourmet menus, intriguing atmosphere, and girls. On the day of a fashion show, one has to make reservations, the lobby has a waiting line, and the crowd is two-deep at the bar. There is, of course, an observance of professionalism; the apparel is provided by a local dress shop, and the models describe their ensembles, complete with prices, at each table. But the popularity of the fashion show is not due to the eagerness of husbands to buy dresses for their wives. I know of one who actually bought one, and only got himself in trouble. His wife went on a one-woman crusade to get fashion shows banned by the local chamber of commerce; being composed of normal businessmen, it politely ignored her. The real motivation behind the fashion show is revealed in the fact that it is no longer the dress shops but the restaurants that hire and pay the models. The temptation is to call the institution just another girlie show. But this misses the point of the main attraction, which is the opportunity to talk with lovely dolls to whom one has not been introduced—a kind of noncommittal adventure which pretty well defines the romantic prowess of the average California male adult and brightens his otherwise dull day.

All this is not to say that the California organization man is a daydreamer or shirker. But competition for promotion is decidedly low key. In this milieu the ambitious schemer is too conspicuous to be effective. Even at these levels, job security and fringe benefits are as important as the chance for advancement. I have heard at least three men in the middle-executive level say, "I never asked for a raise in my life." When the National Aeronautics and Space Administration started recruiting engineers in San Francisco, the following were among the reasons given by applicants for seeking employment: "I'm interested in career employment, and this is one of the larger outfits"; "I like working in federal service—you know, the vacations and all." Some companies accustomed to shifting their executives around the country have found it dangerous to send them to California. Once they fall into the California pattern of life they may resign the company rather than leave for another assignment.

One of the major exceptions is the private entrepreneur who runs his own concern. In the Western tradition, he is a self-starter who derives much of the zest in life from commercial success. But since he operates strictly for himself and his family, rather than as a unit in a group, he is the exception proving the rule.

Typically, the California man has withdrawn from the co-operative life. He has abdicated self-government. And while he is in the business world, he is not of it. The life of service or of achievement is rejected. The Californian turns to what he believes is the only alternative—the life of fun. Having fun becomes not only an acceptable end, but in fact the only realistic goal of life. The theme of Walter Kerr's book, *The Decline of Pleasure,* might be valid for the rest of the country, but not California. There is no noticeable guilt felt by Californians while they are having fun; on the contrary, anyone not having fun is suspected of being a malcontent.

Not that Californians are shameless hedonists. Their fun is not particularly decadent; most of it has to do with sunbathing, sports, barbecues, picnics, camping, boating, travel; it is wholesome, and those not participating are somehow thought to be unwholesome.

4.

The California male, therefore, pursues his sports and his hobbies as though they were the sum of life. The same survey showing that only 30 percent of men in one suburb belonged to any club also revealed that these were largely hobby groups.[5] I know one resident of Manhattan Beach who was transferred to a branch twenty-five miles inland, but who is so committed to beach volleyball that he wouldn't think of moving away from the coast. Indeed, there is something refreshing and unsophisticated, like the barefoot boy with the willow fishing pole, in the Californian's pursuit of his sports. Many are not content with one; one couple has accumulated four activities—skin diving, bicycling, folk dancing, and finally, parachute jumping. Without realizing it, many Californians are like a cousin of mine who acknowledges, "I take up one sport until I've mastered it, and then I go on to another."

Many of these diversions are not unique to California, but the Californians have, by sheer devotion, dominated them for years. Golf, tennis, skiing, bowling, bridge, auto racing— these are some of the games and sports in which Californians are often among the national champions. Another is the national quick-draw contest, in which grown men dress as frontier gunfighters and compete with each other against an electronic timer to see who can get off the quickest shot. They have reduced it to such a science (anybody who can't draw and fire in less than a third of a second isn't even in the running) that they could undoubtedly beat any of the old hands, not excepting Wild Bill Hickok and Wyatt Earp. Whether they could hit anything, however, is another matter, since the guns are mercifully loaded with blanks to prevent the loss of miscellaneous toes, heels, and kneecaps. Considering the importance of the costume (complete with long sideburns) and the inscrutable facial expression (an essential in any sixshooter showdown), it is not certain whether this activity is a sport, a hobby, or a therapy. But in the national contests, Californians arc often the winners and always among the finalists.

California may also be said to have been the original scene of the bowling craze that swept the country in the 1950's. Until then, bowling alleys were considered on a par with pool halls; they were generally uninviting—the hangout of teenage boys and of idlers who should be home with their wives and families. In 1951, an enterpriser in Covina, east of Los Angeles, built a bowling alley of attractive decor—plenty of plate glass and chromium trim—that was obviously aimed at the women. This, together with the onset of automatic pinspotting, brought on the bowling boom.

Since then bowling has gone respectable, with pastel interiors, adjoining fountains, and cocktail lounges with nightclub entertainers. Some, catering to the daytime women's groups, have nurseries to care for the tots while mothers line the alleys with appropriate names on their club shirts: "Time Offs," "Escapees," "Should Be Cookin'." These plush, new establishments (called bowling centers rather than bowling alleys) became almost a way of life in many communities. Within three years, Orange County alone increased the number of bowling lanes from eighty-eight to 322. By 1960, California had twenty-one huge establishments with more than forty lanes each, including one monster of sixty-four lanes in Downey. Some of these are operated around the clock seven days a week; in one, the management once decided to turn off the lights and no one could remember where the switches were—they had never been doused in eight months.

While the latest wrinkle is to install bowling lanes in the basements of colleges and churches, the prevailing social aspect of California bowling is the company league, which offers the principal mode of fraternizing among fellow workers. In one California telephone company, bowling leagues date from 1911; another company in San Diego started up a league and signed up 50 percent of the employees.

On bowling night at most any business office, the end of the working day finds the rest rooms filled with people changing into their bowling costumes; and on the morning after the postmortem conversations dominate the talk around the coffee machines. Some company bowlers belong to two or even three leagues, and a few hopeless cases bowl four or five nights a week.

Not all the participants are as interested in the game as in the side benefits, including the opportunity to follow up on office flirtations. Plenty of happy romances began in the bowling leagues. On one train ride to Sacramento following a bowling tournament in Los Angeles, three bowling couples met and were later married. Others use the game to disguise a weekly night on the town. One friend of mine, a serious bowler, angrily complained that his teammates kept the drinks coming so fast they couldn't hit the pins—and didn't care. A woman actually managed to bounce her ball off the man who was winding up in the next alley.

But it is the outdoor sports, particularly those connected with water, that are more characteristically Californian. The state's 426,000 pleasure boats are second only to the total for New York. And the craze is rising faster than California lakes can accommodate it. In many places, the California landscape is being facelifted to provide new lakes for the boaters. And on the old ones the whizzing outboards are enough to frighten the amateur to the shore. New subdivisions on San

Francisco Bay, the Sacramento River, and the Southern coast feature boat slips as well as garages. To many a family the boat has become the focus of activity—often involving more work than play. One friend of mine labored for years building and outfitting a cabin cruiser only to sell it just before it was completed. Another dedicated couple spent so much time working on their boat, repairing it, maintaining it ("several hours getting it launched, several hours afterward wiping it down"), besides pouring all their spare money into it, that it had made slaves of them. When the wife ventured to suggest that they sell it, the husband lost no time doing so.

But to most owners the pleasure boat means a kind of freedom. When the old man puts his mariner's cap on and takes the helm he has joined the worldwide fraternity of yachtsmen. He is as far away from his office image as he can get and still look civilized.

Allied with boating is water skiing, which has grown so fast that when one speaks of skiing one has to specify "snow skiing" or "water skiing." On a good weekend day, the skiers turn the lakes of California into what can only be described as happy chaos. For the speedboat-water ski team considers itself the royalty of the water. Slower craft will have to get out of the way, and when skiers are coming at you from all directions, this can be a problem. Commenting on one reservoir crowded with skiers, an enthusiast declared it was "like having several thousand cars in one eighty-acre parking lot and all going in different directions at forty to fifty miles per hour. It's mad!"

Still other Californians—an estimated 300,000—go for skin diving in various forms. The primitive type is nothing new—Catalina kids have been diving for coins as the ships come in for two generations. But modern equipment—the faceplate, snorkel, and flippers—have opened up new facets; skin divers are divided into those who fish for abalone armed with an old tire iron, those who go for regular fish with a mechanized spear, and those who simply enjoy the beauties of the deep.

Even technology has invaded the field. Californians are donning rubber suits and air tanks to explore the ocean floor down to sixty feet (a few experts go down 200 feet). Technically, this is called scuba diving, after the phrase "Self-Contained Underwater Breathing Apparatus." Turning thousands of amateurs loose in deep water with this kind of gear can mean trouble (twenty-six California deaths in a seven-year period). But beginning in 1954, Los Angeles County has had a training program which has become a prerequisite for the purchase of scuba equipment. Trained divers, operating always in pairs for mutual help in case of emergency, can explore the deep with very little risk. Latest idea is to dive for gold in the rivers of California's Mother Lode. Using a portable dredge that operates something like a vacuum cleaner, the veteran operator can make several dollars an hour (a few have cleared as much as $100 a day).

Nor do California's sportsmen ignore their state's vast store of other physical features. In the white-water rivers of Northern California, they shoot the rapids in kayaks. On the granite cliffs of the Sierra, they climb up with rope and piton, sleeping at night while hanging in a self-made basket hundreds of feet from oblivion. In the sand hills of the central coast and the Colorado Desert, they race with dune buggies, which are bodyless chassis equipped with balloon, low-pressure tires; with these wide-track jalopies one can scamper over the wasteland with an exhilarating freedom that can only be fully appreciated by a refugee from the stop signal and the parking meter.

Thus, one of the main characteristics of the new generation of young Californians is that they are the first to make the most of their state's physical advantages. Previous generations arriving up to the war were happy to enjoy the climate and take in the outdoors, but they continued to follow the Eastern patterns of life. Older Californians currently in their sixties or above never learned to ski and many never became swimmers. In California, they simply devoted more time to what they already knew—golf, camping, hunting, and fishing. They had California, but they really didn't know what to do with it.

The postwar Californians, armed with better equipment and more imagination, are plunging into adventures in California's varied geography that would raise the hair on their grandparents' heads. They are not content, for example, to go camping; to them camping is a means to some far more exciting end, such as cliff-scaling or exploring subterranean caves.

The marvel is that they are doing these things in comparative safety. If there is one thing Californians will join, it is a hobby or sport club through which they can further their private activities. The expertness fostered by these associations has been the saving feature of what must otherwise be the Californian's postwar quest for danger.

All of which helps to explain some California sports, which, to ordinary mortals schooled in other eras, might appear to have serious effects on one's life expectancy. A seat of pioneer aviation, California has 13 percent of the country's private pilots, 14 percent of the private planes, and a sizable fleet of powerless gliders. It was no coincidence that when nine new astronauts were picked from among the nation's expert pilots, seven were Californians. Three of my friends, otherwise quite sane, are Sunday pilots. You don't have to own a plane to play the game. Many belong to flying clubs that own one or more planes in common, pay the insurance, and provide the maintenance. Not a few aerospace engineers and executives commute to work by private plane; a subdivision in Santa Cruz provides an airport for commuters to San Francisco. Near Vacaville in Solano County, a restaurant maintains a landing strip for flying customers, who can reserve a table and receive landing instructions by radio contact with the dining room. One woman from Los Angeles logged in with the comment: "Just flew up for lunch."

Some one was sure to think of jumping out of airplanes as a sport, and in the mid-fifties, skydiving began with formation of a parachute club at Livermore. Since then, jumping clubs have sprung up in San Joaquin Valley and Southern California; through the triumph of judgment over enthusiasm, members are not permitted to jump until they have passed a thorough course of instruction. Not content just to reach the ground safely, the jumpers hold competitions to see who can land within a target ring, or they will drop from as high as 15,000 feet and wait two minutes before pulling the rip cord. At such moments they do various acrobatics, achieving the ultimate in personal freedom from all encumbrances, which of course is the real goal of any true Californian. Says one, the women's world champion chutist, "You feel so free, you even forget about bills."

Apparently, women are as susceptible to the chuting bug as men; one married couple met on a jumping flight and once kissed each other while falling through space at 125 miles an hour. Another couple was so devoted to chuting that when the 1962 jumping championships were held in Massachusetts, they sold their home and airplane "to further our jumping and to pay off bills so we could go to the contest without any financial worries." Zealots will tell you, with the holy light in the eye that marks the true believer, that parachuting is one of the safest sports in the country. Said one devotee, "One time I sprained my ankle—skiing."

Indeed, as daredevils, no group is in the same class with California's conspicuous corps of motorcyclists. If it is possible for a sport to be controversial, theirs tops the list. The difference of viewpoint divides neatly between those Californians who ride motorcycles and those who don't. The latter would contend, in fact, that organized cycling is not a sport at all but a mobile insurrection.

This view is based on a number of historic engagements between cyclists and local yeomanry at various motorcycling conventions since World War II. The first, commonly known as the Battle of Hollister, occurred in July, 1947. For forty hours several hundred cyclists held downtown Hollister captive while they raced through the streets, drove their cycles into bars and restaurants, and littered San Benito Street with thousands of beer bottles. Overwhelmed, the seven-man police force was reinforced by forty California highway patrolmen, who helped put nearly 100 in jail. Said the local hospital superintendent, "We treated at least fifty patients and collected only $2, all told."

Explained one of the cyclists, "It's a convention. We're just having a convention."

Shortly afterward, thousands of cyclists descended on Riverside. They used traffic lights for starting signals in races through the main street. They blocked traffic while some of them spun circles in the intersections. When police tried to interfere, they were outnumbered and beaten up. When one motorist blew his horn they attacked his car, breaking the windows and trampling in the top.

At these outrages California opinion rose so vehemently against the cyclists that they went down below the border, threw Ensenada into bedlam, and then laid low for several years.

But in 1957, 3,700 cyclists roared into the sleepy little mining town of Angel's Camp and left a toll of three deaths and twenty-three injuries in their wake. In May, 1961, a thousand cyclists invaded Tecate, Mexico, for another convention in which the main order of business was racing in the streets, wrecking bars, and fistfighting. When the twenty-five man police force was unable to save the town, a hundred

Mexican soldiers arrived and escorted the Gringos to the border.

The following August some eighty knights of the road arrived in the staid and respectable city of Santa Barbara and participated in its annual fiesta by holding street races and interfering with the costume dances. A posse composed of city, county, and state lawmen escorted them out of the city and stationed itself on the south county border to repel any further invasion.

After this catalog of behavior it would be understating the case to say that California motorcycling as a sport is in ill repute. But it has been said in defense of the cyclists that most of the disturbances have been perpetrated by maverick groups not connected with the American Motorcycle Association. Not all the news about what Californians call the "motorcycle crowd" is bad news. In 1960, twenty-five Los Angeles cycle clubs collected some 400 used radios, phonographs, and television sets, worked together putting them in good order, and gave them to children in local hospitals.

Indeed, the cyclists may be called California's most alienated and least understood minority group. Living in a world of their own, they even have their own customs, jargon, and clothing styles (white helmet, black leather jacket, blue jeans, black boots). Contrary to general belief, they are normally not teen-agers, but young men in their twenties and thirties (some are considerably older); many are married, with the wives riding double or driving their own bikes.

The situation is further complicated by several types of cyclists, including the pavement riders, the trail riders, and the dirt riders. Most of the clashes with the public have been by the pavement riders, though only a fraction of these are responsible for all the trouble. The trail riders are those who use their bikes (usually light, lower-powered models) to get deep into the mountain country on fishing and hunting trips, or into the desert for rock hunting, amateur archaeology, or

229

just plain exploration. "We are not after speed," says one. "We want something to pull us up the side of a mountain." Dirt riders (of whom there are some 25,000 in Southern California alone) are the ones who draw crowds to watch motorcycles climb up the side of a mountain or run proficiency courses over rugged terrain. Many dirt riders are so particular about their equipment and so uncomfortable in street driving that they haul their bikes to the events in a pickup truck. Explains one, "The average dirt rider doesn't like heavy bikes, night riding, two people on one bike, highway traffic, speeds above normal, or showoffs. You never see an imitation of a cop's uniform or five headlights on a dirt rider's bike."

But to most Californians all motorcyclists labor under a kind of vague suspicion. There is perhaps a touch of envy at the motorcyclist's freedom to race his engine at full blast, giving out a wonderful roar uncurbed by the muffler required on mere automobiles. There is more obvious envy of the cyclist's ability to move through bumper-to-bumper traffic by skirting between the cars. Finally, there is resentment over the time one loses by having to slow down on seeing a cyclist in the rear-view mirror and thinking he might be a cop. Apparently on the principle that the bike rider takes up less space, the motorist generally feels entitled to more rights on the highway; cyclists are not thought to be fellow travelers who are simply using another type of transportation but rather are considered nuisances to the car drivers, for whose benefit the highway was built.

5.

All of which leads to the whole field of automobiling in California, which is not ordinarily considered a sport, but is nevertheless the principal source of excitement and self-expression in the life of the typical California male. It is no coincidence that in recent years, most of the Indianapolis winners are California men; they got their start the hard way as competitors on California's public highways. One Indianapolis winner who had just returned from one of many cross-country trips had a few things to say about the "wool-gathering" drivers he had encountered elsewhere, "We drive faster out here, all right, but it is something of a comfort to be wheeling along with drivers who know what they're doing."

To understand California carsmanship, you have to start with what have been called the West's Magnificent Distances. Since the days when it was forty miles between neighbors, Californians have been used to traveling. The automobile not only grew up with the state, but in many ways made growth possible. For without it the myriad towns and cities situated off the railroad and trolley tracks would never have been born.

For the Californian distance means nothing in itself; the only question is how long it takes to get from one place to another. If you ask the Californian how far it is to some point, the answer will come out in minutes and will vary depending on the day of the week and the time of day. The collegiate thinks nothing of driving an hour to pick up a date (she would admittedly have to be something special). I know one couple who, once every few months, drive nearly two hours from Los Angeles to Santa Barbara for dinner. I have heard of another couple who, on the spur of the moment, will go two hours in the other direction to Palm Springs for a cup of coffee. According to one observer, the Los Angeles life "has as one of its tenets the notion that dinner is best begun and ended with a sixty-mile drive."

Though the average commuter time is something like thirty-five minutes for the Los Angeles area and twenty-five minutes for San Francisco Bay, many commuters travel an hour without complaining. One production foreman drives an hour-and-a-half from Calabasas to Ontario, while an electronics engineer is on the road the same time from San

Gabriel to Woodland Hills; they pass each other on the way.

I suspect that many commuters average considerably more time than they admit, since driving time is a point of pride with most California males. Nobody wants to be considered sucker enough to have settled *too* far from work, even though he is. Also, there is a deal of manly virtue in knowing one's way around town—all the cutoffs and precise turns to avoid tie-ups and beat key signals. Actually, traffic is such that if one set out to drive to work in a straightforward manner, without resorting to strategy, he would have to double his driving time. As one commuter put it, "You just can't get to work on time without breaking the law."

This air of urgency pervading the commuting hours can only be likened to large migrations of animals. The cars press upon one another so closely as to frighten the newcomer. At some stop signs anyone making a complete stop runs the risk of being hit from behind. When traffic jams up ahead there is a frantic search for escape routes. I have seen drivers remove a construction barrier and take off through a work road, followed by the main herd. In such cases even the police hesitate to interfere. At one point on Sepulveda Boulevard in San Fernando Valley, residents of a new tract waited minutes at a time to get into the stream of commuter traffic whizzing by. When their petition for a signal was denied, they wrote to the police department requesting a traffic officer at the intersection. The reply came back, in effect: "Are you kidding? He'd be killed!"

Thus, driving to work is not simply motoring; it is a continual adventure, in which the hero is always on the lookout for a shortcut—not shortened in distance, but in time, for the Californian thinks nothing of driving considerably out of his way at a substantial cost in gasoline if it will save him a minute or two, or even to avoid some congestion without any time-saving. The California driver is so constituted that, after several days of passing a likely looking road, he will pick a day when he is ahead of schedule and try it out. He is also constituted so that if he sees a few cars darting into a side street he will suspect it is a better route to his own destination and will fall in line to find out. Adding zest to the game is the air of secrecy surrounding any discovery; for no experienced commuter is going to tell others about his route and eventually defeat himself, except perhaps in a moment when pride of accomplishment gets the best of him. One of the surest signs that a fellow commuter has accepted you as a true and lasting friend is when he confides his favorite shortcut.

In solving the problem of California's distances, the auto has also created another—the fractionation of community life. The person who lives, works, shops, and attends church in the same community is an exception. The mobility won by the auto has multiplied the possibilities in all these activities, until one's commitments are spread in several directions. Many people do their banking near their place of work, rather than in their home community, which may be twenty miles away. Others who establish church connections in one town may, after moving to another, drive half-an-hour back to their old church every Sunday. Still others who are "shopping" for a church will decide to join one in another community fifteen miles distant. California life so thoroughly presupposes car ownership by everybody that the few without a car are often amazingly inconvenienced. I know two elderly sisters living together who have to call a taxi when they want to go to the supermarket.

It is no wonder, then, that for a number of years California has had more automobiles than any foreign country. From their first stirrings of consciousness, California babies are aware of and fascinated with automobiles. At two years of age our youngest was collecting toy cars, spending considerable time pushing them around the floor with appropriate sound effects, putting "gas" in his kiddie car, experimenting

233

with the knobs on the dashboard of the family car, and demanding that he take his turn driving it. It is unsafe to leave one's keys in the car when one arrives home—not because it might be stolen but because one's children might drive it away. I know of one two-year-old girl who got the car started and was trying to get it into gear when she was discovered by her horrified mother. A five-year-old boy went further, got the car in gear, and drove it through the garage door. A three-year-old scored even higher; he roared out of the driveway, stopped when a passing police car halted behind him, shifted into reverse, and caught his opponent broadside.

Thus, to the Californian the car quickly becomes, as one writer observed, "an extra, highly essential part of the human anatomy." Like the proverbial frontiersman who wouldn't cross the street without climbing on his horse, the Californian will hardly walk more than a block without driving. When he does walk he feels strangely uncomfortable, as though he had forgotten something and would be helpless in case of trouble. I have known people who lived two or three blocks from work and still commuted. A Canoga Park woman actually drives across the street to work.

In fact, along many California highways the pedestrian is an object of suspicion; police cars will slow down, eye the culprit as if he were up to no good, and if it is after dark, may stop and question him. The hitchhiker is all right; he is at least expressing a desire to ride in a car. But in a society on wheels, the deliberate pedestrian may be considered some kind of malcontent.

California's mobile society might work reasonably well if it would stop growing long enough for the facilities to catch up. But the car population, already nearing 9,000,000, is currently growing at the rate of 1,000 a day and is estimated to be more than double by 1980. With 10 percent of the nation's cars, California has only 4 percent of the streets and highways.[6]

234

The strain on this system is obvious. Since the dawn of the gasoline era more than 100,000 Californians have been killed by automobiles, and the grim figure rises by about 3,800 per year.[7] The breakdown is most apparent in major cities, where commuter traffic is usually bumper to bumper. Though the state's growing freeway system has provided massive relief, stop-and-go traffic at a snail's pace is still the unfortunate lot of most commuters in Los Angeles and San Francisco and often in such other cities as San Diego and Sacramento. Even on the freeway, rear-end collisions are the most common form of accident. The person wearing a neck brace is assumed to be the victim of a whiplash accident; one such victim spotted another on the highway and called, "Join the club!"

For most commuters the big parade every morning has all of the disadvantages and none of the advantages of train or subway commuting. They can't read the paper, play cards, or talk with anybody. Car pools are not unknown, but the typical Californian will not make the accommodations necessary for such cooperation; besides, he really doesn't trust anybody's driving but his own. And so he sits there in his isolation booth, prevented even from quiet contemplation by the demands of stopping, starting, and watching for any unpredictable maneuver by one of his mobile neighbors. There is always the car radio—considered a necessity in California. One long-distance commuter hears three hours of news a day and calls himself "the most informed highway traveler." A friend of mine believes he has solved the bumper-to-bumper waiting periods by reading a book held in his hands over the steering wheel.

"I tried that once," I said, "and ran into the lady in front of me. How do you know when to move ahead?"

"When the guy in back of me honks."

Just finding enough space to park the cars is a problem that is changing the whole face of California communities.

Across the state, new developments founded since the war put primary emphasis on parking space, with acres of pavement surrounding the shopping center. Many supermarkets have their main entrance facing the parking area, and the main market in the town of Westchester has no door at all facing the street. San Francisco, Oakland, and downtown Los Angeles all lost population during the 1950's because they were becoming impractical as living areas in comparison to the more roomy suburbs. In Long Beach, chain-store business was cut in half within six years, while office-building occupancy fell at the same rate. Complained a merchant's association official, "Downtown Long Beach is becoming a ghost town."

Nor is California's car consciousness confined to the populous areas. The whole state runs on gasoline; small- and medium-sized cities are choked with traffic, driving shoppers to the new suburbs, which have supplied their own parking. On an average weekend, Palm Canyon Drive in Palm Springs is jammed with thousands of cars. Fresno found some of its streets increasing in traffic by 340 percent in five years, and turned to pedestrian malls as the only solution. Many small counties of Northern California have a higher per capita car ownership than Los Angeles County. Even in a remote section like the redwood country, traffic on narrow, winding roads finds a special hazard in the logging trucks that are either going too slow when loaded or too fast when empty.

Naturally, California adopts extraordinary methods to ease the strain. Radio stations maintain helicopters over some freeway systems at the busy hour to observe the flow of traffic, warn of accident tie-ups, and broadcast route suggestions to the commuters below. Some city police officers provide cruise cars to help stranded motorists and prevent bottlenecks; these highway samaritans will help get the car started, send for a tow truck, and even send a telephone message to the victim's wife or boss. Los Angeles has installed a central computer to receive data on the flow of traffic and automatically regulate the timing of some forty traffic signals on Sunset Boulevard. On a number of highways throughout California, state patrolmen police the traffic by means of helicopters; errant drivers are spotted from the air and pinpointed for the benefit of the other policemen in patrol cars; on the San Bernardino Freeway, speeding motorists are even warned by loudspeaker from the helicopter—a kind of California version of George Orwell's "Big Brother" in *Nineteen Eighty-Four.*

In many areas, congestion has reached the point where the police are just as busy keeping traffic moving as in slowing it down. For many years it has been legal to pass on either the right or left in California—a situation most California drivers take full advantage of to the utter horror of newcomers. But a newer law requires that autos going slower than the rest of the traffic must get as far to the right as possible. As one highway patrol official puts it, "If cars are passing you on the right, you're in the wrong lane." The result is that anyone in the left-hand lane driving slower than the flow of traffic is liable to be arrested. A friend of mine was pulled over for this offense and pleaded that he was going the speed limit. This made no difference to the cop, who said, "Let 'em go by at ninety if they want; I'll catch 'em when they go through." In such a predicament the California motorist isn't sure where he stands. He's afraid to go too fast and afraid to go too slow. Once while highballing along in the left-hand lane, I saw a motorcycle cop at the side of the freeway and instinctively slowed down; a minute later he was arresting me for holding up traffic.

There is a theory that these crowded conditions make California drivers nervous and account for the state's high accident and violation rate. However, considering the energy and determination in the California temperament, the truth is that the Californians themselves make the situation even more impossible than it would otherwise be. This has been effectively noted by the neighboring state of Nevada, where all eleven persons killed in traffic on one July 4 weekend were visiting Californians. Numbering around 8,000,000, California drivers get more than 5,000,000 traffic tickets a year; one of the fringe benefits offered by some large California companies is that they will process your traffic tickets so you won't have to stand in line to pay your bail. A State Department of Motor Vehicles counselor estimates that for every traffic ticket there are probably about seventy-five other violations.[8] California firms are finding traffic accidents second only to the common cold as a cause of absenteeism. On some commuter routes, particularly in the evening run, it is an unusual day when traffic is not held up by an accident. One long-distance commuter reports seeing an accident an average of once a day.

Curiously, this kind of experience does not particularly frighten the Californian, who regards his moments on the road as a kind of competitive venture. The first point to note on joining the highway cavalry is that driver chivalry is dead. There are no Alphonses and Gastons on California freeways. The polite motorist literally gets nowhere; if he slows to let merging traffic in front of him, there is no end to it. He soon realizes that everyone will take advantage of him. Out goes the Golden Rule; with curled lip and narrowed eyes, he goes primitive. Some of the most modern highway facilities in the world are thus the avenues for Stone Age behavior. One of the commonest sights in California is a car trying in vain to enter a line of creeping traffic from a side street. Letting the driver in line would involve no measurable disadvantage to anyone, but so callous has the driver become that literally scores will pass by without performing an act of decency. Indeed, many drivers will speed up if necessary to close the gap before the entering car can wedge in. Our oldest daughter, who has to cross a busy street every day to catch the school bus, once counted fifty cars going by before one would slow down to let her pass. Acts of courtesy are, in fact, so rare that they invariably evoke a wave of thanks. At the same time the benefactor is apt to get a honk from the driver behind for holding up traffic.

Yet even though each California driver regards every other California driver as his natural enemy, there are a few honored observances. For example, the horn is not honked for light or transient reasons and is never used in passing another car unless one has been held up for miles. The reason, apparently, is an unspoken understanding about holding down unnecessary sound. The horn is reserved as a mode of expression in two specialized situations: to protest some dangerous maneuver, such as cutting in (although I have seen many cases of cutting in without a horn response), and to uproot a slow starter at a signal. In fact, the impatience of California drivers makes the slow signal start the most unforgivable offense; the classic California definition of a split second is the time after the signal turns green and before the driver behind you honks.

Allied with the restrained use of the horn is the decline in the fine old custom of hollering out the window. Up to the war, shouting insults at one another was brought to a fine art and was actually a beneficial form of therapy. The slow signal starter could hear the mellow tones of the driver behind him, "It won't get any greener!" Since then verbal communication has unfortunately given way to the dirty look or the horn, neither of which provides the same richness of expression.

This unfortunate decay of the motorists' dialogue is caused by the assumed air of anonymity that has pervaded the California highway. Somewhere in the 1940's most Californians discovered they were doing most of their driving outside their own communities. Since the rivals they encountered on the road were strangers, the normal social pressures that enforce human decency and consideration were missing. Because one would never see those driving alongside again, one got to caring less and less about what they thought. This rationale enabled one to do more outrageous things and at the same time to feel less responsibility for them.

The ultimate impersonalization of the highway has been reached in the prevailing attitude that the whole hassle is a battle between automobiles, not people. It is the automobile that cuts in, follows too closely, switches lanes without notice. One does not therefore holler out the window, because this destroys the illusion of anonymity. One may blow the horn, if necessary, since this is the voice of the auto, not the driver.

More significant, one does not look at the faces of other drivers, even in a test of wills when both are contending for the same lane or are trying to beat each other at the dig. There are only two exceptions to this rule: if another driver is a girl with a promising profile, or if one has been grievously wronged by another (in which case it would be craven to continue hiding in anonymity). Instead, one pulls alongside and delivers the Dirty Look, accompanied by the mouthing of short Saxon words which the other does not have to be a lipreader to recognize. Some would go farther and cut in on the other for revenge. There are, of course, occasional vendettas on the freeway, in which two cars driven by men in a rage will be racing in order to get in each other's way. But this is frowned upon as unprofessional, since it tends to personalize the highway.

Normally the privacy of the isolation booth is honored. Even when traffic is at a standstill, one looks straight ahead and does not idly survey the neighboring drivers; this might be construed as the Dirty Look for some forgotten trespass a few blocks past. Besides, one might have to contend for position with the other automobile at the next turn, and there is no sense recognizing the fact that there is a human being in it. Chances are that even after the jockeying, bluffing, and maneuvering develop and the contention becomes obvious, neither driver will look at the other. They may be sitting in their glass chambers fuming, but they will not even sneak a glance. The winner of the contest will not want to rub it in, and the loser will want to pretend that he is not even aware there was any kind of difficulty.

On rare occasions this game of anonymity can backfire. A friend of mine employed in a large California company used to wear a beard; one day while driving to work he found himself trying to beat another driver to a one-lane bottleneck ahead. According to custom he didn't look at the rival driver. Both, however, were clearly conscious that a race was on, both were accelerating rapidly, and neither was about to yield. At the last moment my friend found it necessary to cut in on the other in order to avoid hitting a parked car. As he slyly looked in the rear-view mirror he saw that the loser was the president of his company. Next morning he shaved off his beard.

The highway dialogue still persists, however, through the silent medium of the bumper strip and the rear-window sticker. Organizations with axes to grind long ago discovered the value of the rear of an auto for advertising, since most of the time California drivers are following so closely that they can read the smallest print. In fact, there is one strip that says, "If you can read this you're too damned close."

Though the strips blossom in profusion during election campaigns, they are a year-round institution that provides, among other things, a continuing comic dialogue. During one campaign with an abundance of ballot propositions, motorists were so bombarded with "Yes on 4" and "No on 21" signs that somebody came out with the clincher, "Yes on No." When newcomers from Texas began appearing on California streets with the window stickers, "Made in Texas by Texans," they provoked a rash of counter-stickers: "Made in California by Texans," "Made in Pasadena by Little Old Ladies," and on the backs of Volkswagens, "Made in der Black Forest by Elves." In response to the popular strip, "The only ism for me is Americanism," another sticker announces, "The only ism for me is abstract expressionism." Industry has gotten into the act with so many messages ("Eat Lamb, Wear Wool") that the conscientious consumer should carry pad and pencil to list the things he should buy. Some advertisers even provide a reason: "Buy a record and help stamp out TV."

Thus the California automobile is actually more than a "part of the human anatomy"; it is a projection of the individual's personality. The very tradition of anonymity tends to make the projection genuine; for as accountability fades, truth appears. Many a Milquetoast becomes a tiger the moment he roars out of his driveway. If it were not for the possible hazards, the psychiatrist could throw away his couch and simply take an hour's ride with every patient.

The fact is that the Californian, while he may be fun-loving and easygoing the rest of the day, reverts to his aggressive male instincts behind the wheel. In California's blissful idyll of togetherness, male domestication is nearly complete. It goes beyond the state of "quiet desperation" in which Thoreau assumed most men live. The California male is happy, or thinks he is happy, in his role. But as the English have demonstrated, the most civil and mannerly people can on rare occasions erupt with the most brutal crimes. The auto could therefore be considered a safety valve for subhuman instincts that might otherwise build up more dangerous pressures. Like the dog whose hair rises when he hears the howl of the coyote, the Californian reverts to his primordial ancestry when he joins the pack on the freeway. Afterward, refreshed by the therapy of the steering wheel, he returns to his particular slice of California life.

More and more the focus of this life, for the male as well as the female, is the California home. "Prestige Homes" are advertised with such headlines as "Resort Living," "Seashore Living," "Country Club Living." One subdivision is named Leisure Hills, while another land development is dubbed Fun Valley. Of course, the ads for these happy subdivisions show smiling people romping on the beach, standing with poised meat fork by their barbecue, lolling beside their pools, or getting into their motorboats at a backdoor dock. The home is, indeed, becoming a luxury resort suite with emphasis on dazzling appointments—the great picture windows, the sunken baths, the private patios or lanais, the interior atriums lush with tropical growth. The yard is, of course, a veritable funhouse of equipment for young and old. And the whole is framed with exotic verdure that speaks of some South Seas paradise.

While this description holds fairly true for the newer middle-class neighborhoods, both on the San Francisco peninsula and in Southern California, the undoubted bliss capital of California is Palm Springs. This sun-happy community—one of the world's largest oases—owes its success to a freak of geography and climate, parlayed by California promotion. I have seen it raining at San Gorgonio Pass and as I rounded the last jut of mountain before entering Palm Springs, the rain ended and the sun began as though they were separated by an invisible wall. Palm Springs, in brief, offers more sunny days for having fun. On this seemingly ephemeral base it has built a winter population of 50,000 and an annual tourist turnover of 500,000. Since the war it has acquired golf courses at about the same rate that Las Vegas has acquired luxury casino-hotels; with fifteen finished and more planned, Palm Springs calls itself "the winter golf capital of the world."

In this hedonist's paradise, the whole tone of life is geared to the funlover. Police don't give traffic tickets—just polite warnings. Natural fertilizer is barred by law as a possible offense to the nostrils. On any day that the sun fails to shine, one hotel serves free champagne to its guests.

Actually, the Springs is no longer just a tourist center, but a permanent home for the wealthy, the retired, those who operate a business not requiring regular hours, and those who can commute by plane. The hundreds of hotels and inns(it is unlawful to name an establishment a motel) have been joined by thousands of homes (mostly air-conditioned) and thousands of pools (mostly heated). There is a sumptuous health spa in which the customer is treated with servile attention unknown outside the Orient and a variety of physical treatments that recognize the body as a new California god. At one home the host has constructed chaise longues on an automatic turntable, which keeps sunbathers continually facing their deity. To people accustomed to more work than play, the Springs has an edgy unreality—like the fear that a good dream will end. One is somehow reminded of the incredulity of archaeologists as they uncovered the purlieus of Pompeii.

This is not to say that Palm Springs is wicked in the classic sense. Its obvious pleasures—sunbathing, swimming, golf, horseback riding—are wholesome enough. Indeed, its denizens can't even be called lazy, since they can hardly avoid getting involved in strenuous exercise. The Springs has one of the world's finest collections of physical specimens and may also be considered the nation's winter girl-watching capital. The question is whether frank hedonism can stop at mere idle diversion. So far it appears to be doing so in California, and perhaps even in Palm Springs. But as one permanent resident observes, "The good people stay OK. The ones who can't take it go bad—faster."

Palm Springs is only an extreme projection of the California playground mentality. The home-turned-resort is a characteristic of big-city suburbs; it is even cared for by a husband who has been convinced that wielding a shovel, trowel, and paintbrush is also fun. Otherwise he could never explain to himself why he hasn't time to relax and enjoy the home. Indeed, the place requires such maintenance that the California suburbanite has gone mechanized, like the farmer. Some of these motorized gadgets, such as the power mower, he owns outright. But mostly he rents his equipment from one of 150 do-it-yourself rental companies in California.

Actually, the do-it-yourself craze started in California just before World War II, when the first rental yards made their appearance. Their historic contribution was to centralize in one place all the varied rental equipment needed by the homeowner. Since the war both the do-it-yourself movement and the rental yards spread to the rest of the country, but as one operator says, "There are more rental yards in Southern California probably than the rest of the nation combined." You can rent anything from a power saw to a cement mixer, a power crane, or a bulldozer. Most of this equipment is passed out (one rental yard has up to 700 transactions on a Saturday or Sunday) without operating instructions unless specifically requested—the assumption being that every self-respecting Californian knows how to use practically everything.

One aspect of the do-it-yourself craze—the garage power tool equipment—reached a peak and went into a well-deserved decline in the early 1950's. So many suburbanites were buying power tools for home carpentry work that neighborhood parking problems were created by the cars that couldn't be squeezed in the garages. It got so you couldn't be invited anywhere without having to take a tour of the host's hardware shop. As doctor's offices began to be swamped with emergency cases of missing fingers, the fad came to a merciful halt.

A much safer phase of the do-it-yourself movement is the male preoccupation with lawns. For a time after the war, any group of two or more men was almost certain to be discussing the fine points of putting in a lawn—how deep to prepare the soil, whether or not to rake it after spreading the seed and fertilizer, how to keep dogs and small children out of it. The advent of dichondra grass about 1950 opened up whole new realms of conversation. I have seen men standing over martinis at a party arguing earnestly whether it is better to plant dichondra from seed—mixed with clover, of course—or set out in clumps of mature dichondra grass from nursery flats. By the 1960's, nearly any head of a family has put in at least one lawn, and many are veterans of four or five. Something of the newness has worn off, but one can still get into discussions on which brand of fertilizer has the fewest weed seeds, or the best way to get rid of crab grass.

The lawn has, in fact, earned a kind of reverence that is given to few California institutions. In most tract settlements, there is a silent understanding that everyone will plant grass rather than ivy—except in the parking strip, where anything goes. There is some belief in a clean view, down the whole block, that should remind one of a mountain meadow or a golf course. To the individualist caught setting out ivy, neighborhood pressure can be overwhelming. In one San Francisco peninsula subdivision, there is a deed restriction requiring grass, and one nonconformist planting ivy is being sued by his neighbors. Ivy is supposed to be reserved for out-of-the-way spots or slopes where mowing the grass would be impractical.

The same attitude applies to front-yard fences, which are somehow considered an eyesore and an affront to the neighborhood. Curiously, this never applies to the backyard, where fencing is taken for granted in California. These are not just the short rail or picket variety, but five- or six-foot redwood fences, or if one can afford it, concrete block walls. It is not just a matter of privacy for one's personal resort, though this is important. It is also a matter of enclosing one's domain, like a feudal lord with his turreted ramparts, and reflects the Californian's unusual preoccupation with possessions.

But one result is that, unlike Eastern communities where backyards are generally open, privacy is not at a premium. Precisely because of the fences, one does not feel obliged to ignore the neighbors while one is in the backyard. The fence is considered privacy enough. In fact, one cannot go into one's backyard when the neighbor is also outside without feeling obliged to strike up a conversation. This can prevail even when the fence is six feet high—a situation that can lead to some weird predicaments. A woman friend of ours was sunbathing in her backyard and carrying on an intermittent conversation with her neighbor on the other side of the fence. At this point her minister called and found his way to the backyard. He was just settling into a conversation with his sunbathing parishioner when the neighbor lady spoke up from behind the fence, "You sure parked your car at a crazy angle when you came in last night. Were you drunk?"

The etiquette of California fences also includes joint financing by the neighbors on both sides and rear, as well as placing the fence along the property lines. On moving into a new subdivision, one does not just put up a fence to one's liking. Nor does one say to a neighbor, "I'm going to put up a fence; would you like to go in with me?" Besides sounding arbitrary, this tips one's hand prematurely; some neighbors would conclude that if you are going to put up a fence anyway, why should they help pay for it? The proper method is as follows: during a conversation with the neighbor, you steer the discussion around to fences and ask whether he has thought about it at all. He will allow that he has, and you gradually converge on an agreement for joint financing. Then comes the problem of agreeing on height and style, in which the wives are consulted. When one triples this process for the neighbors on the other two sides, each of whom may have a different idea on style, the complications multiply. The man who is able to display to his guests a fence of uniform style and height all the way around is considered a master of diplomacy.

At the opposite extreme, two neighbors in Compton couldn't agree on a fence; one put up a four foot wire fence; the other fastened bamboo shoots to it on his side. The first then put up a redwood fence to hide the first fence. The second built a concrete block wall a foot higher, so that it showed over the fence. The first then constructed a different-color block wall higher than the first wall. This was the status of the battle at the last report, but it serves to show the seriousness with which Californians take their fences. I have heard of two neighbor women engaged in a water fight with their garden hoses over a difference of opinion on the fence. Once it is built, however, Californians agree with Robert Frost that "Good fences make good neighbors."

Actually, the California fence effectively symbolizes the compartmentalization of California society, in which the family tends to shut itself from the world and live its separate life. The fence around the house is hauntingly parallel to the fence around the self. For to be uncommitted is also to be, in the long run, unconcerned. One has the feeling that the dynamic issues of the day are rushing headlong past the Californians; their faces are inclined inward to their own games while the truly exciting and consequential events in a dramatic era are occurring over their shoulders.

The result is that a people with a potential for greatness—with energy, zest, imagination, and freedom of mind—are busying themselves in small things. The California male is not only "together" with his family—certainly a commendable condition in itself—but is often assuming a domestic role that leaves no clearcut domain for the female. It is a common California sight for men to be stuffing clothes in the washer at the laundromat, and then waiting in pathetic silence on a chair by the window. More and more, husbands are accompanying their wives at the supermarkets, slowly pushing the shopping cart while Mama stows it with goods. Rather than reject this role outright, the more assertive males tend to dominate the shopping session, deciding what items to buy and playing havoc with the wife's grocery budget. I have heard women complaining that they couldn't get up to the meat counter because it was monopolized by men carefully choosing their favorite cut of steak. There is even a trend toward the inclusion of husbands at wedding and baby showers—an obvious recognition of male equality in things domestic.

Is the Californian happy in this self-imposed microcosm, this supertogetherness? The assumption has generally been that California life is the good life—healthy, carefree, purged of social oppression and class consciousness, full of opportunity and variety, and especially rich in the homely values. Most California men appear content; workingmen from other regions probably never had such equality, ease, and personal freedom as that afforded by the tract house and the auto. To many, California Living is synonymous with creature comforts; this is perhaps the first society that genuinely offers such comforts to practically all.

Yet at the edges of this picture there appear some disturbing facts. Some of the yardsticks of a healthy society do not measure particularly well for Californians, and especially for California men.

In California, the rate for major crime per 100,000 population is the highest in the United States and approximately double the national average.[9] California has about one-eleventh of the nation's population and about one-sixth of the major crime.

The suicide rate is second only to that of Nevada. While the San Francisco rate is the highest among major cities in the country, the Los Angeles County rate is also substantially above the national average.[10] As elsewhere, the rate for men is noticeably higher than for women.

More acute, since it touches many more lives, is California's drinking problem. With about 9 percent of the national population, California has about 12 percent of the known alcoholics. Depending on the particular county, drunk arrests account for 30 to 50 percent of all criminal arrests. Alcoholism is by far the largest category for mental patients in California.[11] Many large companies take an active responsibility in the problem with thorough-going programs of help and rehabilitation; one firm has had a full-time man on this assignment since 1945. In Los Angeles, both pastors and psychologists indicated in a wide survey that alcoholism topped all other mental health problems. Governor Pat Brown has called it the state's chief health problem. Nor are the increasing rates necessarily associated with crowded city conditions. San Fernando Valley, conceded to be the epitome of suburbia, is estimated to have about 40,000 alcoholics, or about one for every twenty persons. This is higher than the ratio for both the state and Los Angeles County.

These figures do not necessarily indicate a bacchanalian atmosphere in California. Except perhaps on New Year's Eve, the sight of a drunk on the street is an extreme rarity. Private parties are generally moderate; drinks are still considered primarily as a social grace, rather than as a means to intoxication. Among the middle classes there is a noticeable tendency to serve wine at dinner, in an air of decorum that at times approaches snobbery. Wine-tasting parties are even employed as fund-raising devices for charities. The desire to be known as a wine connoisseur necessarily rejects intemperance as unprofessional. When a friend of mine was discussing the merits of wine-tasting parties, I baited him by asking whether there was any limit on the amount consumed and drew a righteous reply that would have done credit to a temperance worker.

But while heavy drinking has no place in California's social tone, it is apparently more widespread—judging by the figures—than the observer would suspect. How do these and other unhappy statistics square with California's happy faces?

The crime rate has been explained by the state attorney general with the observation: "Mobile getaway techniques and facilities in a transient and migrant population have increased the opportunities of those with criminal tendencies . . ." But suicide and alcoholism—two diverse escapes from the realities of life—may well have something to do with the Californian's self-orientation. The high incidence of alcoholism is not surprising among people who tend to be overly interested in themselves; the person who takes an alcoholic escape from personal problems is often one with an almost childlike concern for self. Something of the same comment can be made on the high rate of suicides. The world is bound to be disappointing if one expects too much out of it.

But still more devastating is the obvious challenge in these figures to the "fun" philosophy. What Lin Yutang calls "the satisfaction of wants" may not, after all, be the essence of happiness. In the end, the Californian, no less than other people, hungers first of all for meaning in his life. If there is such a thing as personal happiness, a more plausible basis for it is surely one's significance to one's environment—more simply, one's genuine value to others. But in California one's community is held at such an arm's length that one's significance is confined to the home.

Yet man is, as Spinoza assures us, a social animal. The retreat to the home is a startling retrogression back before society, even before the tribe. Ironically, the fence that the Californian has erected around himself may be the real source of the discontent that reveals itself on the statistical fringes of his society. He has narrowed his area of commitment to the point where, if something goes wrong in this

251

small domain, there is no room for adjustment, but only for escape.

In defense of the California male, he must be acknowledged as one of the world's true individualists in an age when individualism is in retreat. He seizes and exercises as much personal freedom as any common man on earth. The question is whether he puts this precious possession to purposes worthy of his manhood.

CHAPTER X

Californians Never Die ...

1.

As San Francisco's Powell Street cable car approaches the end of the line at Market Street, it is the custom for passengers to hop off some eighty feet short, in order to facilitate maneuvering on the turntable. One day a little old lady refused.

"I've paid my fifteen cents," she insisted, "and I intend to ride to the end of the line."

The conductor and the motorman tried to reason with her. As nine more cable cars jammed up the hill behind, other conductors, motormen, and even passersby joined in the polemics. Hundreds of would-be passengers, many carrying packages, filled up the intersection. Other hundreds gathered just to watch the fun; it was said to be the biggest crowd at that corner since the celebration of V-J day.

Still the little old lady refused to get off. When two policemen tried to plead with her, she hit one on the head with her umbrella. As they packed her into a taxicab amid the cheers of the crowd, she pronounced her valedictory, "I just wanted to ride to the end of the line."

This, in capsule, is the story of California's older people.

They are going to get everything that's coming to them in life. They are not going to settle down in a rocking chair because they have reached their sixties. They didn't come to California just to resign from life. They are going to ride clear to the end of the line.

Maybe this is why so many of California's elderly hold their age so well. They don't think old, and they certainly don't act old. In fact, they refuse to be considered old; in California the terms "old folks" and "the elderly" are frowned on and are going out of usage in favor of the euphemism, "senior citizens." I have one friend in his sixties who appears in his fifties and is now on his third successful professional career. Educated and widely experienced as a mining engineer, he came to California and naturally became a real estate developer. After retiring, he turned a hobby into a business by making educational slide films for the public schools—a profession full of pressures, deadlines, and long hours. In his spare time, he and his wife take trailer trips several weeks or months at a time into some of the roughest country of the United States and Mexico.

Another friend is a great-grandmother in her seventies who conducts a baby-sitting business, takes care of chickens and turkeys, regularly puts on large dinners for her many descendants, and at least once a year goes with her husband on a long automobile trip.

There are plenty of other examples to show that Californians don't know when to quit. In Ojai, a carpenter retired at the age of sixty-eight and couldn't stand it; so he went back to work as a mason tender, pushing wheelbarrows full of cement or carrying thirty-five-pound concrete blocks in each hand; at seventy-five-and-a-half he is still at it.

A seventy-five-year-old blacksmith has been following the strenuous California county fair circuits, shoeing race horses, since 1936. When he retires from the road in a few years, he expects to settle down and open a hardware store. "I know I'll have to do something," he says. "I can't just sit still."

At a hotel in Ocean Park, a ninety-year-old bellhop named David Epstein has been sponsoring essay contests (on Americanism) for high schoolers since 1952. Besides giving away several hundred dollars a year on this project, he once figured out his share of the national debt ($1,600) and sent a check to the United States government for that amount. As for his bellhopping chores, "I do errands for old people who can't do things for themselves."

In Los Angeles, a veteran second-story man with a fifty-three-year police record was arrested for picking a pay telephone at the age of ninety-three.

Actually, most Californians retire in their sixties, the same as any other people, but the difference is that they don't slow down much. The idea is that in California you can retire and really start living. It is nothing to see bowlers and golfers in their seventies, ocean swimmers and even skin divers in their sixties. In Glendale, a seventy-year-old is one of four members of the world's champion lawn bowling team, and claims to be "the oldest athlete holding a world's title." In San Diego's Balboa Park, one of the most accomplished roque players is one hundred years old. A spry Coronado woman in her eighties learned she was a great-grandmother and celebrated by riding her bicycle all over town spreading the news. In Venice, an eighty-one-year-old woman divorced her husband (only fifty-nine) because he took her out dancing five nights a week. Said she, "I like to dance two nights, once in a while three, but every night was a little too much."

A Los Angeles man, seventy-seven years old, gives figure skating exhibitions across the country. He was inspired to try it at the age of seventy while watching the graceful maneuvers of a young girl who was a former national figure skating champion. He stepped up and asked if she would skate with him, and soon they were a regular team at the rink.

"At my age you don't have to hesitate about asking the pretty girls," he explains. "Younger fellows, fifty and sixty, may be misunderstood as to motive."

Yet even romance is no stranger to California oldsters. I have yet to know a California male of any age who will not turn his head at a cute figure. Older women, no less than their daughters and granddaughters, watch their weight, generally dress stylishly, keep their age a secret, and use makeup to good advantage. One woman with nine grandchildren was complimented by a male admirer who said: "You've sure got a good figure for an old gal." In a public park in West Hollywood, women over fifty can enroll in a glamour class that includes instructions on makeup, hair styling, posture, and poise. A graduating class had several ladies over seventy (one of them started using lipstick for the first time in thirty years).

One result of all this maintenance work is a profusion of December romances—not a few with whirlwind courtships and elopements. I have known of several widows or widowers in their sixties who, in a remarkably short period after their loss, remarried. It is not unusual for persons consigning themselves to a quiet life in an old folks' home to strike a romance there and start over. In Glendale, a man eighty-eight years old moved into a home for the aged, caught a look at a woman ninety-three, and proposed ("It was love at first sight."). In San Diego, an eighty-six-year-old and an eighty-four-year-old met at a church social and eloped to Yuma, Arizona. Not quite so impetuous were two others—a ninety-seven-year-old and a seventy-seven-year-old—who were married after a two-month courtship. Their explanation: "We were sick of the lonely years."

This touches one of the chief reasons why California old people keep going so long. The custom of several generations living under the same roof—standard practice in much of Europe and still widely observed in parts of the United States—was never imported to California. There is little or no social pressure to open one's home to widowed grandparents or great-aunts. They live alone, or with another relative of their generation, or else they remarry. The exceptional cases help to prove the point, since they evoke attitudes of pity or disapproval by others. Nor is it simply a question of the younger generation resisting its filial duty; the older generation is just as determined to keep its independence.

As a result, for example, a widowed grandmother is not living out her days sitting around the house, expecting to be waited on, feeling sorry for herself because she isn't, and serving as a glorified baby-sitter for a second brood of infants. Nor are her own children living in silent resentment over an alien presence and hating themselves for wishing the presence might end. Such self-imposed misery is minimized by Californians. They have discovered, through what might be considered shocking callousness in other places, that both generations are happier living separately.

This solution still leaves the question of aged loneliness, but Californians have other ways to solve that. The solutions are, in fact, what makes California life for old people so distinctive. For the oldsters, no less than the youngsters, tradition and sentiment have given way to the pursuit of a good time.

2.

Originally, older people did not come to California for fun. Some are still coming simply because California, as one observer puts it, "is a better place to die; their old bones don't ache so much in the warmer weather." The motivation was largely negative: life was not hard in California. There, one could vegetate in peace and comfort.

Beginning in the late 1880's, Southern California in particular came to be considered a vast sanitarium for the afflicted. Resort hotels were not, as they are now, centers of entertainment. Many of them were simply oversized rest homes with a view. Their verandas, crowded with elderly guests stuffed into armchairs under a blanket, resembled the deck of a transocean liner. The atmosphere had the silent expectation of a hospital, but without the bustle. The most exciting event of the day was winning a game of Parcheesi or filling the last hole in a jigsaw puzzle.

Not that California had more than its share of old people. The state had a bigger percentage of people sixty-five or older in the 1960 census than in 1890, or any other census since then, and the percentage is still under the national average.[1] The proportion seemed higher to many people because the elderly congregated first in Southern California, and then in particular communities. Even today some California cities—Santa Cruz, Pasadena, Glendale, Santa Monica, Long Beach—are noted for a larger-than-average elderly population. One of these, with 17.6 percent of its population sixty-five or over,[2] has produced a legendary figure, the "little old lady from Pasadena," which is California's answer to Paul Bunyan.

Upon these communities the stamp of age is unmistakable. In politics, they are conservative, except as regards old-age pensions. In appearance, they are most pleasant, with such mature shrubs and trees that they appear to have been there forever. In public policy, they are terribly respectable, with Sunday blue laws, strict control on bars and liquor stores, and an efficient police force whose principal duty is the maintenance of silence. There is a lot of land in public parks, and a lot of well-filled benches. On national holidays, there is an unusually high proportion of flags on display in front of the homes, and a few earnest citizens keep theirs flying the year round. There are excellent and well-patronized libraries, where one is apt to open a book and find therein an anonymously placed religious tract.

But there is little or none of the negativism that once pervaded the haunts of California's aged. There is still a higher ratio of doctors to population (175 per 100,000) in California than in the country as a whole, and there are seventy-six health food stores in Los Angeles alone.[3] But there is not the obsession with health—an almost corporate hypochondria—that once pervaded Southern California. Time was when the main object of older Californians was to get well and stay well. They were so preoccupied with the quest for good health that they didn't know what to do with it if they got it. By contrast, health is no longer an end in itself, but simply a prerequisite for the enjoyment of life.

There is likewise a noticeable evolution in the California attitude toward death. Visitors from the East are shocked to see funeral homes advertised on billboards and TV commercials. Like everything else in practical California, death appears to be something sold on the installment plan. Says one newcomer from Ohio, "You get the feeling the next thing they'll offer is trading stamps." But this is somewhat beside the point, which is that in California—or at least in Southern California—death has been vastly upgraded. As one writer observed, "Dying in Los Angeles is something to be anticipated."

The man who changed Southern California's attitude toward death was Hubert Eaton, who conceived a cemetery without headstones, a funeral service without a procession, and for that matter, death without sting. In place of finality, he emphasized continuity. He created at Forest Lawn a burial ground that did not look like a burial ground but rather like a classic green pasture, sanctified by works of art. He called it "a place where the sorrowing will be soothed and strengthened because it will be in God's garden." As

259

Aldous Huxley described such a Los Angeles mortuary in his *After Many a Summer Dies the Swan:*

Statues wherever you turned your eyes. Hundreds of them, bought wholesale, one would guess, from some monumental masonry concern at Carrara or Pietrasanta. All nudes, all female, all exuberantly nubile. The sort of statues one would expect to see in the reception room of a high class brothel in Rio de Janeiro, 'Oh, Death,' demanded a marble scroll at the entrance to every gallery, 'where is thy sting?' Mutely, but eloquently, the statues gave their reassuring reply.[4]

To support this tender illusion, Eaton's staff developed a new lexicon of the trade: the deceased became The Loved One; the mourners, The Waiting Ones; the funeral, The Leavetaking; death, "being out of sight"; the cemetery, Memorial Park. As Eaton told his salesmen, they must always remember that they were selling immortality. More than this, they were really selling a piece of heaven. To the prospective customer who comes as a Waiting One or as a tourist, the California cemetery is an advertisement for the hereafter. Spoofing the Los Angeles morticians in his *The Loved One*, Evelyn Waugh told of The Dream that motivated the founder of Whispering Glades:

There amid all that Nature and Art could offer to elevate the Soul of Man I saw the Happy Resting Place of countless Loved Ones. And I saw the Waiting Ones who still stood at the brink of that narrow stream that now separated them from those who had gone before. Young and old, they were happy too. Happy in Beauty, Happy in the certain knowledge that their Loved Ones were very near, in Beauty and Happiness such as the earth cannot give.[5]

And so Forest Lawn set the tone for other Southern California mortuaries—the streamlined service, eliminating the long funeral procession and thus increasing the turnover; the sylvan slopes with the idyllic perfection of a Watteau painting; and finally, since death had become a good word, a frankly hard-sell promotional program. Death was nothing final, but simply an important ceremonial milestone in an ongoing life, like birth and marriage.

Cemeteries such as Forest Lawn are therefore not merely upgraded graveyards; it is not just a question of banishing the morbid in favor of beauty and dignity. They are really an apotheosis of immortality, a capturing of life after death under glass. These classic glades are supposed to be Valhalla (as one cemetery is actually called). To accept the pious jargon of the plot salesmen is to believe that this is truly a physical home for disembodied spirits; somehow they reside here and enjoy its green (always green) serenity.

Here, too, the living are able to mingle with the dead in some mysterious union. Entering one of these memorial parks is like stepping through the mist into the Green Pastures; and if one only had eyes to see, surely one would glimpse departed Loved Ones. Indeed, if the spell were not broken by traffic lines of finite automobiles filled with mortal tourists, one would feel a strange uneasiness until one returned back through the gates into the profane world.

Thus, for all the satire heaped upon it, the Southern California mortuary should not be judged simply by the commercial motives of its operators. What has been the harm if, in Southern California, death has become a beautiful thing? The forests of macabre gravestones have been abolished; they belong to the era of the all-night wake and the year's mourning in black. There is, in fact, no real death, but merely a change of abode to an Elysian Field where, in the language of the undertaker, the Loved One is simply "out of sight."

There yet remains in this approach a cosmic presumption. It has long been impossible by law to die in California without falling into the hands of the undertaker. But if we take seriously the stage he has set, the undertaker is also presiding over the afterlife. He has the Keys to the Kingdom, and he will sell you a piece of it at nothing down and a few dollars a month.

Thus, the idea has been that death is a beginning of a new

261

life—not a dreaded subject to be shunned. But a new attitude has been developing among older Californians; they do not look to death for their reward. Instead they are living as though the present existence is what counts.

Symbolically, funerals are becoming simpler; the ostentatious production is often considered in bad taste. An organization, the Los Angeles Funeral Society, has even been formed "to provide decent funerals at reasonable rates" for its members by securing special prices from the mortuaries. There is a recognizable tendency for the aggrieved family to suggest a charitable donation in lieu of flowers; long funeral processions are becoming passé. Two older friends of mine died having left instructions against any funeral whatever. In such cases there is little feeling that they have died at all; it simply seems as though it's been a long time since you've seen them.

There is even a small but growing trend to forestall the morticians altogether by leaving one's body to science. Indeed, many medical schools have a waiting list so long they won't accept new offers (300 at UCLA Medical Center). I know of one man, enthused with the idea, who spent a good part of a day on the telephone trying to get a reservation somewhere before he was finally accepted.

At the same time there is less supersentiment and more practicality on the subject of death. In offering sympathy to someone for the loss of a parent, one is less likely to encounter an emotional expression of grief than a sober declaration, "Well, you know, it was really a blessing this way—no long illness." There is no longer an accepted time for a period of mourning; in some cases following a death in the family, people will change the pace of their life very little; they will explain, piously and probably quite sincerely, "She would have wanted it this way." Once while I was consoling a friend on the phone about the loss of his mother, he said, "By the way, I understand we're going to the same party tomorrow night. Why don't we go together?"

The point is that life is for living; dying is something one just doesn't think about. For all you can gather from their behavior, you get the impression that Californians never die.

This also accounts, partly at least, for a comparative decline in the religious cults for which Los Angeles was once famous. Not that there is any serious loss of original theology in California. The great evangelists and spiritualists of the hectic twenties and thirties have left their movements in the Foursquare Gospel, the Vedanta, I Am, and Self-Realization. The church page in a Los Angeles newspaper picked at random contains four display ads for evangelists who at least imply healing powers:

> "2 days of Dynamic Miracles. . . . Bring the sick, lame, blind and deaf. 'With God, all things are possible.'"
>
> "Entire Service Directed to Healing the Sick."
>
> "Special Miracle Service. The blind see, the deaf hear, the lame leap for joy."
>
> "Prayers for the sick and afflicted. The Lame Walk! . . . Cancer Melts Away!"

More than 100 different churches of the salvationist, Pentecostal, spiritualist, or occult types are listed in the Los Angeles classified phone book. These include such denominational names as Greater Works Church, Lighthouse Full Gospel, Savior's Crusaders, Temple of Spiritual Logic, Agasha Temple of Wisdom, Aquarian Church of Chirosthesia, Institute of Thought Control, Pillar of Fire, Sky Pilot Revival Center, Scientology, Totality, and one that seems to include everything, Pentecostal Spiritual Church. In a 1959 survey of ten Los Angeles communities, 10 percent of those interviewed stated they belonged to a group that could formally be called a cult.[6]

Little wonder that Californians, having left behind the pressure of conformity to traditional worship, and showing an adventurous spirit in the very process of migrating, would experiment with new religious thought. Little wonder, too, that the followers of most California fringe religions have tended to be older people, who might be nearer to their Maker than others. Those without a firm faith gravitate to the tent that makes the most promises. It is almost as though the fearful soul, believing that salvation comes through a demonstration of faith, deliberately chooses the most preposterous doctrine available: "Look, God, how much I believe!"

In this atmosphere, Los Angeles is still the nation's crucible for original theology. It was there, for example, that the flying saucer craze assumed all the aspects of a religion. As late as 1949, a man arrived at Los Angeles International Airport, barefooted and dressed in Biblical robes. Standing on the steps at the door of the plane, he told reporters, "I may as well say it. I am Christ." Within nine years, Krishna Venta had founded his Fountain of the World center in San Fernando Valley, claimed thousands of followers, and achieved martyrdom in a dynamite blast at his headquarters.

Still, Southern California is growing out of its religious adolescence. By far the majority of Californians, including the elderly, are either adherents of the traditional denominations or are unattached. The new churches of the major faiths rising and growing in the suburbs are the most conspicuous religious activity in postwar California.

Even more important, however, is the secularization of the old people. They are too busy leading a full life to worry about dying. They are not going to spend valuable time hollering and wiggling their hands in a revival tent just to get on the good side of God. It is as though, philosophically, they had long ago come to terms with death and had discounted it in their plans. Consider two examples:

In Placer County, an eighty-one-year-old was getting out of his car in the garage when he was accosted by two robbers. Drawing a revolver, he whirled and shot the gun—a toy pistol—from one bandit's hand. Both of them ran off—saved only by the old man's fear of hitting a neighbor's house. When a policeman arrived and told him he was lucky to have hit the gun, he snorted, "What do you mean, 'lucky'? I meant to hit the gun."

In San Francisco an eighty-three-year-old was riding up in an elevator when another passenger suddenly put a knife to his neck.

"Give me all your money!"

"I've only got ninety-three cents," snapped the old man, "and you can go to hell!"

The intruder got off at the next floor.

The point is that these California oldsters act as though they are going to live forever. They may be forced to retire at sixty-five, but that doesn't mean they have to stop living. In fact, contrary to the attitude of previous generations who came to California to die, these senior citizens take the positive attitude that life begins at retirement. As one older gentleman, who decided to retire earlier than he had previously planned, told me, "I don't mind dyin', but I'd sure kick myself for dyin' before I do some of the things I've wanted to do all my life."

Not all older Californians have adopted the new, or active, school of thought. Killing time is still among the main objects of some. You can still walk through the south side of MacArthur Park in Los Angeles, or two of the city parks in Long Beach, and see table after table filled with old folks playing cards. At Pershing Square in downtown Los Angeles, or at the "University by the Sea" on the Long Beach pier, you can see them sitting on benches listening blankly to

265

religious or political orators. But these idle pastimes are of another era. Most of the elderly do not confine their outdoor diversion to the parks; in house trailers and camps, they are making all outdoors their park. More and more the city parks are the province of the foreign born, mostly from the cities of Europe where the public park is a social institution. They, too—or at least their children—will discover that the city park is too restrictive for Californians. The park smacks too much of an era when leisure was something to be grasped lightly and momentarily—never with enough sureness for big plans. To the modern Californian, leisure is a lifetime goal and a weekend reality. The elderly are not pitied for their infirmities or their uselessness; they are admired and envied for having the freedom to do all the time what everyone else must try to do only part of the time. One woman friend of ours, whose in-laws have taken trips to every continent and around the world, once exclaimed, "I can hardly wait till I'm middle-aged and can really start living!"

3.

How do the California oldsters do it? The first step out of loneliness is to join a club. At first glance this would appear to contradict the California penchant for going it alone. But most of the thriving organizations are concerned with the members' private interests rather than with civic or cultural affairs. In fact, the only organizations in which Californians may be accused of being joiners are the hobby and sports clubs on the one hand, and the youth-service organizations on the other. It is a further measure of California individualism that most special interest clubs—camera clubs, garden clubs, writers' clubs, various collectors' clubs—are heavily populated by older people. Without meaning to, many consist almost exclusively of the middle-aged and the elderly, while the few young members are legacies brought along by a strong parent. From time to time these groups will take stock of themselves and launch a membership drive for "younger blood," without realizing that it is simply the older people who are interested in joining. They are interested for several reasons—the desire for companionship, the availability of leisure time, and simply the fact that they are products of an earlier day when "joining" was the ruling custom. The difference is that the popular organizations of former times were groups of general interest—fraternal orders for the men, women's clubs for their wives—while the present-day groups are specialized. In fact, the California city can be dated according to the types of clubs that are thriving; if they are hobby and parent-child groups, the community is just getting started; if they are merchants' service clubs, the town is in its prime; if they are women's clubs, the city is mature; if they are fraternal lodges, the place is getting old.

In effect, the special interest club is a sort of California lodge. It is organized more sensibly than the lodge, in that it brings together people with a common pursuit. In fact, the interests sometimes cut across all class distinctions in California. Company presidents may rub shoulders with retired pensioners in a camera club or an antique car club. Proficiency in the group activity, or at least enthusiasm, is all that counts. The result is some competitive effort that becomes almost professional in many fields of self-expression. In Southern California alone, there are sixty-four camera clubs competing with each other in exhibitions of color slides and black-and-whites. The judging processes are such that the individual can't help learning from the others. California is probably the nation's leading center for amateur still photography; it has become everyman's art form.

In another sense the gregariousness of California old people is simply a remnant of a clubbier generation. They still get together in vast annual state picnics, attended in the tens of thousands, which are superorganized to the point of separating the picnickers by home counties. It is the older women, generally, who are the mainstay of community women's clubs. Indeed, those who are worried about the antics of California's bare midriff crowd can always take comfort in the nearest woman's club, garden club, or historical society, where Midwest propriety still reigns. During a luncheon at one of Southern California's oldest and largest women's clubs, the lady next to me confided, "When I came out from Michigan two years ago and saw all these people in shorts and dark glasses, I thought I was in the wrong place. Then [she sighed, triumphantly] I found the Ebell Club." Keepers of all that is sound and certain, the good ladies of the women's clubs constitute California's other half—the part that came out of the Victorian Middle West.

It is no coincidence, either, that the senior citizens constitute one of the best organized political blocs in California. Individually, they are heirs of a day when politics was a continual dialogue in every community. Collectively, their organizations got their training in the heyday of pensioneering—the 1930's—when California spawned its brood of crackpot political-economic schemes (Townsend Plan, Utopia, Epic, and Ham 'n' Eggs).

But while stabler times demand stabler systems, the pension and aged-welfare organizations are as potent as ever—operating not so much as separate movements but as powerful pressures upon the political parties. Old people in California seem to have an acute sense of what is coming to them, possibly because so many came West to retire, and they want to be able to afford it. But their biggest political ally is the prevailing custom of older and younger generations living separately. The younger folks, who are not anxious to have the grandparents move in, are willing to support plans to help them live alone.

Nor are older people limited in their politics to aged welfare. Some are of the old school of intense party loyalties learned in other states. I know one older woman who enthusiastically addressed envelopes all day long for a candidate of her political party, but didn't know a thing about him and a few hours later couldn't remember his name. Splinter movements, from the economic cure-alls of the thirties to the rightist dispensation of the sixties, seem to have an affinity for oldsters—possibly because their views were jelled in an earlier era of absolute values. There was, for example, a basic truth in the state attorney general's quip that the John Birch Society was composed of "wealthy businessmen, retired military officers, and little old ladies in tennis shoes."

While little old ladies are among the best political properties in California, the active ones really constitute a small fraction of their kind. Most older people are too busy enjoying their retirement to exercise a respected voice in the community. They seem to feel that they have retired, not only from their occupation, but from society. Nor does society expect them to carry a role as elder statesmen. Upon reaching sixty-five, or preferably sixty, the Californian is supposed to become decently inactive in his relations with others. Unlike Europe, and many American communities, California does not look to age for either leadership or wisdom. Age is instead a period for personal isolation. One is expected to take up a hobby and remove one's self from the active world.

This is not an enforced fate, but rather a happy agreement between all concerned. After all, California has been the goal of retired people for so long that the idea of living out one's old age here has taken on some special value, in and of itself. How one spends one's later years is no one else's business; it is enough to be in California. The ultimate goal of most people seems to be that of getting in a financial position to retire—the earlier the better.

The interesting point, however, is that California oldsters no longer retire to the rocking chair and the daily paper. They are not particularly "old" in their choice of activities.

One Palm Springs woman celebrated her 104th birthday by going out with her friends to a nightclub; said she, "A cocktail now and then never hurt anybody." Among the most ardent devotees of professional wrestling are sweet old ladies, who seem to derive some vicarious exhilaration from the muscle contests between the Good Guy and the Bad Guy.

Older folks' penchant for gambling is so obvious in California that one Nevada casino owner operates a fleet of buses to bring them from Northern California cities (up to twenty buses a day from Oakland alone) to his establishment on the Nevada side of Lake Tahoe. According to a Stanford Research Institute report, the typical passenger is "elderly, in a low occupational status, unmarried, a renter rather than homeowner, and without a car." [7] As soon as they arrive at the casino their bus fare is refunded and they are given a "free cocktail and free meal," plus "continuous free entertainment." For many, a weekly or monthly trip is a standing procedure, while some women's clubs and service clubs go up in a body. In Las Vegas, older women are among the best customers at the roulette table and the slot machines. I recall, upon landing at the Las Vegas airport, seeing one elderly woman passenger scurrying to the one-armed bandits in the airport lobby and stuffing coins into them as though she was afraid someone would stop her. As I left for town she was still there, and for all I know never left the airport. One ex-employee in a Tahoe casino reports, "Women would play two slot machines at once, pumping in coins with both hands, and anybody who tried to get at either machine would catch a handbag in the face."

Most important of all, the old folks are determined to settle down where they can make maximum use of "California Life." They got the idea from the younger folks, who were obviously preoccupied with sun fun. But with unlimited leisure and unhampered by the necessity of living near a job, the old people are setting the pace for California action.

Many of them are leading more strenuous lives than their children.

4.

The movement for retirement action first began with the house trailer craze immediately before and after the war. With a house hitched behind, older people found they could go camping without drudgery, could actually go traveling as cheaply as staying at home. Gradually, the trailer became the home itself. Some couples simply squatted in state and national parks on a semipermanent basis, preempting scarce campsites, until time limits were imposed to uproot them.

Meanwhile, the commercial trailer park came along to offer utility connections, telephone service, rules against children and pets—all at low rentals. The idea caught on so quickly that by the 1960's there are some 2,000 trailer parks in Southern California alone; [8] as a way of life, trailerism has been refined until the major emphasis is not on the trailers, but on the recreation facilities, including swimming pools, shuffleboard, horseshoes, billiards, dancing, and even such fast action as basketball, tennis, and volleyball. Some trailer parks provide boat slips; others located along the coast offer surf swimming and skin diving. In San Jose and Sacramento, one company operates parks providing every conceivable recreational and shopping facility under the name of Mobile Country Club.

Indeed, as the parks have expanded, so have the trailers; many are sixty feet long, expandable to a twenty-four-foot width, and no longer called trailers (a term speaking of limited living) but "mobile homes." Actually, their mobility is only achievable by a major engineering effort. Judging by the permanent gardens, patios, and verandas around many of the trailers, mobility is but a memory. A few couples even have two trailers—one to live in and a truly mobile one for outings. One two-trailer wife, who had recently moved from

271

a nonmobile home to a trailer park, explained, "We're not so tied down. On weekends, we don't have to worry about getting home to cut the grass or water the flowers."

Such people have obviously achieved the ultimate in California rootlessness. They can take off for anywhere on the spur of the moment, without making reservations; and if they don't like their neighbors at home, they simply phone for a tow truck. The uncommitted Californian could ask no more.

Most older Californians have not gone this far; they do not yet believe that the only way to live is out of a suitcase. One of the reasons is the new movement to bring to the home every conceivable hobby or sport, complete with recreation director, through the device of the retirement community. In the process, the social life of California may be undergoing the biggest revolution since the invention of the freeway.

Special living facilities for oldsters, or for any other minority group, is nothing new in California. Shutting one's self off with one's own kind is an old California custom. Thus, there are apartments or communities exclusively reserved for girls who came to Hollywood to be movie stars, for visiting company executives, and for displaced people who have been rooted out of their homes to make way for freeways, schools, and so forth. Now, however, the trend is to get all the old people out of sight in isolated, self-contained communities where they no longer have to set an example for the younger generation.

At first, this movement was approached cautiously. After the war, there was a definite effort to dignify the traditional nonprofit "home for the aged" by such devices as charging more money, building new buildings, providing croquet and other safe sports, and adopting names (Casa de Mañana, Royal Oaks Manor) that had nothing to do with age. Many of these communities were church sponsored and some required a flat entrance fee (ranging from $10,000 to $30,000

272

depending on the scale of living and one's age) in return for lifetime care including meals and medical costs. Most of them maintained a full range of activities: one went so far as to offer "continuous social and recreational programs," which ought to be enough for just about anybody. Some tried to locate near the beach, mountains, or another recreational locale. As a California state pamphlet puts it, "A well-located home tends to become a beehive."

Still, these institutions seemed to imply growing infirmity on the part of the participants—at least the emphasis on care seemed to say that if one didn't become infirm one wasn't getting one's money's worth. And there was the disagreeable matter of the flat fee for a lifetime, which was a kind of wager that you would live longer than they expected you would.

Californians being hopeless gamblers, the life-care community is still popular, but the biggest trend is toward the huge community (either cooperatively owned apartments or individually owned homes) launched by a private developer. In 1959, builder Del Webb opened his Sun City near Phoenix, Arizona. It was restricted to older people, it emphasized recreation, and to prove it the golf course and swimming pool were finished before the first house was sold. To Webb's surprise, 100,000 people visited Sun City the first three days, and the place was sold out faster than it could be built. Most of those who visited and most who bought were from California.

Since then, Webb has built two more in California—Kern City near Bakersfield, where 55,000 people turned out the first four days of sales, and Sun City near Riverside, which will eventually be a vast metropolis of 150,000 people. Also rushing to emulate Webb's success are other big developers in Sacramento, Fresno, Carmel Valley, Long Beach, San Diego, Palm Desert, Redondo, and Seal Beach.

In most of them the bars have been lowered to admit those

273

who are as young as fifty. It took no great promotional genius
to realize that an age requirement of sixty-five or even sixty
was putting an undue limit on the market. Besides, lowering
the age restriction to fifty takes away the stigma of an old
folks' home while still keeping out the little monsters and
preserving a calm atmosphere. Actually, so long as one
spouse is at least that age, the other may be as young as she
wants. This very gallantly permits the wife to lie about her
age. One development for "mature adults" has an age requirement of forty-five for one spouse, which is pushing the
limit about as far down as it can go while still assuring peace
and quiet for the oldsters. The key restriction is, of course,
no children under eighteen; they may visit but they may not
live there. Nor does there seem to be much encouragement
for visiting; to my knowledge, only one retirement community advertises guest quarters. Apparently if one of the resident couples happens to bear a child they must move out.

5.

Once inside these privileged precincts, the senior citizen
is confronted with an almost frightening array of activities.
For the sportsman there is lawn bowling, shuffleboard, arch-
ery, swimming ("Olympic-size pool"), fishing (at one place,
an artificial lake stocked with bass), horseshoes, badminton,
square dancing, folk dancing, and golf ("championship
eighteen-hole course"). For the hobbyist there is the Arts
and Crafts Center with all the facilities for photography, including dark rooms and processing equipment; leatherwork;
stone and jewel cutting; ceramics; painting; and, of all things,
sewing and "light gardening." One community has more than
sixty clubs for various sports and hobbies. Some have a fully
equipped stage for variety shows, and one has a Greek theater ("modeled after the world famous Hollywood Bowl").
Another has a "complete Town Hall," apparently for civic

meetings, though it is impossible to imagine any public issues arising for discussion inside these Utopias. Others organize tours to major league baseball games and rock-hunting or shell-collecting expeditions, while one has its own bird-watching society.

But these forays outside the sanctuary are not essential, since the whole concept is to meet every need within. Indeed, to make sure that no one misses anything, the bigger communities have continual free transportation operating throughout the park. The retirement community is, in short, a kind of resident Disneyland for old folks.

While inactivity is clearly frowned upon, there is sometimes a provision for the more thoughtfully oriented. Most large communities have at least one church, some have one "for every major faith," a few have a library, while one church-sponsored project has a "meditation and prayer room" as well as a "men's television and smoking room."

However, most of the developments do not cater to the passive or contemplative types. They might tend to drag down the others; besides, the presence of quiet rooms smacks too much of old age. If one wants to be quiet, one can stay in his own apartment or home, which in one community is fully equipped with a "Leisure Room." The senior-citizen project, according to a Sun City ad, means the "Active Retirement Way-of-Life."

The fact is that in a retirement development, which restricts admission to senior citizens, one does not hear the words "retirement" or "senior citizen." Thus, even the words that were once considered euphemisms for harsher terms are in themselves taboo, because they are still reminders of the special nature of the community. The effort is to pretend that the community is not special, that it is "normal." The real world is so effectively shut out that one could doubt that it exists; inside the magic walls, life is timeless and one never

275

ages because one is too busy to think about it. George Mc-Lain, long-time leader of old-age pension movements and founder of two senior-citizens villages, explains, "It's got to be like a long vacation on a cruise ship—never a dull moment." A professor of social work declares, "Give them a well-supervised program and something to look forward to and they'll live longer. The quickest way to kill a person is to retire him to a life of nothingness." And as the resident of one life-care home puts it, "Out there [out there is always the legendary other world left behind] I had a constant doctor's bill for high blood pressure. Now I don't have high blood pressure. I believe I'd be dead if I stayed on my own."

Just in case, however, the communities have a staff of trained nurses and doctors on call; in varying degrees, this service is offered free of charge, along with the recreation, as part of the monthly payments. There are other concessions appealing to those who are frankly aware of their age. Curbings are rounded, presumably to lessen toe-stubbing; stairs are eliminated in favor of ramps (one development has eliminated even these: "Everything ground level"); hallways have low-burning safety lights; plug-ins are two feet off the floor to minimize stooping; bath tubs are eliminated in favor of showers with seats to prevent slipping, or else they are equipped with sturdy grab rails. But these are simply provided, not advertised, and the merciful illusion is preserved in the forward-looking names of the communities (New Horizons, Leisure World) and in the unexceptional decorum of the advertising copy:

> "Step out of the sidelines and into Sun City."
> "Sun Citians are people with ACTIVE minds who feel they've earned the right to live exactly as they please, with all of the things that make life worth living at their fingertips."

276

".. . Your years of freedom and independence should
be, and can be, the happiest years of your life! How?
Have fun! Live in fabulous Palm City."
"Leisure World—America's Prestige Community for
Happy People Over 52."

One might ask a few nasty questions about the personal
and social consequences of the retirement community movement. What happens to the tax burden for schools and other
local essentials when those over fifty withdraw to their own
special-purpose city? Are "all of the things that make life
worth living" really to be found in sun deck, fairway, and
the Arts and Crafts Center? What becomes of a society in
which experience and wisdom are culled out and isolated?
Do children have the sense of social continuity and the depth
of family attachments when Grandma and Grandpa become
mere myths, like Santa Claus? Do the elderly retain their
most precious achievement—that of deriving pleasure from
the happiness of others—when they are committed only to
themselves? Is the isolation of the older generation a more
drastic step in the splintering of California society? And can
a people who are turning their backs on one another really
maintain, in the long run, a society at all?

A faint and hesitant answer may appear in the few who
have left retirement communities because, as they confess,
they "miss the contact with younger minds," or simply "miss
the children." Another answer may be seen in the tendency
of some church groups to sponsor retirement apartments in
the cities, where the residents can be close to their families
and to major cultural life.

Yet there is no exodus from the self-contained senior cities;
indeed, many life-care homes have a long waiting list, and
each new retirement community is sold out within weeks.
More communities are being born that further divide the
retirees into smaller fractions—homes or communities for re-

tired military, retired union members, retired Jewish couples, retired Methodists. There are even efforts to create an appendage of light industry at some retirement cities to provide jobs for the "younger" residents between fifty and the normal retirement age of sixty-five—a curious reversal of the traditional rise of cities in which it is industry that draws the people.

Construction of new senior cities goes merrily on in the confidence that the market is barely tapped. Indeed, many of the buyers are newcomers to California; it is conceivable that the state, with its retirement communities, its favorable climate, and its liberal pension laws, will attract an increasingly larger proportion of older people. This will in turn constitute a growing segment that does not contribute to the California society, and that can use its political strength to maintain its immunity.

Yet so long as the retirement community offers improved living conditions, attacking it is like attacking the American Dream. As Del Webb puts it, "We can realize a way of life unprecedented in America." Since it is obviously a progressive step over the lonely flats and old-age homes of other days, who would be mean enough to turn back the legions of "happy people over 52"? Let them ride first class clear to the end of the line.

CHAPTER XI

The Unassociated Society

1.

One evening I was present at a dinner of the management club in a large California corporation. Among the hundreds attending, few were acquainted with any others besides those they came with. In an effort to find a topic of conversation, I asked the fellow across from me, "What's your department?"

He answered, proudly, "Twelve."

I was impressed, of course, with this manager's loyal acceptance of the system. It was not so much that his department had a number, but that he would think of it first as a number. To me his answer has epitomized the estate to which the Californian has attained in his relation to society. He has achieved total anonymity—a kind of Nirvana in which he is wholly identified with his environment. He is nothing, and everything.

But in California this ultimate impersonalization represents only half the man. At those moments of the day or week when he is on his own, he is the total individualist. He does as he pleases, thinks as he pleases, dresses as he pleases, and also believes in letting others do as they please.

279

Indeed, it is precisely because of this freedom that he so willingly removes his face on company time. He can afford to be anonymous in the one life because he can escape every day to another.

This other life of near-complete freedom, made possible for the Californian by the mildness of the climate and the mobility provided by his car, is what contemporary observers praise as California Living. The Californian is a successful refugee from the tyranny of Eastern tenements, of stifling weather, of hereditary occupation in company towns, of the 8:15 Limited and the Crosstown Local.

That this freedom is good, and an American social advancement, is one thing. That it is leading automatically to a better society is quite another. For in their present pursuit of this freedom, the Californians are turning their backs on each other. Physically as they roar down the highway with the top of their cars decorated by surfboards or skis, they may clearly be termed outgoing. There is a more zestful affirmation of life than is noticeable, even possible, elsewhere. But in its orientation this life is actually ingoing, withdrawn. It is a rejection of society, in favor of the self. The rolling isolation booths on the highway, the fences around each yard, the absence of sidewalks between houses in the newer subdivisions, the tendency toward specialized communities of young marrieds or senior citizens, are all symbolic of a society of strangers. Observes Leo Rangell, a Beverly Hills psychoanalyst, "Our modern culture fails to encourage the deep friendships between man that occurred in ancient times." There are, to be sure, circles of friends in California. But many of the friendships are of questionable depth, and the contacts of pathetic infrequency. Yet as Dr. Rangell emphasizes, "True friendship is a human trait which goes along with and makes possible civilization."

The point is that the California society is losing communication—at least horizontal communication among its members. There is ample volume of vertical communication, from leadership elements to the general public via newspapers, television, and radio. The quality of this vertical communication may be no worse and is probably no better than its quality elsewhere. Although the mass-audience TV shows are even more debilitating to the human mind in the 1960's than they were in the 1950's, there is a heartening improvement in the perception of some news reporting. Among some metropolitan newspapers there is also a noticeable advancement in objectivity and reportorial initiative, due in part to competition from three Eastern-based journals of superior quality—the *Christian Science Monitor*, the *Wall Street Journal*, and especially the *New York Times*—which have all established Western editions. The brightest phenomenon in California journalism has been the newspapers of medium-sized cities, some of which have shown exceptional vigor and have even, at times, picked up the lance of the old-time crusading editor.

Yet no matter how commendable the mass media—and California's are perhaps average—a society responding automatically to data fed into it by the linotype and the video tube is a travesty of the democratic ideal. Vital to the free society is the unprofessional, uninhibited dialogue between its members; it is the only means of developing a true public opinion, rather than a conditioned response.

In California, this dialogue is thin and halting; the lack of it gives the outbursts of the extremists an importance all out of true proportion. Apparently noting the shrillness of their cries against an almost silent background, John Gunther once wrote, "If either Fascism or Communism should ever smite this country, it is more likely to rise first in California than in any other state." But actually, the dogmatists of both right and left are driven to their extremism by the disconcerting tolerance and happy indifference of the California mentality.

They demand finality out of what is essentially an open and uncommitted mind.

The alarming thing in contemporary California is not the rise of the Far Right, which is entitled to its opinion, but rather the general willingness to let the Far Right define the terms and frame of reference for the public dialogue. There is thus a rather wide belief that social justice means socialism; that government is the enemy rather than the instrument of society; that there is no such thing as the public good, outside of what private individuals consider to be their own good. If anarchy and selfishness are enshrined by such a dogma, this is precisely the appeal to many Californians, who may not be rightists by nature, but who like to have a philosophical justification for their pursuit of private pleasure. Thus, while the Far Right offers little threat of assuming political control in California, it does exert a subtle influence on the California mind, particularly in providing a doctrinal vindication of the self-oriented life and the neglect of the public business.

2.

Not that the forms of government are missing in California. It is only that the machinery is abandoned to the organizations of special interest. In 1961, there were four lobbyists for every legislator at Sacramento. During the 1960-61 legislature, they spent approximately $1,000,000 to influence legislation. Some of them averaged $3,000 to $4,000 per month in expenses for food, lodging, liquor, and incidentals.[1] Some of the top spenders are the private utilities, the oil industry, the horse racing interests, and the wine manufacturers. Among other significant lobbies are the veterans, the teachers, the senior citizens, the labor unions, the morticians, the trucking industry, the railroads, the commercial fisheries and canneries, and the real estate business. Many of these maintain lobbies at the larger county seats and city halls.

These groups are not, in themselves, sinister. They have a right to present their viewpoint to the lawmakers. It is simply that their influence is unusually strong in a state where the citizens themselves are preoccupied with their private affairs. Legislation becomes a tug-of-war between the special interests, and nobody speaks for the public interest. So while tirades have been aimed at California's "Third House," it is hypocrisy to leave out of the equation the default of the California citizen.

The harsh fact is that the Californian's long neglect of community affairs can destroy the very environment that spawned his individualism. Already he is reaping some serious results of his naïve belief that the community will run itself.

In the two largest metropolitan areas, growth has been fostered with too little consideration for human values. The flight to the suburbs—a national phenomenon—has been permitted in California with almost no reservation for local parks and playgrounds.

Another public offense has been committed in the private subdivision and unrestricted commercialization of the California shoreline. Of the 271 miles of coastline in Southern California, less than eighty are accessible for beach recreation to a regional population of ten million. A similar blight has been allowed to vandalize the shores of Lake Tahoe, one of the world's superb resort resources.

The same absence of public policy has permitted whole cities to rise without many of the basic municipal services. San Fernando Valley—larger in population than San Francisco—is so lacking in storm drains that when it rains many street corners are clogged with stalled automobiles and the whole pace of activity is turned back to the pre-auto age.

When it rains hard and long, people in the lowlands are evacuated in boats.

In public transportation, San Francisco and Los Angeles are equally backward. The freeways have not solved the commuter bottleneck; the worker spends an important part of his income on individual transportation by auto, and an important part of his day in nerve-rending, bumper-to-bumper traffic. The San Franciscans have at least voted the bonds for a rapid transit system. The Angelenos have done little more than talk about it since their Metropolitan Transit Authority was first established in 1951.

Meanwhile, the smog created by the mass of motor exhausts is a threat to public health. And while Los Angeles County has spent more money than either the State of California or the federal government to combat smog, the best that can be said is that the evil is getting no worse. By now it has also reared its insidious gray head in San Francisco, San Diego, and parts of the San Joaquin Valley.

These are not just minor shortcomings. They tend to crowd in upon the individual, limiting his capacity for the very freedom that California supposedly exemplifies, forcing him to spend a growing part of his days in the elementary job of surviving.

In his various local governments, he has the instruments for action, but there is no dynamic push behind local government in California; in many areas the void has of necessity been filled by chambers of commerce. For decades, public policy in Los Angeles has been created and largely implemented by the Chamber of Commerce. The rehabilitation of downtown Los Angeles and San Francisco owes its inception and its vital push to business groups. In this respect, California exhibits a curious phenomenon; its business community is not a brake against change, but rather the spearhead for change. And while these progressive businessmen are not without personal motive in seeking community improvement, they are at least ahead of the average Californian, who does not even seem to recognize his own interest.

In still another dimension, California Living is threatened. Crudity, cheapness, and commercialism is allowed to offend and finally to harden one's sensibilities. Increasingly, California's rich variety of scenery is hidden behind a screen of billboards. In most cities, there is no aesthetic restriction on architecture or advertising. Some of the most-traveled thoroughfares (Sepulveda Boulevard in Los Angeles is an example) are a gantlet of ugly business signs fighting for the attention of motorists. Along some of the few attractive drives in Southern California that are free from such eyesores, weekend drivers are assaulted with the portable signs of candy salesmen and peddlers of "Guide Maps to the Stars' Homes" who squat by the roadside. Many communities have been made nearly insufferable by the roar of trucks passing by on elevated freeways; more adequate mufflers to suppress the noise are available, but they are not required by law.

3.

Throughout its development, California has suffered various forms of such human indignities; the values observed in pioneering communities have been practical, not aesthetic. Until the massive influx of population following World War II, most Californians had enough elbow room to overlook these offenses.

But there is getting to be no place to hide. The west and east shores of San Francisco Bay contain a continuous "long city" curving eastward as far as Vallejo with a population of four million. Southern Californians are now predicting a 200-mile megalopolis extending from Santa Barbara to San Diego. San Joaquin Valleyites are talking about a "string of beads" city stretching another 200 miles from Bakersfield to Modesto. Even the charming city of Palos Verdes Estates, which still looks like a Neapolitan resort, is split in two every weekend as crowds drive through on the main highway to sightseeing attractions down the coast. The ultimate surrender occurred in Los Angeles when a freeway interchange completely surrounded a hundred apartment dwellers. With typical optimism, the owner of the Castle Hotel viewed it as "a stroke of luck" and made plans to modernize. "Why, people will stay at the Castle just for the novelty of it!"

Throughout California, farmers have been in retreat before the onslaught of the tract developer. On the San Francisco peninsula, they got zoning rules against housing projects until the land became so valuable they couldn't resist sale. To block subdivision, dairymen in Los Angeles and Orange counties have incorporated cities whose population is numbered in cows rather than people. In Ojai, a group of ranchers optioned property at $8,000 an acre to keep it from being subdivided. A chicken rancher in San Fernando Valley opposed zoning variances for subdivisions on both sides of his place and lost out. When the land value went up enough he petitioned to get his own property zoned for residential use, knocked down the chicken coops, and took a regular job.

"What else can I do?" he said at the zone hearing. "I have to follow the trend."

In short, while the Californian has been able to indulge his civic irresponsibility up until recently, the relentless population growth is crowding in upon him. He will either have to fight for his way of living after making an extraordinary change of character, or he will succumb to the faceless existence that has overtaken man in other crowded cultures.

When California realized it would soon pass New York as the most populous state in the Union, exuberant Governor Pat Brown called for "the biggest party this state has ever had to celebrate." But on his desk lay an official report reproaching California for failures in planning "to meet the crisis problems of California growth."

"We still sing in praise of the Golden State," it observed, "notwithstanding the smog, the water pollution, the crowded roads, the dirty, blighted cities, the disappearing open space. Perhaps we sing out of nostalgia—for the old uncrowded ways of life . . ."

To this the *Fresno Bee* added, "Bigness itself is nothing. It is what you do with your prestige and your position of strength. It is bigness of mind, of character, of vision, that counts, not bigness of body."

Thus, as California became the most populous state in the Union, and therefore inherited a position of political and social leadership among the states, there was serious question whether she was ready for it. And there was an even more ironic question whether the Californians had not enjoyed the good life so much that they were in danger of losing it. Indeed, they are driving headlong to a society of the unassociated, which means either a rise to, or a decline to, no society at all in the accepted sense. The only anarchy man has actually experienced is in the state of savagery. Some philosophers, notably Confucius, have postulated an ideal civilization of superior men, in which there is no need for formal organization, since all have a supreme sense of station and of duty. This civilization, if it is attainable at all, is not the one toward which the Californians are headed, since one of their characteristics is a rejection of duty except to themselves and their families.

Actually, the compartmented existence of the Californians takes place within, and depends upon, an ordered political, social, and economic framework. Such a framework must continually be kept in order. And it is not at all clear that the Californians have reached a state of perfection that does not require the framework.

287

Yet it appears that within the California character are traits that might eventually match its "bigness of body" with "bigness of mind, of character, of vision." California is, after all, a young society; it is perhaps natural that it would be preoccupied with physical achievement. But in the so-called Art Boom, Californians are showing a fascination for cultural values that is probably not just another fad. As art is a search for truth, the results may be more than a new cultural enrichment. The flowering of art has, in the past, often stimulated a general pattern of reexamination and inquiry; more than one Golden Age in art has preceded a Golden Age in philosophy. Through this process, Californians who have always been in too big a hurry to question where they were going might dredge up some badly needed insights.

Further, California's intellectual base is broadening as never before, and as in no other state outside of the North Atlantic Seaboard. California's mammoth system of public and private universities, colleges, and junior colleges is providing campuses and faculties for communities throughout the state. The entertainment business has gathered to Southern California what Niven Busch calls "the greatest collection of playwrights, performers, and producers living anywhere." The aerospace industry has attracted to San Diego, Los Angeles, and the San Francisco peninsula probably the largest body of advanced scientists in private employment. It is no coincidence that California has more people with the designation of scientist (22,800) and more Nobel Prize winners (nineteen) than any other state.[2] California also has tens of thousands of engineers and other technical people holding degrees in many different disciplines, with hundreds of practical applications. The climate, the varied scenery, and informality of life have brought to California several thousand serious artists, as well as inspiring many of the native born. This is no surprise so far as Northern California is concerned, but finally, as the curator of the Metropolitan Museum of Art has observed, "In Southern California you have the greatest group of young painters in America."

This large and variegated intelligentsia is not necessarily the seat of all wisdom in California, but it vastly increases the chances of wisdom breaking the surface. Nor is it yet a cohesive force, since communication is inhibited by the magnificent distances and the difficulties of community identification in much of California. For example, there is not a high degree of social life among the faculty members at UCLA, or much faculty participation in the college community, because real estate prices in Westwood and vicinity are so high that few faculty members can afford to live there.

But such barriers to communication are also a function of a society's youth. As the communities develop social patterns, communications will follow. Already in Los Angeles —as has traditionally been the case in San Francisco—there is a meeting of artists and the art-minded through some sixty commercial galleries. Study and discussion groups, both formal and informal, are part of a genuine intellectual ferment appearing not only in the big cities, but in the smaller cities as well. Out of this growing exchange of minds must come original ideas, new systems of thought, fresh values.

Fortunately, these seeds fall upon fertile earth, for among the Californian's most salutary characteristics is an open mind. In the crucible of the frontier, and among pioneers who had more nerve than education, trial and error was a way of life. There is in California a willingness to give an idea a sporting chance to prove itself, rather than condemning it out of hand. California voters are inclined to support a ballot proposition to "give it a try" as a substitute for studying it. In the words of Kimmis Hendrick, the *Christian Science Monitor's* veteran Pacific correspondent, California "has an experimental attitude toward the nature of society."

Still further, California is literally full of people who have rejected tradition in the very act of coming West. Rutted social patterns have been left behind. Once in California, they have no heritage to anchor their minds. While this very condition has led Californians into some wild and worthless causes, it also puts a premium on the present and the future. Except in some localities treasuring their history, Californians spend little time in nostalgia. "The good old days" have little meaning to them. On the contrary, they have that unblinking confidence in progress that was once possessed by all Americans. Californians operate on an almost arrogant assumption that they are doing things better than their parents did, and better than people are doing them elsewhere, and that they will be doing them still better tomorrow. In short, new concepts find an open market, relatively free of restraint, in which they can compete on their merits.

Finally, by its very bigness California still offers opportunities for dramatic social innovations. For example, it provides a chance to build cities primarily for people, taking humanitarian considerations into at least as much account as haphazard commercial growth. Much violence has been done to the California landscape through private greed and official blindness. But some private developers and public planners are launching whole new communities with attention to aesthetics, living space, and the other factors that offer means of extending what Lewis Mumford calls "the dimensions of the human personality."

5.

California therefore contains not only a great danger, but a great hope—which is what might be expected of a free society, and which has always been its obvious risk. Nowhere does the conflict between individual freedom and social responsibility have a more open arena or show a more advanced stage of struggle. This conflict is the essence of the democratic experiment and hence finds in California an exceptional laboratory. Unlike some other parts of the world, where success of the experiment is threatened by extreme want, it is threatened in California by the very abundance it has created. It is the good life itself, developed under free institutions, that is seducing the Californian into a neglect of them.

What is all the more insidious is that the good life is not, in itself, decadent by ordinary standards. A lapse into classic debauchery would be so easily recognized that it would perhaps generate its own reaction. But California Living is not depraved; it is generally wholesome, as family devotion and physical exercise are wholesome. What mechanism is there for sounding an alarm at the decline of man's noblest achievements—the exercise of justice and the elevation of the human consciousness?

This is the haunting California fear—that a people who appear to be moving on the frontier of American culture are quietly abrogating what Rousseau called the Social Contract, with its basic premise, "for every right, a duty." Instead, to the simple human pleasures, in Tocqueville's words, "the heart, the imagination, and life itself, are unreservedly given up; till, in snatching at these lesser gifts, men lose sight of those more precious possessions which constitute the glory and the greatness of mankind. . . . By these means, a kind of virtuous materialism may ultimately be established in the world, which would not corrupt, but enervate, the soul, and noiselessly unbend its springs of action."

Notes

CHAPTER 2

1 Thompson, Warren S. *Growth and Changes in California's Population*. Los Angeles, 1955.

2 Report, State Department of Public Health, cited in *Los Angeles Times*, August 3, 1958; *San Francisco Chronicle*, January 21, 1962; *Los Angeles Times*, September 12, 1957 and June 5, 1960; *Holiday*, April, 1961.

3 *Los Angeles Times*, June 5, 1960.

4 *Pacific Citizen*, February 23 and March 16, 1962. The *Pacific Citizen* is the newspaper of the Japanese-American Citizens League.

5 Hearings before the United States Commission on Civil Rights, Los Angeles and San Francisco, January, 1960. Washington, 1960.

CHAPTER 3

1 Cleland, Robert Glass. *California in Our Time* (New York: Alfred A. Knopf, Inc., 1947), p. 163.

2 Morales, Dionicio. *The Need for a Social Agency to Serve the Mexican-American Community*. Los Angeles, 1962.

3 Los Angeles Classified Telephone Book, August, 1962.

4 *Los Angeles Times*, October 5, 1957.

5 *Life*, October 19, 1962; *Los Angeles Times*, June 24, 1962.

CHAPTER 4

1 California Raisin Advisory Board, cited in *Los Angeles Times*, December 22, 1961; *Fresno Bee*, January 14, 1962.

2 Population Reference Bureau, cited in *San Francisco Chronicle*, January 14, 1962.

3 *Fresno Bee*, December 31, 1961.

4 *Sacramento Bee*, December 17, 1961.

5 *Los Angeles Times,* August 5, 1962.
6 *Fresno Bee,* January 7, 1962.
7 Council of California Growers and Stanford Research Institute, cited in *Fresno Bee,* January 28, 1962.

CHAPTER 6
1 *Los Angeles Times,* July 16, 1961.

CHAPTER 7
1 *New York Times,* Western Edition, January 3, 1963.
2 1960 Annual Report, Bureau of Criminal Statistics, Department of Justice, State of California.
3 *Los Angeles Times,* July 6, 1961.
4 *Pacific Citizen,* March 23, 1962.
5 Narcotics Arrests and their Disposition in California—1960. Bureau of Criminal Statistics, Department of Justice, State of California.
6 *Ibid.*
7 *Ibid.*
8 *Ibid.*
9 *Los Angeles Times,* February 5 and 12, March 26, October 5, 1961.
10 Vincent, Clark E. *Unmarried Mothers.* New York, 1961, p. 71.
11 *Los Angeles Times,* November 28, 1960.
12 *Los Angeles Times,* March 15, 1960.
13 *Los Angeles Times,* February 21, 1960.
14 *Sacramento Bee,* December 3, 1961.
15 *El Mustang,* November 10, 1961. *El Mustang* is the college newspaper of the California State Polytechnic Institute.

CHAPTER 8
1 Thompson, Warren S. *Growth and Changes in California's Population.* Los Angeles, 1955.
2 National Council of Churches. Churches and Church Membership in the United States: An enumeration and analysis by counties, states, and regions. Series B, No. 5 (1956) and Series C, No. 58 (1957). This source gives a California church membership of 40 percent of population. However, membership is for 1952, while population is for 1950, so that the percentage does not allow for two years of population growth. The *Los Angeles Times,* November 15, 1961, gives a California church membership of 20 percent of population.
3 Berger, Bennet M. *Working Class Suburb.* Berkeley and Los Angeles, 1960, p. 113.
4 *Los Angeles Times,* June 21, 1956.
5 *Los Angeles Times,* March 24, 1962.
6 Berger, *op. cit.,* p. 118.

294

7 Security-First National Bank. Monthly Summary of Business Conditions in Southern California. Vol. 41, No. 4. April, 1962.

8 *Los Angeles Times,* March 18, May 10, and July 24, 1960; June 18 and 29, 1961.

9 *Sacramento Bee,* January 14, 1962; *Los Angeles Times,* February 23, 1958, and June 5, 1960.

10 *Los Angeles Times,* February 17, 1960.

11 *Ibid.*

CHAPTER 9

1 Berger, Bennet M. *Working Class Suburb.* Berkeley and Los Angeles, 1960, pp. 59, 64.

2 *Wall Street Journal,* October 31 and November 5, 1962; *Los Angeles Times,* October 26 and 31, 1962.

3 *Los Angeles Times,* October 22, 1962.

4 Berger, *op. cit.,* p. 17.

5 *Ibid.,* p. 61.

6 *Modoc Record,* February 15, 1962; *Los Angeles Times,* September 20, 1961.

7 *Sacramento Bee,* December 31, 1961.

8 *Los Angeles Times,* September 8, 1961, and April 15, 1962.

9 *Los Angeles Times,* September 3, 1959, and July 25, 1961.

10 Farberow Norman L., and Shneidman, Edwin S. Eds. *The Cry for Help.* New York, 1961, p. 4.

11 *Fresno Bee,* January 28, 1962; *Los Angeles Times,* November 26, 1959.

CHAPTER 10

1 *Los Angeles Times,* September 18, 1962.

2 *Ibid.*

3 Los Angeles Classified Telephone Book, August, 1962.

4 Huxley, Aldous. *After Many a Summer Dies the Swan* (London: Shatto & Windus, 1939, and New York: Harper & Brothers, 1939).

5 Waugh, Evelyn. *The Loved One* (Boston: Little, Brown & Company, 1948), p. 39.

6 Mathison, Richard R. *Faiths, Cults and Sects of America.* Indianapolis and New York, 1960, p. 130.

7 *Harper's Magazine,* January, 1962. "The New Gambling King and the Social Scientists," by Keith Monroe.

8 *Los Angeles Times,* October 29, 1961.

CHAPTER 11

1 *Sacramento Bee,* September 10, 1961.

2 *Los Angeles Times,* December 3, 1961, and May 27, 1962.

Index

299

Negroes, 31-33, 42ff., 54, 73, 146, 166
neighborliness, 3-4, 59, 92, 95, 98, 217, 247-48
Newhall, 60
Newport Beach, 136-38
New York Times, 38, 118, 217, 281
Nineteen Eighty-Four, 237
Nob Hill, 14, 19
nonconformity, 5, 27-28, 33, 129, 140, 166, 200, 209-11, 264, 290
Norris, Frank, 72
North Beach, 126
North Hollywood, 120, 168
North Island, 119

Oakland, 14, 17-18, 154, 236, 270
Oakland Art Museum, 17
Oakland Bay bridge, 21
Ocean Beach, 13, 30
Ocean Park, 40, 55, 162, 255
occultism, 6, 263
Octopus, The, 72
Ojai, 254, 286
Okahara, Bee, 44
Ontario, 203, 231
open-mindedness, 5-6, 30, 282, 289-90
Orange County, 36, 112, 193, 222, 286
Orange County State College, 157
Orientals, 31-33, 42-45
Orwell, George, 237
Owen, Wilfred, 36
Owens Valley, 97-98
Oxnard, 54, 155

Pacoima, 147
Palm Desert, 273
Palm Springs, 57-58, 64, 137-38, 231, 243-44, 270
Palo Alto, 19
Palos Verdes Estates, 3, 113, 123, 286
parachuting, 205, 221, 227
Paradise, 203
Parent-Teacher Associations, 98, 113
"parking," 151ff.
Pasadena, 16, 22, 36, 47, 51, 110-11, 121, 198, 205, 242, 258

peninsula, the San Francisco, 14, 16, 18-20, 32, 102, 112, 243, 246, 286, 288
photography, 266-67, 274
physical fitness, 50ff., 139-40
Piedmont, 17, 191
Pierce College, 159
Placer County, 211, 265
Plumas County, 91
poetry, 27, 176
Point Arena, 97
politics, 5-6, 30, 46, 96, 164-66, 171-72, 212, 214ff., 241, 258, 268, 278, 281ff., 289
pools, 2, 4, 8, 19, 61-62, 124, 139, 243-44, 271, 273-74
Popenoe, Dr. Paul, 203
Portuguese, 73, 205
postwar boom, 18, 41-42, 47
premarital relations, 151ff.
press, the (*see* journalism)
pretense, 33, 123, 190ff., 199
"privatism," 3, 7, 59, 174ff., 212ff., 247ff., 251, 280ff.
promiscuity, 154, 163
prostitution, 24, 154
Puente, 197

quick-draw contests, 221-22

racial discrimination, 31-33, 42ff., 73, 166, 183-84
Ramirez, Isabel, 170
Rangell, Dr. Leo, 280
real estate, 6, 35, 36, 38-40, 45, 63-65, 68, 93, 104, 191ff., 243, 254, 290
Redondo Beach, 134, 273
Redwood Coast, 6, 87, 91, 95-97, 236
religion, 5, 42, 115, 164-65, 169, 178ff., 259, 263-64
retirement, 47, 94, 104, 218, 254ff., 265ff.
retirement communities, 272ff.
Riesman, David, 178
Right, the, 30, 165-66, 269, 281-82
riots, 148-49, 210-11
Riverside, 228

301

303